Foundations of Modern Information Security

A Vendor-Neutral Guide to Securing the Cloud, Data, and Identity in the AI Era

Ankit Gupta
Shilpi Mittal

Apress®

Foundations of Modern Information Security: A Vendor-Neutral Guide to Securing the Cloud, Data, and Identity in the AI Era

Ankit Gupta
Little Elm, TX, USA

Shilpi Mittal
Little Elm, TX, USA

ISBN-13 (pbk): 979-8-8688-2557-6
ISBN-13 (electronic): 979-8-8688-2558-3
https://doi.org/10.1007/979-8-8688-2558-3

Managing Director, Apress Media LLC: Welmoed Spahr
Acquisitions Editor: Susan McDermott
Project Manager: Jessica Vakili

Cover image from Pixabay.com

Distributed to the book trade worldwide by Springer Science+Business Media New York, 1 New York Plaza, New York, NY 10004. Phone 1-800-SPRINGER, fax (201) 348-4505, e-mail orders-ny@springer-sbm.com, or visit www.springeronline.com. Apress Media, LLC is a Delaware LLC and the sole member (owner) is Springer Science + Business Media Finance Inc (SSBM Finance Inc). SSBM Finance Inc is a **Delaware** corporation.

For information on translations, please e-mail booktranslations@springernature.com; for reprint, paperback, or audio rights, please e-mail bookpermissions@springernature.com.

Apress titles may be purchased in bulk for academic, corporate, or promotional use. eBook versions and licenses are also available for most titles. For more information, reference our Print and eBook Bulk Sales web page at http://www.apress.com/bulk-sales.

Any source code or other supplementary material referenced by the author in this book is available to readers on GitHub. For more detailed information, please visit https://www.apress.com/gp/services/source-code.

If disposing of this product, please recycle the paper

To our families, whose steadfast support, understanding, and encouragement sustained us throughout the writing of this book.

Table of Contents

About the Authors

Ankit Gupta is a cybersecurity leader with over 15 years of experience across enterprise risk, identity governance, and cloud security. Holding a master's in Cybersecurity from NYU, he has earned advanced industry certifications including CISSP, CCSP, ISSMP, CISM, CRISC, CISA, and TOGAF. He leads strategic initiatives in AI governance, data protection modernization, and cloud security architecture within the financial services sector, securing large-scale digital infrastructures and mission-critical systems.

He actively contributes to the cybersecurity community through published technical analyses, research on AI-driven and quantum-era threats, professional certification development, and service as a judge for international cybersecurity programs and conferences. This book reflects his vendor-neutral, architecture-driven approach to modern information security.

Shilpi Mittal is a cybersecurity professional with extensive experience in application security, cloud security, and modern secrets management. She holds a graduate degree from the University of Utah and is pursuing a PhD in Information Science at the University of North Texas, where her research focuses on advanced cryptography, API security, and emerging technology risks.

Her contributions span technical writing, academic research, and community engagement. She actively supports the security field through conference presentations, peer reviews, and mentoring. Her interests include post-quantum security, API protection, and the growing impact of artificial intelligence on modern security practices.

This book reflects her commitment to making information security clear, accessible, and practical. It is written for readers who want to understand the foundations of modern security in a way that supports real-world decision-making and long-term professional growth.

About the Technical Reviewer

Matt Bunch is the VP and Global CISO for Tyson Foods, Inc., where he is responsible for cybersecurity, privacy, and IT mergers and acquisitions. He has over 29 years of experience and holds a BS in Computer Systems Engineering and a master's in Information Systems from the University of Arkansas and has a CISSP certification.

He is on the advisory board of Forge Institute, a nonprofit facilitating cybersecurity workforce programs; serves as the cybersecurity chair for the Meat Institute, an industry association; and serves on the board for the Food and Ag-ISAC, advisory boards for the Computer Science and Computer Engineering departments of the University of Arkansas and Sam M. Walton College of Business enterprise systems programs, and on advisory boards for multiple security technology and service providers. He is also a startup mentor for the Northwest Arkansas-based Fuel Accelerator program and is an active startup mentor and advisor.

Acknowledgments

We thank the Apress editorial and production teams for their guidance and professionalism throughout the development of this book. We are especially grateful to the technical reviewers whose independent evaluation and detailed feedback strengthened the clarity and rigor of this work.

We also acknowledge the broader community of cybersecurity researchers, conference peers, and industry practitioners whose ongoing dialogue, research, and collaboration continue to advance the field of modern information security.

CHAPTER 1

Rethinking Information Security for Evolving Threat Landscapes

Information security now stands at a crossroads. Rapid technological change, from the expansion of artificial intelligence to the shift toward cloud-centric and identity-driven technology environments, has exposed the limitations of traditional, product-centric security approaches. At the same time, cyber threats have grown in scale, speed, and sophistication, demanding a fundamental rethinking of how organizations protect themselves. In response, business and security leaders are increasingly treating cybersecurity not as a siloed technical problem, but as a strategic enterprise concern woven into risk management, technology governance, privacy, operational resilience, and digital trust. The old security playbook of reactive defenses and isolated point solutions is no longer sufficient. Instead, foresight, agility, secure design, and integrated governance are becoming the foundation of effective information security programs.

Note This chapter is written for a near-term operating horizon and a durable strategic outlook. The aim is vendor-neutral guidance that leaders can operationalize across the full technology stack, including traditional IT, cloud, OT, data platforms, AI systems, and third-party ecosystems.

This chapter explores how organizations are reshaping their security strategies for a more distributed, AI-enabled, identity-driven, and governance-heavy operating environment. We first examine the shift away from product-centric security toward holistic, architecture-driven, risk-aligned, and governance-focused security strategies. Next, we discuss the growing convergence of AI, privacy, data governance, and digital

A. Gupta and S. Mittal, *Foundations of Modern Information Security*,
https://doi.org/10.1007/979-8-8688-2558-3_1

trust, and how the interaction of these domains is redefining cybersecurity priorities across modern technology environments. We then analyze the continued transition from network-perimeter-based defenses to identity-first and context-aware security models in an era where identity is widely viewed as the primary control plane for enterprise security. Throughout the chapter, we highlight emerging threats, strategic changes in how security leaders manage enterprise risk, and evolving regulatory, operational, and technological developments shaping the near-term security operating environment. The goal is to provide a forward-looking, vendor-neutral perspective on how information security is evolving as organizations work to build resilient, adaptive, and trust-centered security programs in an increasingly complex threat landscape.

Beyond Product-Centric Security: Strategy, Architecture, and Risk

For years, many organizations approached cybersecurity primarily through the lens of technology products, deploying the latest firewalls, antivirus tools, or intrusion detection systems as silver-bullet solutions. It is now clear that product-centric tactics alone are inadequate against modern threats. Security leaders are pivoting toward a more strategic posture that emphasizes architecture, risk management, technology governance, data governance, AI governance, and policy over any single vendor tool. In practice, this means embedding security into system and process design, aligning security initiatives with business objectives, and focusing on fundamentals such as identity, application security, resilience, secure operations, and defensible governance rather than chasing every new product category.

Security As a Strategic Business Driver

One hallmark of this shift is treating cybersecurity as a strategic business enabler rather than a mere compliance requirement or IT cost center. Organizations that "meet the moment and weave cybersecurity into their strategic planning" are finding they can actually gain competitive advantages. Organizations that treat cybersecurity as a strategic differentiator, rather than only as a compliance obligation, are better positioned to earn customer trust, satisfy partner requirements, and support resilient digital growth. Leading enterprises now reframe security investments as business investments: for example, strengthening cybersecurity can yield returns in the form of avoided incident costs, lower cyber insurance premiums, or even winning contracts by meeting stringent security requirements. In other words, robust security postures increasingly influence customer and partner trust, becoming a factor in who wins business in sectors like defense and critical infrastructure. This mindset shift requires executive-level attention across the CEO, CIO, CISO, CTO, Chief Data Officer, privacy leadership, legal, risk, and business leadership functions. Notably, about 60% of business and technology leaders worldwide now rank cyber risk among their top three strategic priorities amid ongoing geopolitical and technological volatility. Security has risen to the boardroom agenda as a core component of enterprise risk management and continuity planning, rather than a narrow technology operations issue.

Note As I've seen in discussions with CISOs over the past quarter, the most significant security gaps are often not technical but strategic. Leaders who treat cybersecurity as a line item rather than a business enabler usually miss the signals until it's too late.

From Reactive to Proactive and Risk-Focused

Another strategic adjustment is moving from reactive security (cleaning up after breaches) to proactive risk management (preventing breaches and minimizing their impact). Many organizations still split resources between reactive incident response and proactive prevention, but mature programs increasingly rebalance toward preparedness, continuous validation, and resilience. Those few who have achieved a proactive tilt represent the "ideal spend ratio," and others are being encouraged to follow suit. The rationale is straightforward: responding to incidents after damage is done is more costly and unsustainable than hardening systems in advance. In fact, reactive costs often extend beyond IT budgets (e.g., legal fees, reputation damage), whereas proactive spending is more visible and controllable. Forward-looking security leaders are therefore pushing for resilience-by-prevention – integrating continuous monitoring, threat hunting, testing, and drills into their programs so that attacks can be thwarted or contained before escalating. As one industry expert observed, "moving from reactive defense to proactive resilience is a real opportunity" to not only improve security but also drive business growth, so long as C-suite stakeholders commit to the effort. This includes leveraging advanced technologies (such as AI and cloud-driven analytics) to help security teams work smarter, not just harder (see Figure 1-1).

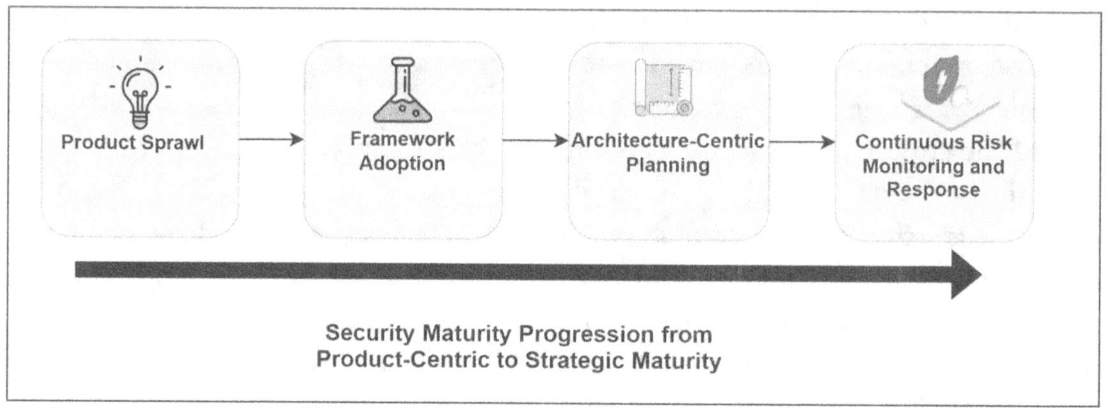

Figure 1-1. *Security maturity progression: from product-centric to strategic*

Crucially, a proactive, risk-driven approach means concentrating on the most critical risks to the organization's mission. Rather than buying every new security product, leading CISOs are mapping their security investments to the top risks in their specific context - whether that be securing a supply chain, protecting customer data, or ensuring the uptime of critical systems. Frameworks and standards have become valuable tools in this regard. Organizations increasingly rely on cybersecurity frameworks such as the NIST Cybersecurity Framework, ISO 27001, and risk assessment methodologies to systematically identify gaps and prioritize controls. Notably, the US government's Cybersecurity Maturity Model Certification (CMMC 2.0) for defense contractors has transitioned from concept to requirement, forcing companies in the defense supply chain to implement tiered best practices and undergo assessments. Such frameworks are reshaping how organizations approach security - with greater emphasis on governance, documentation, and architectural maturity and less on ad hoc tool deployment.

Embracing Secure Architecture and Design

In the current threat environment, security architecture and system design choices matter as much as individual security products, if not more. This is reflected in guidance from agencies such as the US Cybersecurity and Infrastructure Security Agency. CISA's strategic guidance stresses hardening the terrain by minimizing systemic vulnerabilities, including strong authentication, secure cloud configurations, and segmentation to limit lateral movement. In practice, organizations are advised to build security into the fabric of their technology environments from the outset, rather than bolting on tools later. This includes secure cloud architecture, network and identity segmentation, application security, secure code development, DevSecOps, and security checks in the software development lifecycle and CI/CD pipeline. For example, an enterprise might redesign its network with internal micro-segmentation, refactor an application to enforce stricter access controls, add automated code scanning to the development pipeline, and require security testing before production release.

The CISA plan and others advocate for secure-by-design and secure-by-default principles, meaning that technology providers and users should ensure products ship with security safeguards enabled by default and that security is considered at the architectural phase. An illustration of this philosophy: multi-factor authentication (MFA), cloud security configuration, and network segmentation are cited as "proven, effective measures" that yield good results and should thus be universally implemented as baseline controls. Indeed, many attacks in recent years have succeeded not because of ultra-sophisticated zero-day exploits, but because basic measures were missing - such as an admin account protected only by a weak password or an unpatched known vulnerability. By focusing on strong architecture (e.g., Zero Trust network designs) and sound policy (e.g., enforcing least-privilege access), organizations significantly reduce the "soft targets" that attackers might otherwise exploit.

To support this, there's a growing emphasis on measuring security posture and risk reduction. Rather than unquestioningly trusting that a product improves security, organizations are developing metrics to gauge their resilience. CISA's road map calls for tools and services that help measure risk exposure and track improvements over time as threats evolve. Business and IT leaders want to know: Are we more secure this quarter than last? Are our most critical assets properly safeguarded? Metrics such as mean time to detect/respond, percentage of systems with up-to-date patches, and results of regular penetration tests are increasingly reported to boards and executives as key performance indicators. This measurement culture aligns with treating security as an ongoing process of improvement - analogous to quality assurance or safety in other fields - rather than one-time deployments.

Mastering the Fundamentals: A Risk and Resilience-Oriented Mindset

Perhaps the clearest sign of moving beyond a product-centric mindset is the renewed focus on cybersecurity fundamentals. High-profile incidents and industry studies continue to reinforce that many breaches can be prevented or mitigated by getting the basics right. As the FBI's Cyber Division Assistant Director noted in a recent cyber outlook report, "In a threat landscape defined by nation-state adversaries and increasingly sophisticated criminal groups, resilience depends on mastering the fundamentals: identity and access management, network segmentation, securing cloud environments, third-party risk management, and building robust response plans... Every investment in prevention, detection, and workforce skills narrows the gaps adversaries aim to exploit." This statement captures the current consensus: success lies in consistently executing core security principles. Identity and access management (IAM) – making sure the right people (and devices) have the proper access and nothing more – is paramount (we explore this further in the identity-first section).

Proper network architecture (segmentation, Zero Trust principles) ensures that a breach of one system doesn't automatically compromise the entire enterprise. Cloud security hygiene, from configuration management to monitoring, is critical as cloud services proliferate. Third-party risk management has gained importance following a series of supply chain attacks, prompting companies to assess vendors and demand stronger security assurances from partners continually. Notably, incident response preparedness is crucial. Having robust plans, performing drills, and engaging in joint response planning with key partners or government agencies helps turn "preparation into muscle memory," enabling the containment of incidents with minimal damage.

Importantly, these fundamentals are as much about people and processes as they are about technology. Rethinking security strategy involves investing in the cybersecurity workforce and culture. Organizations continue to face a shortage of skilled security professionals, creating sustained competition for talent. Strategic leaders are addressing this by expanding training, cross-training technology staff in security, using managed services where appropriate, and applying automation and AI to reduce repetitive analyst workload. The goal is not to replace human judgment, but to help limited teams focus on higher-value investigation, architecture, governance, and response work. At the same time, building a culture of security within the organization is essential. This means top leadership setting the tone that security is everyone's responsibility, regular security awareness training for employees, and incorporating security considerations into daily business decision-making. For example, development teams are being encouraged (or required) to adopt "DevSecOps" practices so that software code is reviewed for vulnerabilities as it's written, rather than after deployment.

Regulators and governments are also pushing organizations to elevate their security posture strategically. In the United States, the National Cybersecurity Strategy and related initiatives continue to advocate shifting the burden for security "to those best positioned to reduce risks," such as software vendors shipping secure products and service providers enabling strong default protections. A concrete reflection of this is that both the US national strategy and CISA's road map emphasize secure-by-default product development and expanded support for under-resourced organizations to implement security basics. Meanwhile, in the European Union, regulations such as NIS2, DORA, and the AI Act have raised expectations for board accountability, operational resilience, third-party risk management, and governance of high-impact digital systems. All these trends reinforce that piecemeal or purely technical approaches are insufficient - what's needed is systemic resilience. Recent guidance and industry commentary continue to reinforce that compliance alone is not enough; customers and regulators increasingly expect security to be built in by default at every level of design and operations.

Proactive Resilience and Business Continuity

A modern vendor-neutral security strategy also heavily emphasizes resilience, the ability to maintain critical operations in the face of cyber incidents. This goes hand in hand with risk management: assume some attacks will penetrate defenses and plan accordingly. Business continuity and incident response planning are thus core parts of security strategy. Enterprises are investing in capabilities such as data backup and recovery, network isolation techniques, and redundant systems to ensure that, even if one part of their environment is compromised or disrupted, the business as a whole can stay afloat. Regular tabletop exercises and cross-functional crisis simulations (often aligning with National Cybersecurity Awareness Month activities each October) are conducted to test these plans. The focus on resilience is evident in the language security leaders use - terms like "when, not if" a breach will occur and "cyber resilience" as an outcome. Industry trend analysis increasingly frames cybersecurity as a business enabler through resilience, with CISOs expected to embed organizational and technical resilience so the enterprise can withstand attacks without catastrophic losses. This resilience mindset represents a maturation of cybersecurity from a purely preventive approach to a balanced preventive/detective/corrective approach.

In summary, the strategic shift beyond product-centric security is characterized by a holistic, risk-aligned approach. Organizations are redesigning security architectures for Zero Trust and resilience, strengthening defense-in-depth, doubling down on fundamental controls, and integrating security governance into broader enterprise risk management. Defense-in-depth remains important because no single control, identity platform, AI tool, or monitoring system can fully protect the organization on its own. The modern goal is to layer preventive, detective, corrective, and recovery controls so that the failure of one control does not become the failure of the entire security program. Cybersecurity is being reimagined as a journey, not a destination, requiring continuous adaptation and improvement rather than one-time deployments. Organizations that adapt in this way, treating cybersecurity as a strategic, architectural, and risk-focused discipline, are not only better protected against emerging threats but also better positioned to innovate with confidence.

The Convergence of AI, Privacy, and Digital Trust

One of the defining features of the current cybersecurity landscape is the convergence of artificial intelligence, data privacy, data governance, technology governance, and digital trust. These areas are increasingly intertwined, creating both new challenges and new opportunities for security strategy. Organizations face AI-driven cyber threats and AI-powered defenses while also navigating privacy obligations, audit expectations, regulatory change, and stakeholder trust. Security teams are not only gatekeepers in this model. They are also enablers. By helping define practical AI governance, access controls, logging, data classification, and risk acceptance processes, cyber teams can help the business adopt AI faster and more safely.

AI As Both Ally and Adversary in Security

Few technologies have impacted information security as dramatically as artificial intelligence. On one hand, AI and machine learning are revolutionizing how defenders monitor, detect, and respond to threats. On the other hand, attackers are weaponizing AI to enhance their exploits and social engineering campaigns. This dual-use nature of AI has led to an "arms race" in cyberspace.

The transformative potential of AI for cyber defense is clear. AI-enabled security systems can process enormous volumes of events, identify anomalous patterns faster than human analysts, and support faster investigation and response. In Security Operations Centers, machine learning models are increasingly automating routine alert enrichment, correlating telemetry from multiple platforms, prioritizing incidents based on business risk, and initiating controlled containment actions where policy allows. Incident response is also accelerating through AI-assisted workflows that rapidly gather context, reconstruct timelines, summarize evidence, and reduce analyst fatigue during triage. In vulnerability management and application security, AI-assisted code review, exploit analysis, and software testing are becoming especially important as development cycles continue to accelerate.

Anthropic's Project Glasswing and Claude Mythos Preview illustrate this broader industry shift. The initiative was introduced as a defensive research effort focused on helping qualified security researchers and defenders identify and remediate critical software vulnerabilities more efficiently. Anthropic stated that Claude Mythos Preview demonstrated advanced capabilities in vulnerability discovery and exploit generation, in some cases outperforming many human researchers on complex software security tasks. This is significant because it reflects a larger industry reality: AI is dramatically compressing the time required to discover, weaponize, and potentially exploit vulnerabilities.

For defenders, the implications are twofold. First, AI can materially improve defensive workflows such as secure code review, dependency analysis, patch validation, attack-path analysis, and threat modeling. Second, the same acceleration benefits attackers as well. As AI lowers the cost and technical barrier for vulnerability research and exploit development, organizations must respond by strengthening secure-by-design engineering practices, improving application security testing coverage, reducing patch deployment timelines, and integrating security validation directly into CI/CD and DevSecOps pipelines. The security challenge is no longer simply detecting vulnerabilities. It is responding at machine speed before adversaries can operationalize them.

This discussion is not intended as a recommendation for a specific vendor or model. Rather, it illustrates a defining near-term trend: AI is transforming software security and cyber operations from both the defensive and offensive sides simultaneously. Organizations that fail to modernize governance, software assurance, telemetry, and response processes at the same pace may find that traditional security review cycles are no longer fast enough to manage modern attack velocity.

Yet, the very same AI technologies are supercharging the threat landscape. Attackers are leveraging generative AI to craft highly convincing phishing lures, malware, and social engineering scripts. A few years ago, phishing emails were often riddled with spelling errors or odd phrasing, but AI-generated messages can now be fluent, personalized, and contextually believable. Social engineering has also moved beyond email. Groups such as Scattered Spider have shown how effective voice calls, SMS messages, help desk impersonation, and MFA reset manipulation can be when attackers understand enterprise identity workflows. Deepfakes add another layer of risk because attackers can mimic voices or video appearances to pressure employees, service desks, finance teams, or executives into taking actions that appear legitimate. A documented case involving a deepfake video call led to a fraudulent transfer of about $25 million, illustrating that the trust problem is no longer limited to suspicious links or poor grammar. Beyond phishing and impersonation, AI is also helping attackers automate vulnerability discovery and exploit development. The result is a threat landscape where identity, human trust, application security, and AI governance must be defended together.

This dynamic has made AI governance a pressing issue. Many organizations admit they adopted AI tools faster than they secured or regulated them. Enterprise AI adoption has accelerated faster than many governance programs. As a result, organizations may expose sensitive data, create unapproved automation paths, or deploy AI-enabled workflows before security, privacy, legal, and audit teams have defined appropriate guardrails. One cautionary tale occurred at Samsung: employees reportedly fed sensitive source code into ChatGPT for coding help, only to inadvertently leak confidential data through the AI service. After the breach, the company moved to ban or strictly limit the use of external generative AI. This kind of "shadow AI" - employees using AI tools without oversight - is now recognized as a significant risk in many firms. Without guidelines, staff might input proprietary data into AI chatbots or use AI-generated outputs that haven't been security-tested, leading to compliance violations or hidden vulnerabilities.

To balance innovation with security, organizations are developing AI usage policies and controls as part of their security strategy. Effective frameworks often include (1) a policy-first approach, establishing clear acceptable-use rules for AI before widespread deployment; (2) approved AI tool lists, ensuring that employees use vetted tools that meet security, privacy, and contractual requirements; (3) data classification integration, ensuring AI usage aligns with data sensitivity; (4) access management, ensuring AI systems respect existing user permissions and do not expose data beyond what the user or workflow is authorized to access; and (5) monitoring, audit, and enforcement, including logs that show which AI tools were used, what data was accessed, what outputs were generated, and whether policy exceptions were approved. In more mature environments, AI agents and automation workflows should be treated like unique identities. They should have owners, scoped permissions, audit trails, lifecycle management, and revocation procedures, just like service accounts or privileged automation. Some organizations have formed internal AI governance committees that include security, privacy, legal, compliance, audit, CTO, CDO, technology operations, and business stakeholders. This structure helps ensure AI decisions are not made only as technology decisions but as enterprise risk, data, trust, and accountability decisions (see Figure 1-2).

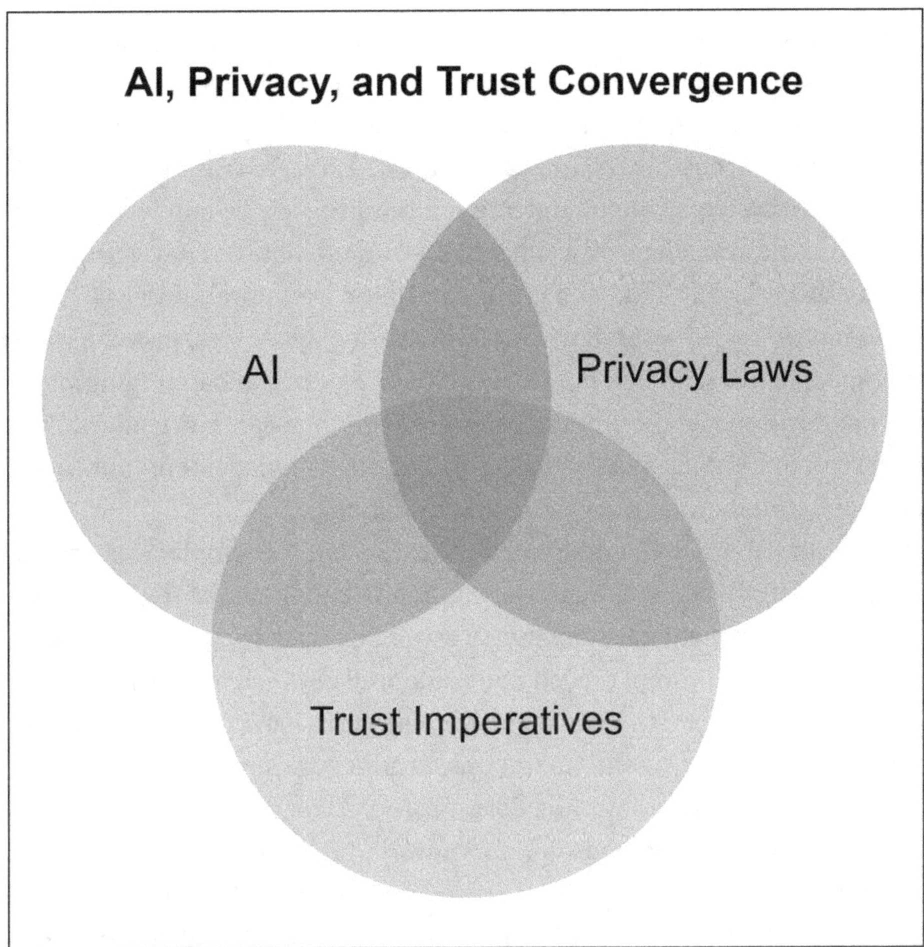

Figure 1-2. *AI, privacy, and trust convergence*

Note If your organization is rolling out generative AI or large-scale automation, establish internal guardrails before adoption spreads informally. AI policy maturity is becoming a core part of security, privacy, and technology governance.

Privacy Regulations Raising the Stakes

Concurrent with the AI revolution, a global wave of data privacy and AI governance regulation is expanding organizations' obligations to protect personal information and manage data responsibly. Privacy and security have always been closely related, since a failure in security often becomes a failure in privacy, but the relationship between the two has become even more interconnected. Security leaders must now ensure that their strategies support not only confidentiality, integrity, and availability but also privacy expectations, regulatory accountability, responsible AI use, and defensible data governance practices. This convergence is part of the broader concept of digital trust: the expectation from users, customers, regulators, and business partners that organizations will handle data, AI systems, and digital interactions ethically, securely, transparently, and responsibly. One challenge, especially in the United States, is navigating a patchwork of privacy laws. Unlike the European Union's comprehensive GDPR, the United States has no single federal privacy law covering all sectors. Instead, state privacy laws, sector-specific rules, breach notification requirements, and emerging state-level AI regulations create a complex compliance environment. For security leaders, this means privacy, AI governance, data governance, and cyber risk management must operate as one coordinated model rather than as separate programs.

Companies operating across multiple states face a complex compliance burden, needing to implement controls that meet the strictest common denominators. For instance, these laws often mandate reasonable security measures for personal data, consumer rights to access or delete data, and prompt breach notification, all of which require robust security practices to support. The state-by-state approach also poses liability risks – a security lapse could trigger enforcement or lawsuits in multiple jurisdictions simultaneously.

As a result, many organizations are elevating their data governance programs, cataloguing where personal data resides and how it's protected, as part of their security strategy. Strong encryption, fine-grained access controls, and data loss prevention technologies are being deployed not just to keep hackers out, but also to ensure compliance with privacy rules that require safeguarding personal information.

Globally, privacy and data protection regulations have continued to tighten. Countries in Asia, Latin America, and Africa are enacting GDPR-like laws, and Europe itself is expanding its regulatory regime with laws addressing specific technologies (e.g., the EU AI Act imposes phased requirements on AI systems to ensure transparency, safety, and absence of bias). In the context of AI, privacy and ethics regulations are converging: the EU AI Act classifies specific AI applications (such as biometric identification and deepfakes) as "high risk," requiring risk assessments and human oversight. As these rules apply in phases, companies must adjust how they deploy AI to remain compliant and trustworthy. Already, concerns about AI-generated synthetic media have drawn regulatory attention, for instance, disclosing deepfakes or securing consent for AI use of personal data are on the agenda.

Another aspect is cross-border data flows. Heightened privacy and national security sensitivities are driving data localization trends, which, in turn, are shaping how global businesses architect their systems. According to industry analysis, over 100 new data localization or sovereignty laws are now in place across 40 countries, fragmenting the once-borderless internet into a "splinternet" of regional networks with different rules. Companies are being forced to keep certain data within specific jurisdictions and implement region-specific cloud instances and security controls. This fragmentation complicates security operations, increases cost, and raises the bar for compliance. Threat intelligence, incident response, logging, cloud architecture, data retention, and legal review may all need to be adapted by region. Security teams must therefore ensure that data protection meets the most stringent applicable law in each locale while also keeping the operating model practical and affordable. As Kris Lovejoy of Kyndryl noted, this effectively turns the digital supply chain into a geopolitical battleground, and state actors are even weaponizing these differences (and using tactics such as AI-driven disinformation targeting populations) to gain an advantage. In practical terms, CISOs at multinational companies now need to be as versed in international privacy law and cyber diplomacy as they are in malware and firewalls.

All these developments mean that security strategies now must incorporate privacy by design. Encryption of data at rest and in transit is increasingly non-negotiable, not only to prevent breaches but to ensure that if data is stolen, it remains unreadable (a requirement under many privacy regulations to avoid liability). Identity and access management practices are being extended to enforce least privilege for personal data access, ensuring that only those with a legitimate business need (and proper training) can access sensitive personal information. Data retention policies are being tightened – keeping data only as long as necessary – to reduce risk exposure. Additionally, incident response plans invariably include privacy-specific steps, such as evaluating if personal data was affected and coordinating communications to users and regulators within legally mandated timelines. The integration of privacy considerations into security operations represents a significant shift from a decade ago, when these functions often operated in silo. Now, privacy and security officers are working hand in hand, and the concept of "digital trust" encapsulates their shared goal.

Building and Preserving Digital Trust

Digital trust is essentially the confidence stakeholders have in an organization's ability to maintain the security, privacy, and integrity of the digital services it provides. In an era of daily cyber incidents and growing public awareness of data misuse, earning and keeping this trust is a core strategic priority. A breach or violation of privacy can instantly shatter customer trust, leading to long-term business repercussions. Conversely, organizations known for robust security and ethical data practices can leverage this as a key selling point and differentiator.

Recently, discussions of digital trust reached new heights. For instance, PwC's annual global cybersecurity survey was tellingly rebranded as the "Global Digital Trust Insights" survey – underscoring that cybersecurity is no longer just about IT defense but about enabling a trustworthy digital society and business environment. Notably, this survey, one of the largest in the industry, draws input from thousands of senior business executives (not just technical security folks), showing that digital trust has become a cross-functional concern spanning leadership from the board, CEO, CIO, CISO, CTO, CDO, and beyond. Their latest findings highlighted a split in confidence: roughly half of organizations feel only "somewhat capable" at best of withstanding current cyberattacks, and a mere 6% feel fully confident across various areas of vulnerability. These sobering statistics, combined with high-profile attacks, have made transparency and honesty part of building trust. Stakeholders expect companies to acknowledge cyber risks and demonstrate preparedness, rather than assume they are invulnerable.

So, how do organizations bolster digital trust? Consistent execution of strong security and privacy practices is the foundation. This includes all the elements discussed earlier (secure-by-default design, rigorous risk management, compliance with standards). Companies that demonstrate adherence to frameworks and obtain certifications (such as ISO 27001 for security, ISO 27701 or similar for privacy, or SOC 2 reports) often find it easier to assure partners and customers. Another key element is transparency. There is growing demand for transparency into software components and the supply chain, which is why concepts like the Software Bill of Materials (SBOM) have gained traction. An SBOM is effectively a list of ingredients in software – by providing it, a software supplier increases trust that they know their components and have vetted them for vulnerabilities. Building on this idea, forward-looking experts are even discussing an "AI Bill of Materials (ABOM)" – a documented record of the data, models, and training process behind AI systems – to provide transparency into AI behavior for assurance and auditing. In late 2025, security leaders recommended measures to "help secure digital trust," including adopting deepfake-resistant authentication methods and instituting internal AI governance to protect AI systems from tampering. These steps are about proactively countering the ways new tech could undermine user trust (e.g., using liveness detection in biometric authentication to combat deepfake spoofing).

Digital trust also involves ethical considerations, transparency, and evolving user expectations. The responsible use of AI, including reducing bias, ensuring appropriate human oversight, protecting training data, and improving the explainability of AI-driven decisions, increasingly factors into whether users trust digital services and platforms. Organizations are therefore developing AI governance and ethics frameworks alongside traditional security controls, recognizing that security, privacy, and trust are now deeply interconnected. A company that provides clear privacy notices, transparent data practices, meaningful user control over personal information, and responsible AI governance will generally be viewed as more trustworthy than one that monetizes data or deploys AI systems in opaque or poorly governed ways. Public awareness of privacy, AI misuse, and digital manipulation has grown significantly. As a result, even a single incident involving hidden data-sharing practices, irresponsible AI behavior, or misleading use of customer data can trigger regulatory scrutiny, reputational damage, public backlash, and long-term erosion of customer trust and brand loyalty. Thus, from a strategy perspective, many CISOs are collaborating with Chief Data Officers, Chief Technology Officers, Chief Privacy Officers, legal teams, and risk leaders to ensure that data governance policies not only secure data but also enable its use in line with customer trust expectations. In some organizations, the CISO is also taking on a dual role or close operating partnership with privacy leadership, especially where AI governance, data protection, and regulatory response are tightly connected.

The Threat to Trust: Deepfakes and Misinformation

A stark example of an emerging threat to digital trust is the rise of AI-generated misinformation, deepfakes, and real-time impersonation. Convincing fake audio and video are no longer edge cases. They are becoming practical tools for fraud, influence operations, executive impersonation, and social engineering. The risk is not only that people will believe fake content. The risk is also that people may begin doubting authentic content, which weakens accountability and trust. Cybersecurity teams have a role in mitigating this threat through verified communication channels, liveness checks for sensitive workflows, phishing-resistant authentication, out-of-band confirmation for high-risk requests, and employee training that treats voice and video as potentially spoofable. The convergence of security and trust is evident here: a breach of trust through a deepfake can have direct financial, operational, and reputational consequences. Therefore, preserving digital trust means staying ahead of such tactics and maintaining user confidence that what they see and hear in digital channels is legitimate.

In summary, the convergence of AI, privacy, data governance, and digital trust demands a multidisciplinary approach to modern security. Security teams must not only defend against increasingly sophisticated AI-enhanced threats but also ensure that their own use of AI is governed, monitored, explainable, and aligned with legal and ethical expectations. At the same time, organizations must protect personal and sensitive data, comply with a growing landscape of privacy and AI-related regulations, and enable the business to use AI and data responsibly and competitively. This creates an ongoing balancing act between innovation, governance, operational speed, regulatory accountability, and customer trust. Overarching all of these priorities is the broader mandate to preserve digital trust: ensuring that customers, employees, partners, regulators, and the public have confidence that the organization handles data, AI systems, and digital interactions securely, transparently, and responsibly.

Looking ahead, regulatory pressure around AI governance, privacy, software assurance, and digital accountability is expected to increase, alongside the emergence of more mature tools and frameworks to help organizations manage these risks. Organizations that successfully align their AI strategy with security, privacy, resilience, and ethical governance practices will be better positioned to operate effectively in the emerging digital trust economy. In the next section, we turn to one of the most important architectural shifts underpinning this evolution: the transition from traditional network-perimeter-based defenses toward identity-first and context-aware security models, where identity increasingly serves as the primary control plane for enterprise security.

Identity-First Security: The New Perimeter

Perhaps the most profound shift in cybersecurity strategy over the past several years has been the transition from traditional network-perimeter-based security toward identity-centric and context-aware security models. In traditional enterprise environments, organizations focused primarily on defending the network perimeter through firewalls, VPNs, and network access controls, operating under the assumption that users and devices inside the corporate network could generally be trusted. That assumption no longer holds. Cloud computing, mobile work, SaaS adoption, third-party integrations, and distributed technology environments have significantly eroded the distinction between "inside" and "outside" networks. The perimeter now exists wherever an access decision is made. As a result, identity, including the verification of users, devices, applications, services, and their permissions, has become one of the central control points of modern security architecture. This section explores why identity-first security has become a dominant strategic model and how organizations are implementing context-aware, Zero Trust-aligned approaches to better protect themselves in an increasingly distributed and perimeter-less environment.

The Dissolution of the Network Perimeter

The legacy perimeter-centric model assumed a defined boundary - typically the corporate LAN and data center - that could be defended. That model has unraveled. Workforces are now highly distributed: employees regularly access company resources from home or on the go, using a mix of corporate and personal devices. Applications have moved to the cloud (SaaS, IaaS) and are accessed over the public internet. Business data is spread across on-prem systems, multiple clouds, and third-party services. In this environment, the old paradigm of focusing defenses on the office network or VPN is insufficient. As one industry CISO put it, "The traditional network perimeter has dissolved, and identity has become the constant in security architecture..." Organizations that have not pivoted toward identity-centric security models are significantly more vulnerable to modern attacks that exploit credentials, sessions, tokens, and trusted access paths rather than traditional network boundaries. This perspective reflects a broader industry consensus that identity has become one of the primary control planes of modern security architecture. No matter where a user, device, application, or workload is located, verifying who or what is requesting access, validating context and trust signals, and enforcing appropriate authorization controls are now among the most critical layers of enterprise defense.

Research and industry forecasts reinforce this shift. Gartner projected that a large majority of enterprises would move away from traditional VPN-centric access models toward Zero Trust Network Access (ZTNA) architectures, which prioritize identity, device posture, and contextual access decisions rather than implicit network trust. This transition is now becoming a standard architectural direction across many enterprise environments. Indeed, many organizations accelerated in this direction during the pandemic and haven't looked back. Instead of implicitly trusting a device because it's connected via VPN or inside a campus, Zero Trust models require continuous authentication and authorization for each session and movement. Every user or system must prove its identity (and sometimes device health) each time it tries to connect to a resource, regardless of network location. This "never trust, always verify" philosophy marks a fundamental change in mentality.

Why Identity Is Paramount: Threat Reality

The emphasis on identity-first security is not simply theoretical; it is driven by the reality of how modern attacks occur. A growing percentage of security incidents now involve attackers exploiting stolen credentials, session tokens, privileged accounts, API keys, or weaknesses in identity and authentication systems rather than directly breaching traditional network boundaries through complex exploits alone. Industry threat reporting consistently highlighted a fundamental shift in attacker behavior: initial access increasingly depends on compromising identities, abusing trust relationships, and leveraging legitimate authentication workflows. Techniques such as phishing, credential stuffing, MFA fatigue attacks, session hijacking, token theft, adversary-in-the-middle phishing proxies, and abuse of federated identity systems have become highly effective because they often provide attackers with legitimate-looking access while bypassing many traditional perimeter defenses.

From an attacker's perspective, compromising identity is frequently faster, cheaper, and operationally safer than developing or purchasing sophisticated zero-day exploits. Instead of attempting to break through hardened infrastructure directly, attackers increasingly focus on manipulating users, stealing credentials, abusing authentication flows, or hijacking trusted sessions that already possess authorized access. This shift has fundamentally changed how organizations must think about defense. Security architecture can no longer rely primarily on network location or implicit trust. It must continuously validate identity, context, device trust, behavior, and authorization at every stage of access.

High-profile attack trends illustrate this. Ransomware crews, for instance, have increasingly relied on stolen credentials to deploy malware - either by purchasing passwords on the dark web or through phishing - rather than using self-propagating worms. Business Email Compromise (BEC), a form of fraud where threat actors steal money by impersonating business contacts via email, almost always begins with a compromised email account password; BEC has cost organizations billions and continues to accelerate. Even nation-state hackers often start by harvesting credentials (through spear-phishing or malware) and then pivot across systems under the guise of legitimate users. The prevalence of Cybercrime-as-a-Service offerings has supercharged this trend – today, anyone can rent a phishing kit or an info-stealer malware that automates credential theft at scale. For example, "phishing-as-a-service" platforms now intercept multifactor authentication tokens in real time by inserting themselves between the user and the actual login page (an adversary-in-the-middle attack), enabling them to defeat basic two-factor SMS or OTP codes. Likewise, advanced malware such as information stealers has evolved not only to keylog passwords but also to lift entire password manager databases, browser-stored logins, and VPN configuration files, a treasure trove of identity data for attackers. The economics favor the attackers: stealing one set of valid credentials can be a one-click path inside a network, so the "return on investment for identity-based attacks far exceeds traditional malware operations". This creates a strong incentive for adversaries to continue focusing on identities.

The implication for defenders is stark: traditional perimeter defenses (firewalls, network monitoring) cannot stop an attacker who has valid credentials. If an attacker logs in as "Alice" using Alice's correct username and password (and perhaps her 2FA code, if intercepted), the network will see that as an authorized session. This is why older security architectures are now viewed as fundamentally insufficient – they often lack the internal controls to detect malicious use of valid credentials. Thus, the best way to combat these threats is to focus protection on identities themselves: harden the authentication process, limit what each identity can do, and monitor identity usage for anomalies.

Zero Trust and Continuous Verification

The practical blueprint for identity-first security in most organizations is the adoption of Zero Trust architecture (ZTA) principles. Zero Trust, as noted, is about not trusting any request by default, even if it comes from inside the network or from a known user – verification is required at every step. Implementing Zero Trust typically involves several key components:

- **Strong Authentication and Access Controls:** This starts with ensuring every user (human or machine) is strongly authenticated via multiple factors, not just a password. It also means incorporating contextual authentication – verifying not only who is logging in but also from where, on what device, at what time, and other relevant factors. Modern identity platforms use risk-based authentication that can step up requirements if something seems off (e.g., unusual location or time). As one industry blog put it, authentication is no longer a one-time event at login, but an ongoing process of continuous verification throughout a session. Technologies such as single sign-on with continuous session monitoring, identity federation with token-based access, and conditional access policies are all integral components of this puzzle.
- **Least Privilege and Adaptive Authorization:** In an identity-first model, users (and applications) are only granted the minimum access rights they need – the principle of least privilege. Fine-grained authorization policies ensure that even if an identity is compromised, the attacker can't leap to the crown jewels easily. Moreover, authorization can be adaptive: for instance, if a user's behavior deviates from the norm, the system might require re-authentication or limit their access until verified. Leading implementations will "monitor user behavior continuously" and adjust access in real time based on risk. This minimizes the blast radius of any single identity breach.
- **Micro-segmentation and Device Trust:** Zero Trust often employs micro-segmentation, effectively creating "micro-perimeters" around individual resources or small resource groups. Instead of a flat internal network where any logged-in user can reach any system, each application or service might have its own access gate. Identity, combined with device posture (is the device healthy, patched, corporate-managed, or BYOD?), dictates whether that gate opens. This way, even if an attacker compromises on one account or machine, they cannot easily pivot to others. Segmentation goes hand in hand with identity-based policies to isolate assets and limit lateral movement.

- **Assume Breach Mentality:** Zero Trust encourages an "assume breach" mindset - designing systems under the assumption that an attacker might already be in or will get in and therefore building controls to mitigate that eventuality (see Figure 1-3). From an identity perspective, this means, for example, assuming some credentials could be stolen and thus heavily monitoring for abnormal usage, as well as having rapid containment processes if suspicious activity is detected on an account.

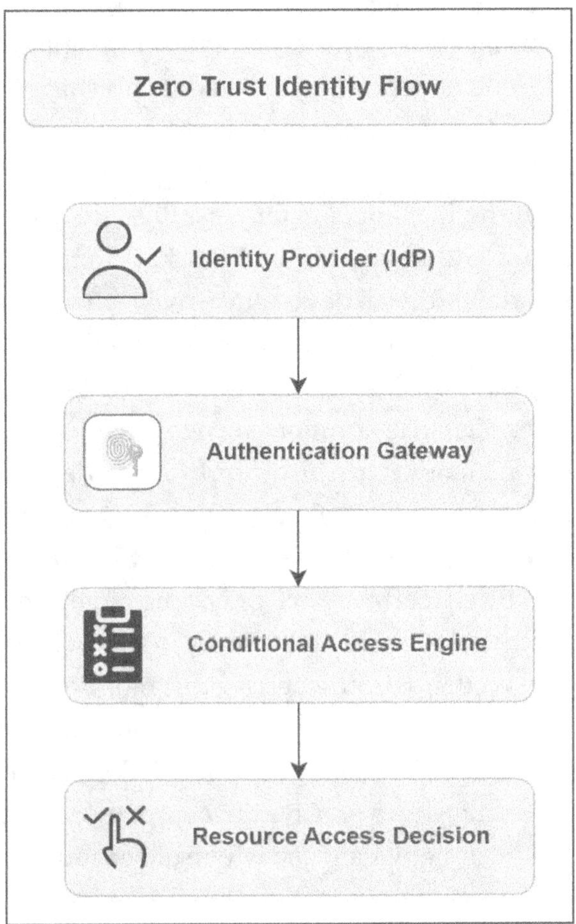

Figure 1-3. *Zero Trust identity flow*

These elements require a robust identity and access management infrastructure. Many organizations are investing heavily in modern cloud-based identity and access management platforms that support capabilities such as federated single sign-on, conditional access policies, privileged access controls, passwordless authentication, integration with device management platforms, and AI-assisted threat and anomaly detection. These platforms increasingly serve as central policy enforcement and visibility layers across cloud services, SaaS applications, hybrid environments, and distributed workforces. The good news is that these technologies are maturing: passwordless authentication (such as FIDO2-compliant security keys or platform biometrics like Windows Hello and Apple Face ID) is increasingly viable at scale, eliminating the weakest link (passwords).

MFA adoption is at an all-time high, but the type of MFA matters. Basic SMS codes, voice calls, and some push-based approaches remain vulnerable to SIM swapping, social engineering, MFA fatigue, and adversary-in-the-middle phishing proxies. This is why the industry is moving toward phishing-resistant authentication, including FIDO2 security keys, WebAuthn, and passkeys. NIST's digital identity guidance states that out-of-band authentication and OTP authentication are not phishing-resistant, while FIDO standards use public key cryptography and domain-bound passkeys to reduce phishing risk. For high-risk users, administrators, service desks, and privileged workflows, organizations should prioritize phishing-resistant methods over legacy MFA wherever feasible. In fact, as of now, government agencies and some regulated industries are mandating phishing-resistant authentication for high-risk accounts, recognizing that basic mobile app 2FA codes may no longer be sufficient against advanced adversaries.

Beyond user authentication, identity-first security also encompasses privileged access management (PAM) and identity governance. Privileged accounts (administrators and service accounts with broad permissions) are prime targets for attackers, so controlling and monitoring their use is critical. Many organizations have adopted PAM solutions that store admin credentials in secure vaults, require just-in-time elevation of privileges (admin access is granted only for a limited time and for a specific task), and log all actions taken with those accounts. Similarly, identity governance processes ensure that when people change roles or leave the company, their access is promptly adjusted or revoked – closing a significant gap where old accounts or excessive privileges linger unaddressed.

Recently, automation was helping here: for example, some companies achieved near-instantaneous deprovisioning of access when an employee exits, whereas previously 28% of organizations took over a week to entirely remove a former employee's access (a risky delay that attackers could exploit). Regular access reviews and certifications, often mandated by compliance, are now considered a security best practice to detect privilege creep or orphaned accounts.

Handling the Wider Identity Ecosystem: Devices, Apps, and Third Parties

A comprehensive identity-first approach extends beyond just enterprise workforce user accounts. It also addresses machine identities (such as service accounts, API keys, and certificates) and the identities of partners or customers who connect to your systems. Of late, machine-to-machine authentication and authorization will be a significant challenge – cloud services spin up ephemeral instances, containers communicate via APIs, and all of it needs to be secured. Often, there are far more machine identities than human ones, and they're less visible. As Gartner noted, a significant portion of breaches now involve non-human accounts that lack proper oversight. Thus, companies are inventorying and managing these identities, rotating credentials, and embedding authentication in application pipelines. The rise of cloud-native architectures has brought tooling for them (e.g., secrets management services, certificate management), but many organizations are still catching up.

Third-party access is another extension of the identity-first mindset. Vendors, suppliers, and contractors – these external users often require access to internal systems but fall outside the normal HR IAM processes. They can introduce vulnerabilities if not managed well (consider a contractor's account that remains active after their contract ends or an MSP whose own network is breached and then used to access clients). The year 2025 unfortunately saw numerous incidents in which third-party breaches led to significant compromises (e.g., an IT service provider being hacked, with attackers using its privileged client connections). No wonder, then, that third-party identity management has gained urgency. Solutions include requiring multifactor authentication and stringent vetting for third-party accounts, setting up dedicated identity federations or portals for external users (to isolate and monitor their access), and implementing more granular controls, such as just-in-time access with automatic expiration for contractors. Some organizations have even begun to insist on specific security measures in contracts (e.g., that partners use hardware tokens or participate in joint incident response drills). The underlying principle is extending Zero Trust to everyone, not just internal employees.

Detection and Response with an Identity Lens

Embracing identity-first security also changes how organizations detect and respond to threats. Traditional SOC monitoring, which focuses on network traffic and endpoint logs, may overlook subtle identity abuses. Now, user and entity behavior analytics (UEBA) and identity-focused monitoring are key tools. These systems establish a baseline of normal behavior for each user or service account (e.g., typical login times, usual devices and locations, normal resource usage patterns) and then raise alerts on deviations that could indicate account compromise. For instance, if an employee who usually logs in from Texas at 9 AM suddenly logs in from Europe at 3 AM and attempts to download large amounts of data from a finance system, an identity analytics system will flag it immediately for investigation. Continuous authentication ties into this as well - some advanced implementations will automatically challenge or terminate sessions that exhibit anomalous behavior.

In fact, a new category, Identity Threat Detection and Response (ITDR), has emerged, reflecting the need to tackle identity-centric attacks specifically. ITDR tools can detect various types of attacks, including Golden Ticket (forged Kerberos tickets in Active Directory), unusual spikes in failed logins (indicating credential stuffing in progress), and signs of directory reconnaissance by an attacker with limited access. Many organizations are augmenting their SIEM (Security Information and Event Management) platforms with identity-focused telemetry from sources such as identity providers, SSO platforms, MFA events, endpoint identity signals, privileged access systems, cloud audit logs, and dark web monitoring for leaked credentials. The goal is to improve visibility into credential abuse, session hijacking, privilege escalation, and anomalous authentication behavior before attackers can establish deeper persistence or lateral movement. The goal is to detect identity misuse at an early stage, ideally before the attacker uses the account to escalate privileges or deploy malware. Given that 90% of ransomware cases that progressed to deployment started with an unmanaged or compromised device (often tied to stolen credentials), the sooner an account takeover is detected, the more damage can be prevented.

Benefits and Challenges of Identity-First Models

The transition to identity-first security is a journey, with both significant benefits and challenges. On the benefits side, organizations that have implemented strong identity-centric controls have been far more resilient during events such as the mass shift to remote work. Since access was tied to user identity and device posture rather than physical network, employees could work from anywhere without weakening security – in essence, the security model travels with the user. Identity-first security also often improves the user experience when done right: implementing single sign-on and consistent authentication across all apps can reduce user friction (fewer passwords to remember, fewer logins per day) even as security is tightened. Furthermore, regulatory compliance is aided by many regulations (from PCI to HIPAA to SOX) that require controls on who can access sensitive data. A robust identity management program provides the audit trail and control needed to satisfy these requirements. It also contributes to digital trust, as discussed, by assuring stakeholders that the organization knows exactly who is accessing systems and can enforce accountability.

However, challenges remain. Implementing Zero Trust and identity-first principles is not just about new software; it often requires reengineering legacy systems and breaking down silos. Integrating multiple identity stores (Active Directory, cloud directories, customer IAM, etc.) to achieve a unified view of identity poses a significant technical challenge. There's also user education – users might resist changes like additional authentication steps or new login procedures unless change management is handled well. Additionally, some advanced attacks can still evade identity-based controls. For example, suppose an attacker manages to infect an endpoint and piggyback on an authenticated user's session (session hijacking). In that case, they might "live off the land" and perform malicious actions without triggering an authentication event. This means identity-first must be complemented by device security and monitoring; it's necessary but not entirely sufficient on its own.

Looking ahead, the identity-first security trend is expected to continue strengthening as organizations expand Zero Trust and context-aware security architectures across increasingly distributed technology environments. The idea that identity serves as one of the primary control planes of enterprise security is evolving from a conceptual model into a practical architectural standard. Organizations are accelerating the adoption of phishing-resistant authentication, passkeys, FIDO2-based authentication, continuous access evaluation, and adaptive authorization models to reduce reliance on traditional passwords and static trust assumptions.

At the same time, many enterprises are modernizing identity infrastructure to support cloud-native operations, hybrid workforces, SaaS integration, machine identities, and AI-driven risk analysis. This includes investment in centralized identity platforms, stronger privileged access management, lifecycle governance, device trust validation, and real-time behavioral analytics that can identify anomalous authentication patterns before attackers establish persistence or lateral movement. Identity proofing and transaction-level verification are also becoming more important in digital business environments where fraud prevention, regulatory accountability, and digital trust increasingly depend on confidence in who or what is interacting with enterprise systems.

In summary, the shift from traditional perimeter-oriented security toward identity-centric and context-aware security represents one of the most important architectural changes in modern cybersecurity. It aligns security with the realities of cloud computing, SaaS adoption, mobile workforces, third-party integrations, and distributed digital ecosystems while directly addressing the techniques most commonly used by modern attackers. Organizations that have embraced identity-first security are often more agile, better positioned to support modern work patterns, and more resilient against credential-driven attacks and privilege abuse. At the same time, this model requires disciplined governance, including continuous authentication and authorization, strong identity lifecycle management, privileged access controls, telemetry-driven monitoring, and rapid response capabilities. These capabilities are increasingly becoming defining characteristics of mature security programs and are likely to remain foundational elements of enterprise security architecture for the remainder of the decade.

Note Among the many cybersecurity investments organizations are making, identity and access modernization consistently delivers some of the fastest and most practical reductions in enterprise risk. It may not always be the most visible or exciting initiative, but it directly addresses many of the attack paths most commonly used by modern adversaries, including credential theft, session hijacking, privilege abuse, and unauthorized access.

Conclusion: Strategic Security for the Modern Threat Landscape

The evolving practices discussed in this chapter, including the shift beyond product-centric thinking, the convergence of cybersecurity with AI, privacy, and digital trust considerations, and the adoption of identity-first security models, all point toward a more mature and resilient approach to information security. Leading organizations increasingly recognize that effective cybersecurity cannot be achieved through a single tool, isolated initiative, or one-time transformation effort. Instead, it requires an integrated strategy that aligns technology, governance, architecture, operations, processes, and people around the shared objective of protecting critical assets, maintaining operational resilience, and preserving stakeholder trust. Looking ahead, this holistic and forward-looking approach will become even more important as organizations continue adapting to rapidly evolving technologies, regulatory expectations, and increasingly sophisticated threat environments.

Several key themes are expected to shape information security in the coming year:

- **Security As an Enabler of Digital Transformation:** Organizations will increasingly treat cybersecurity as an integral part of digital innovation, not a blocker. As businesses pursue new digital products, AI-driven services, and cloud initiatives, security architects will be involved from the design phase to ensure new endeavors are "secure by design" and compliant with privacy expectations. This vendor-neutral, architecture-first approach will help enterprises avoid costly rework or breaches down the line and allow them to innovate with confidence. In the words of one global CISO, the aim is to "move forward – securely and responsibly… It's not about blocking progress; it's about partnering with the business to make informed, risk-aware decisions." This mindset will likely distinguish the winners in the digital economy of 2026 – those who can maintain speed and agility while managing cyber risk.
- **Enhanced Governance and Regulation:** We anticipate a tighter governance environment for cybersecurity and data. Regulatory bodies across the world are poised to introduce or enforce rules on AI system accountability (e.g., requiring algorithmic transparency and risk assessments for AI that impacts consumers), on critical infrastructure security baselines, and on software supply chain security. For example, the EU AI Act entered into force in 2024 and applies in phases, with organizations needing to monitor current implementation guidance as timelines and simplification measures evolve. Governments are also focusing on software supply chain risks, with initiatives to mandate SBOMs or hold vendors liable for insecure software on the horizon. Meanwhile, existing regulations

like GDPR, various US state privacy laws, and industry-specific cyber rules will continue to evolve and be enforced with increasing rigor. By necessity, CISOs and compliance officers must work closely together, and cybersecurity programs must be flexible enough to adapt to new legal requirements. The good news is that many of the practices highlighted in this chapter (e.g., Zero Trust, strong identity controls, data governance, incident response preparedness) serve both security and compliance goals - they put organizations in a strong position to meet new regulations when they arrive.

- **Emerging Technologies and Threats:** The technology landscape will continue to evolve, bringing new benefits and new risks. We will see broader adoption of technologies such as extended reality, 5G and early 6G planning, Internet of Things, industrial IoT, and operational technology environments. Each of these introduces unique security considerations, such as securing large device fleets, protecting safety-critical OT systems, validating firmware and supply chains, and ensuring that network slicing or segmentation does not create hidden trust gaps.

  Perhaps most prominently, quantum computing is looming on the horizon as a potential disruptor to current cryptography. While practical quantum attacks are not expected for some years, enterprises, especially in sectors such as finance and government, are now preparing by inventorying their cryptographic assets and exploring post-quantum encryption algorithms. Fewer than 10% of organizations currently prioritize quantum risks in their budgets, and only 3% report having implemented leading quantum-safe measures, but awareness is rising. Organizations are expected to take more concrete steps toward post-quantum readiness, including pilot migrations to quantum-resistant algorithms for VPNs, PKI, secure communications, identity infrastructure, and cryptographic key management systems. Early efforts will likely focus on cryptographic inventory, crypto-agility planning, hybrid cryptographic deployments, and testing interoperability between classical and post-quantum systems before broader enterprise adoption. On the threat side, we expect a continued rise in AI-enhanced attacks, along with the potential emergence of more autonomous malware that utilizes AI for decision-making. Deepfakes and disinformation attacks will likely become more common in criminal schemes and not just nation-state operations. Ransomware may evolve techniques to bypass identity protections, or attackers may increasingly combine extortion with data-integrity attacks (threatening to alter data rather than steal it). Security teams must remain agile, leveraging threat intelligence and advanced analytics to stay competitive.

- **Collaboration and Shared Defense:** As threats grow more complex and cross organizational boundaries, collaboration in cybersecurity will be ever more critical. We foresee greater information sharing between companies within industries (perhaps via industry-specific ISACs, Information Sharing and Analysis Centers) and public–private partnerships with government agencies on threat intelligence and incident response. In the last few years, it also became clear that public–private collaboration cannot be assumed to remain stable. Federal cybersecurity programs, grant funding, and information-sharing models can change with policy and budget priorities. This creates a practical challenge for state, local, tribal, and territorial organizations, many of which operate critical services but may not have the funding, staffing, or specialized expertise to replace federal support quickly. As a result, large enterprises and public-sector partners should plan for a more distributed model of shared defense that includes industry ISACs, state-level coordination, regional partnerships, vendor-supported threat intelligence, and mutual aid arrangements. Joint exercises, intelligence feeds, and collaborative frameworks still remain important, but organizations should avoid depending on a single coordination channel or funding source. Such collaboration also extends internally: the security function will collaborate more with IT, DevOps, data analytics, legal, and executive teams to build a cohesive defense and response capability. A siloed approach is too slow and brittle in the face of fast-moving threats and regulatory pressures.

In closing, rethinking information security means accepting that change is the only constant. The strategies that protected us yesterday must be continually revised in light of new developments. However, the trajectory is clear. We are moving toward security architectures that are intelligent, adaptive, and ubiquitous - from identity-aware networks to AI-assisted analysis - and toward governance models that integrate security deeply into how organizations operate and innovate. The convergence of security with digital trust imperatives means that the absence of breaches will not only measure success but also indicate confidence among users and customers in an organization's digital dealings.

For business and security leaders reading this chapter, the key takeaways are clear: invest in the fundamentals and execute them consistently, since they remain the strongest defense against many modern attacks; adopt a proactive and strategic mindset rather than waiting for incidents to force change; embrace technologies such as AI thoughtfully and with appropriate governance; and make identity, resilience, and digital trust foundational elements of the security program. Organizations that align security strategy with business objectives, operational resilience, privacy expectations, and modern architectural principles will be better positioned not only to defend against evolving threats but also to innovate and grow with greater confidence in an increasingly digital and interconnected world.

CHAPTER 2

Identity Is the New Perimeter

The enterprise security perimeter has fundamentally shifted. In the past, organizations relied on hardened network boundaries – firewalls, demilitarized zones (DMZs), and VPN gateways – to separate "trusted" internal resources from the outside world. Today, that static perimeter has dissolved. Cloud computing, software-as-a-service (SaaS), mobile devices, and remote work mean users and data are no longer confined to corporate networks. Attackers have taken note: rather than trying to bypass firewalls, they increasingly target the digital identities of users, administrators, and applications, knowing that a stolen credential can unlock the same data a firewall once protected. In this context, identity, not the network edge, has become the new security frontier. Every user login, API call, or device authentication is a potential gateway. Modern security architecture, therefore, centers on Identity and Access Management (IAM) as the primary control plane.

This chapter is a comprehensive guide for security architects to implement identity-first security strategies and Zero Trust models across hybrid and multi-cloud environments. We will cover the evolution of identity technologies (federation, single sign-on, multi-factor authentication), the role of conditional access and context-aware policies, and best practices for leveraging identity platforms to reduce the attack surface. Architecture diagrams and configuration snippets (JSON policies, code examples) illustrate how to enforce "never trust, always verify" at every layer. Both human and non-human identities are addressed, since non-person entities, from service accounts and API credentials to AI agents and autonomous workflows, now outnumber user identities in many organizations. By the end of this chapter, you will understand why "identity is the new perimeter" and how to design an IAM-centric security architecture that protects critical assets in a perimeter-less world.

A. Gupta and S. Mittal, *Foundations of Modern Information Security*,
https://doi.org/10.1007/979-8-8688-2558-3_2

From Network Borders to Identity Boundaries

For decades, cybersecurity was built around a network perimeter. Enterprises assumed that threats lived "outside" and that insiders could be implicitly trusted. Security teams focused on fortifying the boundary between the internal network and the internet, deploying firewalls to block unwanted traffic, using network segmentation to create internal zones, and funneling remote users through VPNs for authenticated access. This perimeter-centric model began eroding with the rise of cloud and mobile computing. Employees needed access to SaaS applications from anywhere, not just the office LAN. Partners and contractors required selective access to internal resources. Corporate data moved to public cloud platforms. The COVID-19 pandemic then accelerated remote work at an unprecedented scale, making "working from the internet" the norm rather than the exception. In this new reality, an employee logging in from a home Wi-Fi or a café network is effectively "outside" the old perimeter, yet must be treated as a legitimate inside user. Likewise, cloud-hosted applications are outside traditional network boundaries. As a result, the neat inside-vs.-outside security model has collapsed, and the perimeter is everywhere and nowhere.

Identity as the new security perimeter has emerged to address this paradigm shift. Instead of assuming trust based on network location, organizations now center trust on authenticated identity: who (or what) you are and the context in which you're requesting access. A user's identity, confirmed via proper credentials and multiple factors, becomes the gatekeeper to data and services. If the user's identity cannot be verified or is deemed risky, access is denied - regardless of whether that user is on the corporate network or the open internet. This approach acknowledges that threats can come from any network, including "inside" ones, so each access attempt must be validated anew. As one security expert succinctly put it, *"Identity is now the new security perimeter, and it's crumbling [the old models]."* In practice, this means robust identity and access management is not optional - it is absolutely vital to defend modern enterprises.

Cybercriminals understand this too: stolen passwords, phishing attacks, and abuse of privileged accounts are rampant because identity is the key to the kingdom. Verizon's data breach investigations and others have consistently found that the majority of breaches involve compromised credentials or identity-based attacks. In high-profile incidents such as the SolarWinds and Colonial Pipeline breaches, attackers leveraged valid accounts or software tokens to gain access to systems. The lesson is clear: if an attacker gets hold of an authorized identity - whether an employee's Microsoft 365 login or a cloud API key - they can walk through your front door unchallenged, unless you have additional identity-focused controls in place.

Transitioning to an identity-centric security model requires changes in technology and mindset. Culturally, organizations must stop trusting an access request just because it originates from "inside." Every request should be treated as if it came from an untrusted network. Technically, this demands stronger authentication methods, continuous monitoring of identity signals, and more granular authorization. In the following sections, we'll explore how identity and access management (IAM) technologies have evolved to meet this challenge, from the advent of single sign-on and federation that unified identity across boundaries to multi-factor authentication that strengthens logins and now to adaptive, context-aware policies that evaluate risk at runtime. We'll then dive into implementing a Zero Trust architecture where identity is the core of security decision-making. But first, let's review how we arrived here by examining the evolution of IAM capabilities.

Evolution of Federation, SSO, and MFA

Modern identity-centric security builds on decades of innovation in authentication and authorization. Key milestones in this evolution include the rise of federation and single sign-on (SSO) to connect identity across domains and multi-factor authentication (MFA) to harden account security. Understanding this history will inform why today's IAM strategies look the way they do.

From Directories to Federation: A Brief History of SSO

In the early days of enterprise IT, identity was siloed. Each application kept its own user database and required a separate login. System administrators had to manually create accounts on each system for each user, and users had to manage multiple passwords. This was inefficient and insecure (users would reuse weak passwords) and gave admins no central way to disable or monitor access. Directory services emerged in the 1990s as a solution. Technologies such as LDAP (Lightweight Directory Access Protocol) and Microsoft Active Directory provided centralized identity stores that applications could query. Active Directory (AD), introduced in 2000, became ubiquitous in enterprises for managing Windows domain identities and credentials. Within an AD-managed network, a user could log in to their domain account and gain access to resources without repeated prompts, an early form of single sign-on, albeit limited to the Windows/AD environment.

For web and enterprise applications outside the core AD domain, early SSO was often implemented using Web Access Management (WAM) products. These acted as reverse proxies: a user would authenticate to the WAM proxy (usually backed by LDAP/AD), and the proxy would then inject an authentication token (like a session cookie or HTTP header) for downstream apps. While this provided a better user experience (one login for multiple apps), it was a patchwork solution that had to be custom integrated with each application and didn't scale well beyond a single organization's domain. There was no standard, interoperable way for an identity in one system to be trusted by another. That changed in the mid-2000s with the advent of federated identity standards.

The watershed moment was the development of SAML (Security Assertion Markup Language) 2.0, an XML-based standard ratified in 2005. SAML 2.0 enabled a "circle of trust" in which an identity provider (IdP) could authenticate a user and issue an assertion that other services (service providers) would accept. In practical terms, SAML allowed a user to log in once to an IdP (e.g., a company's corporate login page) and then use SSO to access multiple external applications (such as Salesforce or Workday) without re-entering credentials. The IdP's digitally signed SAML token, containing the user's identity info and attributes, was enough to establish trust. Competing standards and protocols emerged around the same time (WS-Federation from Microsoft, Liberty ID-FF, etc.), but SAML 2.0 became the dominant federation standard across industries. By the 2010s, federation and SSO were widely adopted, enabling partnerships and cloud adoption. For example, an enterprise could federate its on-premises Active Directory with Azure or AWS, allowing corporate users to log in to cloud services using their AD credentials. This was a huge step in breaking down identity silos – instead of separate accounts everywhere, a single corporate identity could access many systems.

SSO and federation significantly improved both security and usability. Users had fewer passwords to remember (and misuse), and account lifecycle events (like termination) could be handled centrally – disabling a user in the IdP would cut off access to all federated apps. However, as cloud and mobile grew, new protocols arose to address web API and mobile app use cases where SAML was cumbersome. OAuth 2.0, introduced around 2012, provided a token-based authorization framework, and OpenID Connect (OIDC) (2014) layered on top of authentication to OAuth, using JSON Web Tokens (JWTs) instead of XML. These modern protocols made it easier to implement SSO for user-facing mobile apps and to delegate limited authorization (e.g., an app getting permission to access a Google resource on a user's behalf). Today's IAM solutions typically support multiple protocols - SAML, OIDC/OAuth - to integrate with both older enterprise apps and new cloud-native apps.

Despite all these advances in SSO, one thing remained a single point of failure: the password. A federated SSO system still ultimately relied on the user's primary credentials (username/password, or a Kerberos ticket in AD, etc.) to be secure. Unfortunately, passwords are easily phished, guessed, or stolen. Thus, the next evolution was to secure authentication itself with multiple factors.

The Rise of Multi-factor Authentication (MFA)

It became evident that "SSO is great - until someone's password is stolen." If one password unlocks everything, that password better be strongly protected. Multi-factor authentication adds additional verification steps so that possession of the password alone is not enough to impersonate the user. Early forms of MFA date back decades (e.g., hardware one-time passcode tokens like RSA SecurID existed in the 1990s), but widespread adoption came much later. In the 2010s, as phishing and credential-stuffing attacks soared, companies began rolling out MFA more widely. Initially, this meant sending OTP codes via SMS or email or using mobile authenticator apps to generate codes. While these methods added some security, they came with user experience trade-offs and remained vulnerable to sophisticated phishing attacks (attackers could trick users into revealing their OTP codes).

The latest generation of strong authentication focuses on phishing-resistant techniques. Standards-based approaches such as FIDO2, WebAuthn, and passkeys use public key cryptography and domain-bound credentials instead of shared secrets, making them far harder to phish than passwords, SMS codes, or OTP-based methods. Push-based authentication can still be useful when strengthened with number matching, risk signals, and prompt limits, but it should not be treated as equivalent to phishing-resistant authentication for high-risk access. Notably, governments and industry bodies (such as CISA and NIST) have begun explicitly recommending phishing-resistant MFA for high-value accounts, due to the rise of "MFA fatigue" and OTP interception attacks. Leading identity providers have incorporated these technologies; for instance, Entra ID and Okta support FIDO2 security keys and certificate-based authentication as MFA options that are harder to phish than SMS codes.

Adoption of MFA has shifted from a nice-to-have control to a mandatory baseline. Industry research continues to show that credential compromise remains one of the most common paths into enterprise environments, yet many organizations historically required MFA only for exceptional cases, such as administrators or remote access. That model is no longer sufficient. The current direction is MFA everywhere, applied consistently across users, applications, privileged workflows, and high-risk access paths. Modern IAM solutions increasingly treat MFA, device posture, risk scoring, and session controls as core identity capabilities rather than optional add-ons. The strongest programs are also moving beyond basic SMS or OTP-based MFA toward phishing-resistant methods such as FIDO2, WebAuthn, platform authenticators, passkeys, and certificate-based authentication for high-risk users and administrators.

Furthermore, identity systems have evolved to support adaptive authentication, changing MFA requirements or authentication methods based on context. This is where conditional access comes in (covered in depth in the next section). At a simple level, adaptive policies may say “do not prompt for MFA if the user is on the corporate network with a managed device, but do prompt if they are remote or on an unknown device.” More advanced implementations incorporate risk scores and behavior analytics: e.g., a user logging in from a new country or exhibiting atypical behavior might get challenged for extra verification or even blocked, whereas a low-risk login might sail through seamlessly. This adaptive approach improves both security and usability by treating each authentication differently. In essence, the system can “step up” authentication when risk is higher.

MFA is not just for human users. When we discuss non-human identities later, we will see analogous mechanisms, such as short-lived tokens, certificates, workload identity federation, and managed identities, serve as layered verification for services and automation. The goal is to ensure that a single stolen API key or service credential is not enough to abuse a workload. The key concept is layered verification. A password alone is one layer; adding a second factor, such as a device check or biometric, is a second layer; verifying device health or user behavior adds yet more layers. The goal is to dramatically reduce the odds that an attacker can present all the required factors to impersonate someone.

In summary, the progression from directory services to federation and SSO to universal MFA has laid the groundwork for identity-first security. We went from isolated accounts to unified identity and from single-factor trust to multiple proof points. But managing identities and policies across a hybrid, multi-cloud enterprise is complex. This is where the concept of Zero Trust comes in – providing an overarching security model to enforce all these checks for every access request systematically. As we move forward, keep in mind these evolutions: they illustrate why simply having SSO or MFA alone is not enough – we must integrate them into a larger strategy that continuously verifies identity and context.

Zero Trust Fundamentals: Identity As the Core

"Never trust, always verify" captures the essence of Zero Trust security. Zero Trust is not a single product or technology, but an architecture and mindset that assumes no implicit trust in any request, whether it comes from inside your network, from a trusted user, or a managed device. Every access request must be verified *in real time* with strict authentication and authorization and allowed only to the minimal resources required (principle of least privilege). The Zero Trust model emerged from recognizing that traditional network perimeter defenses are insufficient to address today's threats and IT environments. Pioneered by John Kindervag around 2010 and later popularized by Google's BeyondCorp implementation (circa 2014), Zero Trust has gained momentum in recent years as organizations grapple with cloud, mobility, and advanced threats.

At its heart, Zero Trust shifts focus from network-centric controls to resource-centric and identity-centric controls. Instead of assuming everything on the internal network is benign, Zero Trust treats it as hostile and scrutinizes each interaction. In practical terms, this means identity plays a starring role: knowing exactly who or what is requesting access, enforcing strong authentication (ideally MFA) on every request, and dynamically evaluating whether that identity should be allowed to do X at time Y from device Z.

Core Principles of Zero Trust

Several core principles (often called tenets) guide Zero Trust architectures. While different sources articulate them slightly differently, we can summarize them as follows:

1. **Verify Explicitly:** Always authenticate and authorize based on all available context (user identity, device identity and health, location, time, sensitivity of data being accessed, anomalies, etc.). Trust is never assumed – it is earned at each request. For example, if a user authenticated eight hours ago on a corporate laptop and now tries to access a sensitive database, the system should re-evaluate that session – perhaps prompting for re-authentication or ensuring device compliance – rather than thinking "8 hours ago they were OK, so they're still OK." Every access attempt is treated as if it came from an open, untrusted network environment.

2. **Least Privilege Access:** Limit permissions and privileges to the minimum required, and grant access on a just-in-time, just-enough basis. In Zero Trust, a user or application should have no more access than necessary, and elevated permissions are temporary and narrowly scoped. This minimizes the blast radius if an identity is compromised. Techniques include microsegmenting networks and applications so that even if an attacker breaches one segment or service, they cannot move laterally to others. An example is restricting a developer's access: they can access dev systems, but have zero access to production systems unless a specific change management process temporarily grants it. Even then, that access would expire automatically.

3. **Assume Breach:** Design as if an attacker is already inside the environment or as if any single control can fail. This mindset leads to layered defenses and monitoring. If you assume an endpoint might be infected with malware or a credential might be stolen, you implement continuous monitoring and anomaly detection to catch misuse. You also compartmentalize systems so that a breach in one area doesn't immediately compromise the entire system. This principle drives investments in activities such as extensive logging, threat detection systems that monitor user behavior (UEBA), and robust incident response processes. It also underpins the idea of continuously re-validating trust – e.g., just because a device was deemed healthy at login doesn't mean it stays healthy; if it starts behaving oddly (e.g., signs of compromise), the system should revoke its access.

4. **Continuous Monitoring and Adaptive Control:** Zero Trust is not a one-time check at login – it requires constant evaluation of sessions and adaptation of security posture as context changes. In practice, this might mean that if a user's risk score increases mid-session (say their account triggers an alert for possible compromise or their device goes out of compliance), the system can automatically challenge them for MFA again, restrict their access, or log them out. This continuous control also involves separating the control plane from the data plane: dedicated Policy Decision Points (PDPs) that evaluate access and

Policy Enforcement Points (PEPs) that gate access to resources on an ongoing basis (more on this architecture shortly). The goal is to limit the duration and scope of trust - credentials or sessions shouldn't be valid indefinitely, and all transactions should be subject to oversight.

These principles collectively ensure that identity is verified strongly, context is evaluated, and trust is tightly scoped for every access. Implementing Zero Trust is a journey - you don't flip a switch and have it overnight. Organizations often start by focusing on identities as a quick win (e.g., enforcing MFA universally, consolidating identity systems for unified visibility, applying conditional access policies) because identity is one of the easiest pillars to tackle and yields immediate risk reduction.

Identity As the Cornerstone of Zero Trust

Identity plays multiple critical roles in a Zero Trust architecture:

1. **Single Control Plane:** By funneling access through an identity provider or identity-aware proxies, you establish a single control plane to apply consistent policy. For example, requiring all applications (on-prem or cloud) to use SSO via a centralized IdP lets you enforce uniform MFA and conditional access policies across them. Identities (users or service principals) become the unit on which policy is applied, rather than IP addresses or physical segments. Microsoft calls this "putting your identity in the path of every access request," meaning no direct access to resources is allowed without going through an authentication/authorization step.

2. **Granular Access Decisions:** Every request is tied to an identity, and policy decisions consider the identity's attributes (role, group membership, security risk level) along with contextual signals (device trust level, geolocation, time of day). For instance, an identity might have a conditional policy: *"Allow login without MFA only if device is compliant AND user risk is low; otherwise require MFA or block."* This is far more fine-grained than old network ACLs. It leverages the rich context that modern IAM can provide - including risk scores from identity protection systems (such as detections of leaked credentials or impossible travel logins).

3. **Unified Visibility:** Using identity as the pivot point for logging and monitoring gives security teams a coherent view. Instead of analyzing raw IP flows or host-based logs in isolation, you can correlate activity by user or service account. You know which identity accessed what resource and when, which is essential for auditing and threat detection. Identity systems often integrate with SIEM/XDR platforms to feed them this information. If an account suddenly accesses data it never has before, that could trigger an alert - a capability that is much harder if you were monitoring network IPs.

4. **Simplified User Experience (when done right):** Zero Trust can sound user-unfriendly ("You're going to challenge me all the time?"), but done correctly, it can improve user experience by eliminating legacy friction (like clunky VPNs) and using smarter, context-driven access. For example, suppose your identity system knows the device is managed and the user behavior is expected. In that case, it can log the user in with minimal prompts (perhaps leveraging passwordless authentication, which is both more secure and faster for the user). SSO means fewer login prompts overall. The key is to align security with context and prompt the user only when needed. Many organizations find that moving to identity-centric access with SSO and MFA everywhere actually reduces the password-related hassles and resets for users and enables more flexible remote work.

It's important to note that Zero Trust is not only about identity - network microsegmentation, endpoint security, and data security still matter - but identity is often the foundation. As one Microsoft identity VP quipped, we must treat identities as "the new control plane" for security. The US federal government's zero trust strategy explicitly lists identity as the first pillar to address (before devices, networks, etc.) because getting identity right enables so much else.

To visualize how identity and policy enforcement come together in Zero Trust, consider the high-level architecture shown in Figure 2-1.

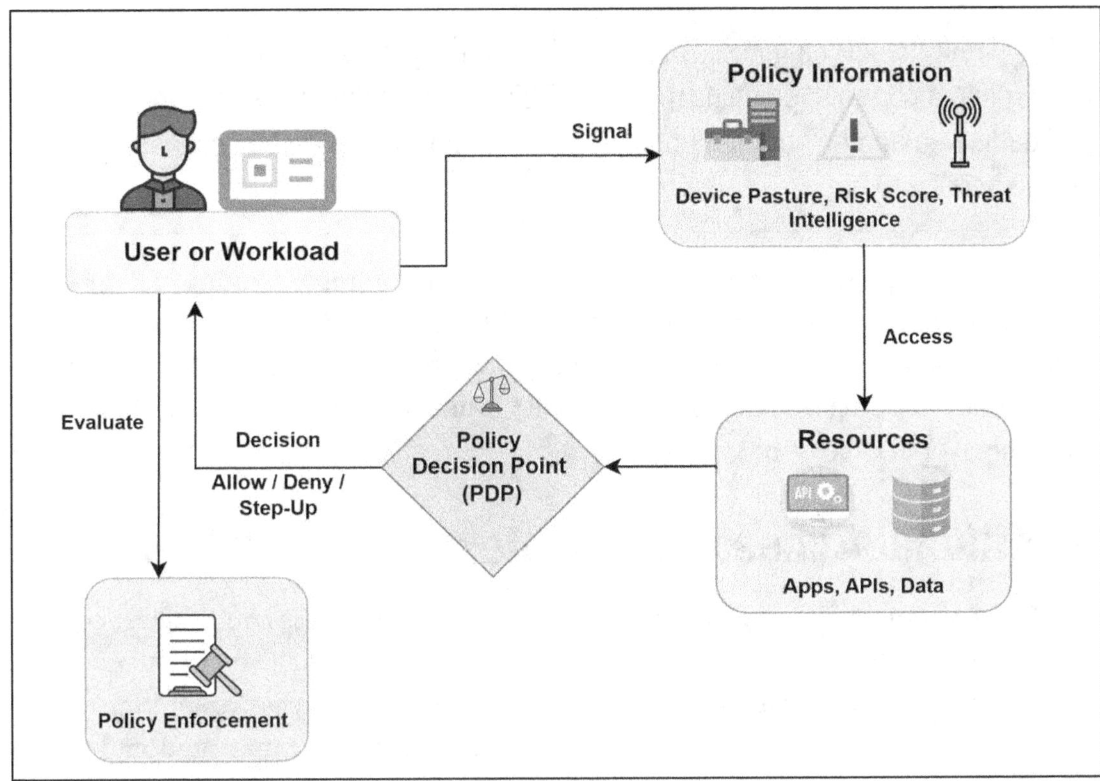

Figure 2-1. *Conceptual Zero Trust architecture enforcing identity-based access*

In this model, identity is central - the user or service account identity must authenticate (preferably with MFA) and is associated with every action. The Policy is essentially an identity-centric access policy (often implemented via an identity provider's conditional access or a dedicated Zero Trust access proxy). The resources on the right could be anything - internal apps, cloud APIs, data stores - but they all rely on the identity-based gate in front of them. This architecture aligns with the guidance in NIST SP 800-207 and other Zero Trust reference models. It's worth noting that, in practice, implementing this might involve multiple integrated systems: an SSO/IAM platform (such as Entra ID or Okta), an endpoint management tool feeding device compliance data, a CASB or gateway for certain apps, and so on. The goal is to integrate them so that, to the user and the resource, they behave as a single cohesive system that enforces security.

Note Treat the IdP, signing keys, and federation objects as Tier-0 assets. Apply the strongest controls (phishing-resistant MFA, HSM-backed keys, change control, and dedicated admin workstations) because a compromise here cascades everywhere.

Next, we'll zoom into one of the most powerful tools for implementing identity-centric Zero Trust policies: conditional access and context-aware policy engines. These are what make "never trust, always verify" actionable on a day-to-day basis by automatically deciding when to prompt for MFA, when to block access, and when to grant limited or full access based on risk.

Conditional Access and Context-Aware Policies

One of the core enablers of an identity-as-the-perimeter strategy is conditional access. This refers to policies that evaluate the context and conditions of a login or access attempt and impose controls (such as requiring MFA, denying access, or limiting the session) based on that evaluation. Traditional access control was binary and static - you either had access or you didn't, often determined just by your role. Conditional access makes it dynamic and risk-aware: the decision can change depending on *how* you're attempting access and what is happening at that moment.

Key Elements of Conditional Access

A typical conditional access policy considers multiple signals. Figure 2-2 shows this decision pipeline at a high level, moving from identity, device, location, application, session, and threat intelligence signals into an access decision such as allow, block, require step-up authentication, or restrict the session.

1. **User or Identity Attributes:** What is the user's role, group membership, or risk level? For instance, is this user flagged as high-risk because their credentials were found in a breach? Identity protection systems today assign risk scores to user accounts (e.g., low/medium/high) based on factors such as password leakage detection or unusual login patterns. Conditional access can use this signal in a standard policy, such as "If user risk = high, block access," to stop potentially compromised accounts.

2. **Location/Network:** Where is the access coming from? An IP address or geolocation can be considered. Access from a trusted corporate network might be treated differently from access from a foreign country where the organization doesn't operate. But be careful: relying on IP is tricky (attackers can come through VPNs or cloud providers). Still, geolocation and IP address detection are useful factors – e.g., "Impossible travel" policies that block logins from, say, New York and then Hong Kong within an hour.

3. **Device Posture:** Does the company manage the device? Is it compliant with security policies (up-to-date OS, disk encryption on, no jailbreak, running an endpoint security agent, etc.)? Device Trust is critical in Zero Trust – an unmanaged or insecure device may be significantly more likely to be compromised, so policies often restrict such devices. For example, allow full access only from known healthy devices, while unknown devices might be granted only minimal access or require extra verification.

4. **Application or Resource Sensitivity:** What is being accessed? Accessing email is one thing; accessing sensitive financial data is another. Conditional policies often apply stricter requirements to more sensitive applications/data. For instance, accessing a confidential HR system might always require MFA, whereas a low-risk app might not under certain conditions.

5. **Session Context:** Time of day, concurrency, and other session info. Unusual times or concurrent sessions from two locations might raise flags. Some systems also consider whether the session token originated from an intact session or was reused illegitimately.

6. **Real-Time Threat Intelligence:** Modern identity platforms can incorporate signals such as "this IP is from an anonymizing proxy or is on a threat feed of known malicious addresses," and then treat them contextually. Or if a particular user's behavior suddenly matches patterns of past breaches (e.g., logging in and immediately downloading extensive data), the system could adapt.

Figure 2-2 shows how these identity, device, location, resource, session, and threat intelligence signals flow into a conditional access decision pipeline. The policy engine uses those signals to decide whether to allow access, require step-up authentication, restrict the session, block the request, or revoke access during continuous evaluation.

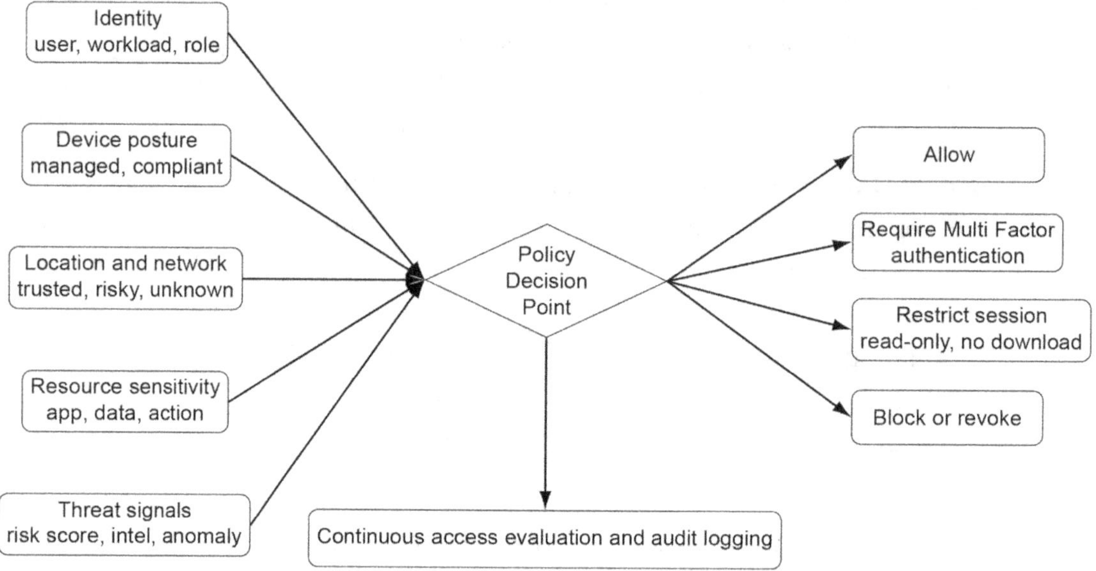

Figure 2-2. *Conditional access decision pipeline*

The conditional access engine then has controls it can impose:

1. **Require Step-Up Authentication:** For example, enforce MFA if conditions aren't ideal. Many organizations have a baseline policy, "if coming from outside our trusted network, or if the device is not a hybrid AD-joined device, require MFA." This ensures that even if a password is compromised, the attacker likely can't get in from an untrusted network without the second factor.

2. **Block Access:** If risk is too high (e.g., user's account marked high risk, or login from a blocked country, etc.), outright deny. It's better to err on the side of safety for anomalous situations. Conditional access provides a granular way to enforce this rather than a blunt one-size network block.

3. **Allow, but with Restrictions:** Some systems can enforce read-only access or limit session length if conditions aren't ideal. For instance, Microsoft's conditional access has a concept of "session controls" - you might allow a login but require continuous re-auth for specific actions or enforce that the session is routed through a Cloud Access Security Broker (CASB) for monitoring. Another example is device-based restrictions: allow access to a web app from an unmanaged device, but through a browser-only session with downloads disabled (to prevent data exfiltration). This is sometimes called "restrict access from unmanaged devices" - the user can view data but not save locally.

4. **Remediation Actions:** For example, redirect to a self-service password reset if login looks like the password might be compromised, or prompt the user to enroll in MFA if they haven't. Some conditional policies integrate with user actions, for example, "if blocked due to risky sign-in, force password change." This ties into identity governance, ensuring that risky events trigger cleanup.

Tip Enable the report-only first to measure impact and exceptions, then switch to enforce policies. Capture helpdesk telemetry to tune prompts and exclusions.

Leading IAM platforms such as Microsoft Entra ID and Okta include built-in conditional access engines. In Entra ID's case, administrators can define policies with conditions (user/group, app, device platform, location, risk level, etc.) and controls (MFA, block, etc.). Okta's Adaptive MFA similarly allows building policies that incorporate device and network context, along with its own risk scoring (Okta's risk engine can analyze factors like new device, impossible travel, known malicious IP, etc., and assign a risk level to the sign-in that the policy can use). The net effect is an adaptive challenge system: low-risk logins get a light touch while high-risk logins get heavy scrutiny (see Listing 2-1).

Example: Conditional Access Policy JSON

To make this concrete, here is a simplified JSON representation of an Entra ID Conditional Access policy that requires MFA for a specific app when the user is outside trusted locations.

Listing 2-1. JSON example of a conditional access policy requiring MFA for Exchange Online when accessed from untrusted locations

```
{
  "displayName": "Require MFA for Exchange Online outside trusted
  locations",
  "state": "enabled",
  "conditions": {
    "users": {
      "includeGroups": ["<GUID of Group of users>"]
    },
    "applications": {
      "includeApplications": ["00000002-0000-0ff1-ce00-000000000000"]
      // Exchange Online app ID in Entra ID
    },
    "locations": {
      "includeLocations": ["All"],        // apply to all locations
      "excludeLocations": ["AllTrusted"]  // except trusted named locations
    },
    "clientAppTypes": [
      "browser", "mobileAppsAndDesktopClients"
    ]
  },
  "grantControls": {
    "operator": "OR",
    "builtInControls": ["mfa"]  // require multi-factor auth
  }
}
```

Caution Some thick clients and scripts silently rely on legacy protocols. Inventory first, communicate change windows, and offer modernized alternatives (e.g., OAuth device code, mTLS).

In this policy, any user in the specified group who accesses Exchange Online from a location not marked as trusted must perform MFA. If they are coming from a trusted location (e.g., company HQ IP range), the MFA requirement is skipped. This is a basic example, but it shows how conditions and controls combine. In practice, one could include additional conditions (like device platform or device state) and controls (e.g., require password change, block legacy authentication, etc.) in the JSON. The policy is enforced by Azure's identity platform whenever a token for Exchange Online is requested. Other platforms express similar logic through their policy configuration, either in identical JSON, via the admin UI, or via scripts.

Such policies enforce the idea that context matters. A login at 3 AM from an unknown device in a different country should not be treated the same as a midday login from the office on a domain-joined laptop. Conditional access gives the flexibility to automate those decisions. It also helps implement regulatory or compliance requirements, for example, by allowing access to specific data only from managed devices to satisfy data protection policies.

Continuous Access Evaluation

A development related to conditional access is the idea of continuous access evaluation (CAE). Traditionally, once a user obtained an access token (say, a one-hour OAuth token after passing conditional access), that token was valid until expiry, and the resource wouldn't know if conditions changed in the meantime. Continuous access evaluation is a mechanism (pioneered by Microsoft and partners) that enables critical events or changes in context to be pushed to relying applications to revoke tokens or re-evaluate sessions in near-real time. For example, suppose during an active session the user's account gets deactivated or marked at high risk or the user signs out. In that case, the system can inform applications to kill that session immediately rather than waiting for the token expiry. This makes the enforcement loop tighter. It relies on a protocol (often using a message bus or direct API calls) between the IdP and apps.

CAE aligns with Zero Trust's continuous monitoring tenet: a session that was acceptable at the time of token issuance should not automatically remain trusted if risk conditions change. It is like a guard that does not go to sleep once someone is admitted. If new information shows that a user account is disabled, a device has become noncompliant, or a session appears risky, access can be revoked or re-evaluated quickly. As more applications and cloud services support CAE or similar capabilities, conditional access becomes less limited to login time and more capable of enforcing policy throughout the session.

Implementing Conditional Policies Across Hybrid Environments

In a hybrid multi-cloud environment, one challenge is applying consistent conditional access across different platforms. You might have identities in Entra ID, workloads in AWS, and apps that don't directly integrate with your IdP. Strategies to extend conditional access include

1. **Proxying Access Through IdP or Secure Gateway:** For example, using Entra ID's Application Proxy to front-end on-premises applications. Users accessing the on-prem app are actually authenticating via Entra ID (with all its conditional access checks), and then the proxy passes the traffic. Similarly, SASE (Secure Access Service Edge) or Zero Trust Network Access (ZTNA) solutions can act as brokers for access to many resources, enforcing centrally enforced identity-driven policies.

2. **Integration with Cloud-Native Controls:** Many cloud providers have their own context-aware access features (e.g., Google BeyondCorp Enterprise, AWS IAM Identity Center with device trust). If using multiple clouds, one approach is to federate all identities to a central IdP and manage conditional access there, while another approach is to configure each environment's native tools in parallel. The former is simpler if feasible: for instance, use a single IdP (Entra or Okta) as the authentication source for AWS, GCP, and on-prem apps via SSO, so that one conditional access policy framework covers all. This requires federating AWS IAM or Google identities to the central IdP.

3. **Conditional Access for Service Accounts:** Human user access can be gated with interactive MFA, but what about API-to-API calls or service accounts? Here, context might include whether the calling service is from an approved host or has a valid certificate. Solutions include using short-lived tokens or OAuth client credentials with policy restrictions. For example, one could require that an Entra ID application token be accepted only if it was acquired from a trusted workload identity (such as a managed identity on an Azure VM). This area overlaps with machine identity management, ensuring that non-human access also respects conditional rules (e.g., deny an API call if the service instance is out of compliance or if an anomaly is detected in its behavior).

Overall, conditional access is the practical engine that makes an identity-first, Zero Trust model work at scale. Administrators need to design policies carefully - too strict and you might block legitimate work, too lenient and you leave gaps. Many organizations iterate on policies, starting with monitor-only mode (just logging what would happen), then moving to enforce mode once they are confident. User communication and training are also important; users should understand, for instance, why they might occasionally get an MFA prompt (e.g., "we noticed an unusual sign-in, so we're verifying it's you"). In our adaptive era, static one-size-fits-all policies are giving way to risk-adaptive IAM, where the system's requirements flex based on the situation. This dynamic approach significantly enhances security without overly burdening users uniformly.

Now that we have covered how identity and context can be evaluated in real time, let's shift to a broader perspective: using identity-focused platforms and best practices to reduce an organization's overall attack surface.

Reducing the Attack Surface with Identity-Focused Security

When identity is the new perimeter, securing identities effectively means shrinking the pathways attackers can exploit. An "identity-focused" security strategy leverages IAM platforms (such as Microsoft Entra ID, Okta, Ping, etc.) and best practices to close standard holes that attackers exploit. This section highlights key best practices - generically described - to harden your identity fabric and thereby reduce risk. Think of these as **high-impact moves** to cut off attacker avenues such as phishing, credential stuffing, privilege abuse, and unattended identities (see Listing 2-2).

Listing 2-2. Attribute-based authorization as Policy-as-Code (Rego)

```
package authz

default allow = false

# Low-sensitivity read with AAL2+
allow {
  input.action == "read"
  input.resource.sensitivity == "low"
  input.subject.assurance >= 2
}

# High-sensitivity write with AAL3, explicit group, and compliant device
allows {
  input.action == "write"
  input.resource.sensitivity == "high"
  input.subject.assurance >= 3
  input.subject.groups[_] == "HighRiskDataWriters"
  input.device.compliant == true
}
```

Adopt a Unified Identity Platform

One fundamental step is to **centralize and unify identity management** as much as possible. Suppose users have multiple accounts across different systems (on-prem AD, separate accounts in AWS, another account for a third-party SaaS, etc.). In that case, it multiplies security challenges - more passwords that could be compromised, inconsistent access revocation, and blind spots between systems. By integrating identities into a single IdP or at least a tightly integrated federated system, you gain a single choke point to enforce security policy and monitor activity. For example, many organizations are now extending their on-prem Active Directory to a cloud IdP (via federation or synchronization) so that cloud services use the same identities.

Others consolidate multiple directories (e.g., after mergers or in a multi-cloud scenario) into a single central directory or use an identity broker to tie them together. The goal: **one identity for each person (or service) that maps to all their access**. This not only improves user convenience with SSO but also ensures that when that identity is disabled or its risk is detected, you can cut off everything at once. Tools like identity governance (IGA) solutions help here by providing a cross-system view of identities and access rights.

Concretely, if you use Entra ID (Entra ID) as your main IdP, try to integrate all critical apps with it - whether via SAML, OIDC, or even password vaulting, if needed for legacy systems. If you use Okta, leverage its app integrations and federations in the same way. Avoid scenarios where, for example, your developers have separate local accounts in AWS or GitHub not tied to corporate SSO - those tend to become weak links (shared passwords, forgotten accounts, etc.). A unified identity platform also makes **consistent logging and monitoring** easier; you can see all sign-ins and admin actions in one place to feed your SIEM.

Enforce Multi-factor Authentication Everywhere

As discussed, enabling MFA for all users dramatically reduces the chance of account compromise - Microsoft famously noted that enabling MFA blocks 99% of automated attacks on accounts. It's therefore a no-brainer from a risk perspective. Use your identity platform's capabilities to require MFA for all interactive logins, especially to any remotely accessible service. This includes not just employees but also external collaborators who access your systems, as well as privileged IT accounts (which might even require more than one factor or a stronger one).

It's worth specifically adopting phishing-resistant MFA methods where possible, such as FIDO2 security keys or platform authenticators (Windows Hello, Apple Touch ID/Face ID via WebAuthn). Standard OTP-based MFA is better than nothing, but it is increasingly being bypassed by targeted phishing (e.g., middleman attacks). If an MFA method can be intercepted or pushed to a user who mindlessly accepts it (MFA fatigue attacks), then it's not fully solving the problem. Many organizations now issue physical security keys for administrators and high-risk users as an MFA method. Even for general users, moving to app-based push or token MFA with number matching (to prevent blind approval) is recommended.

A related aspect is turning off legacy authentication methods that cannot enforce MFA. For example, older protocols like POP3/IMAP for email or basic auth to some web apps might not support MFA and become easy entry points (attackers often try legacy protocols to bypass MFA requirements). Good identity platforms allow blocking legacy auth or requiring app passwords for them (which are effectively another factor). Reducing your dependency on legacy auth and ensuring everything goes through modern auth flows (OAuth/OIDC, SAML) means MFA can be applied uniformly.

Implement Conditional Access (Adaptive Policies)

As covered in depth, conditional access is your friend. Use it to strike a balance between security and productivity. Some concrete best practices:

1. **Block Risky Logins Automatically:** If your IdP has risk detection (like Entra ID Identity Protection or Okta Risk Insights), set policies to block or MFA-challenge high-risk sign-ins or users. There's little reason to allow a login that the system flags as likely malicious (e.g., impossible travel, known leaked password). It's better to err on the side of caution and then have a process to verify the user out of band.

2. **Require Managed Devices for Sensitive Resources:** For specific admin portals or data-sensitive apps, enforce device compliance. For example, require an Intune-compliant (or JAMF-compliant, etc.) device for accessing finance systems. Unmanaged devices are either blocked or allowed via a very restricted session (such as a virtual desktop or browser isolation).

3. **Use Location Wisely:** Define "trusted locations" (e.g., your office IPs or VPN egress IPs) in the system and use them to relax policies slightly for known-good environments, but be careful not to over-trust. Many orgs still use MFA even internally because insider threats and lateral movement are concerns. Still, they might say, not to use MFA for every SharePoint read within the office, but to use it for anything sensitive or for any changes.

4. **Time-Based or Behavior-Based:** Some advanced policies might look at the time of day (e.g., if an employee who typically works

9–5 suddenly logs in at 2 AM, perhaps require MFA or mark it as a risk). And of course, unusual behavior (downloading large amounts of data, accessing uncommon apps) can be policed, though that often falls to UEBA solutions beyond pure IAM. Still, some IdPs integrate behavior analytics to create adaptive policies.

In summary, make access control dynamic. Hard-coding a rule that "user X has access" without context is outdated; instead, "user X has access under conditions A, B, C; otherwise, additional verification or denial occurs." By doing so, you significantly reduce the window of opportunity for an attacker. Even if they steal a credential, the odds of satisfying all the conditions (correct device, location, behavior) are low. If they do, you'll likely get alerted because something will be off.

Embrace Least Privilege and Privileged Access Management

Least privilege isn't new, but Zero Trust emphasizes it even more. Review and minimize which identities have high levels of access. Use a privileged access management (PAM) system or the features of your IAM platform to strictly control admin accounts. This includes

1. **Role Separation:** Administrators should have separate accounts for admin duties vs. regular work, so that phishing their day-to-day account doesn't automatically give the attacker domain admin rights. The admin account should be highly secured (MFA with a physical token, allowed login only from secure jump hosts, etc.).

2. **Just-in-Time (JIT) Elevation:** Instead of permanent membership in privileged groups, use solutions that allow time-bound access elevation. For example, an engineer can request admin access to a production system for one hour to perform maintenance, and the access is automatically revoked afterward. Microsoft Entra Privileged Identity Management (PIM) and various PAM tools do this. This way, if an account is compromised, it defaults to limited access, and the attacker can't do much unless they also manage to elevate the account (which can itself require approvals or additional auth).

3. **Audit and Monitor Admin Actions:** Ensure all privileged operations are logged and, if possible, recorded (session

recording for administrative sessions). Behavioral analytics on admin actions can detect anomalies (such as an admin account performing an action it has never performed before).

Note Maintain two emergency accounts with strong, independent factors and offline recovery. Audit monthly. Prohibit daily use.

Remember that attackers often target the "keys to the kingdom," domain admins, cloud subscription owners, etc. Securing those identities with extra care (dedicated hardened workstations, powerful MFA, continuous monitoring) is a huge part of reducing risk. By limiting what an attacker can do even if they compromise a user, you reduce the blast radius. For example, an attacker who phishes an employee might gain email access but cannot pivot to domain admin because that employee lacks such rights and cannot elevate because of PAM controls, giving you time to detect and respond.

Automate Identity Governance and Lifecycle

Another major attack surface is stale or orphaned accounts - accounts that should have been removed or disabled but weren't or that still have privileges they no longer need (privilege creep). A solid Identity Governance and Administration (IGA) program will continuously address this. Best practices include

1. **Automated Provisioning/Deprovisioning:** Use HR triggers or authoritative sources to create accounts when users join automatically, modify access as they move roles, and deactivate accounts immediately when they leave or no longer need access. Connect your IAM to HR and directory stores so that these events don't rely on manual IT tasks that can be delayed or missed.

2. **Periodic Access Reviews:** Especially for privileged roles or sensitive systems, conduct regular certification campaigns. Managers or system owners should review who has access and attest that it's still needed. Any access not certified is removed. This catches situations where someone changed jobs but retained access rights that are no longer required for the new role.

3. **Removal of Dormant Accounts:** If an account hasn't been used in X days (60, 90, whatever policy), consider turning it off.

Attackers often target accounts that slip under the radar – e.g., a former contractor's account that wasn't disabled, and no one notices the login because that user isn't around. Deactivating unused accounts cuts that off.

4. **Service Accounts Management:** Apply governance to non-human accounts, too. Every service account should have an owner and a clear purpose. Vault credentials for them, rotate passwords or convert them to managed identities if possible, and remove ones that are no longer in use. Tools exist to identify accounts with no recent logins, which may indicate they are candidates for removal (see Figure 2-3).

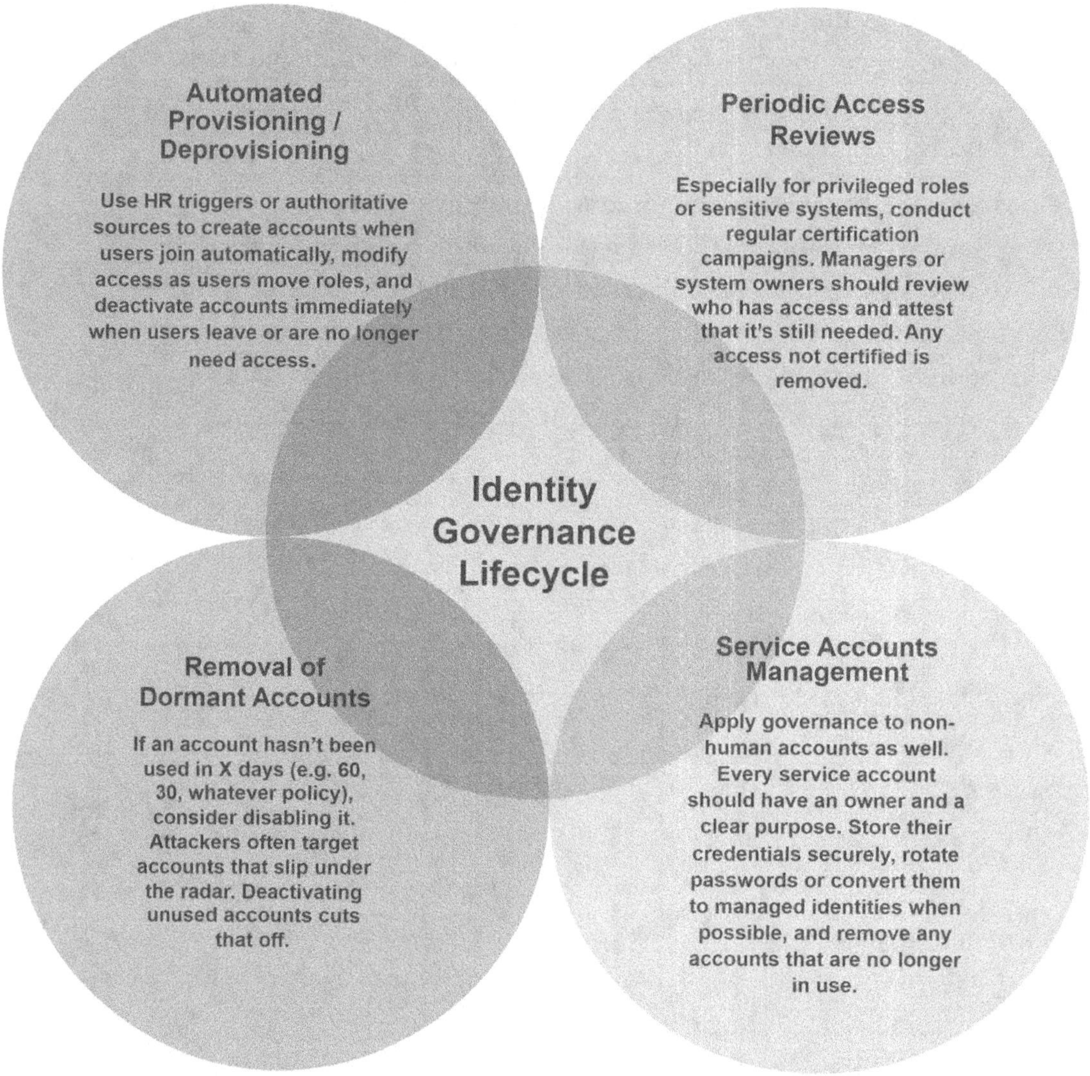

Figure 2-3. *Identity governance lifecycle*

A significant benefit of modern IAM platforms is that they can often serve as a hub for this lifecycle. For example, using SCIM or API connectors, your cloud IdP could automatically deprovision a user from dozens of SaaS apps when their central account is disabled. That closes those lingering backdoors. Identity governance reduces the attack surface by ensuring there is no excess access for attackers to exploit. It also helps demonstrate compliance with standards (many regulations require periodic user access reviews).

Secure Integration Points and API Access

When focusing on identity, don't forget that identities are used in various protocols and integrations. Key areas to lock down:

1. **APIs and Service-to-Service Auth:** Use strong authentication for APIs, prefer token-based auth (e.g., OAuth 2.0 client credentials, JWTs) over static API keys. Where API keys are used, rotate them regularly and limit their permissions. Many breaches occur when an API key with broad permissions is leaked. Using an identity platform's issuance of tokens with conditional access, even for APIs, is ideal, for example, Entra ID issuing an OAuth token to a service that can include conditional policies (such as the service's client cert must be present). Ensure that service identities (such as Azure managed identities and AWS IAM roles) are used instead of embedding credentials in code.

2. **Federation Trust Management:** If you set up federation with partners or between systems, treat those trust relationships as high sensitivity. An attack like "Golden SAML" involves forging SAML tokens if an attacker gains access to your SAML signing certificate. Protect those signing keys vigorously (use hardware security modules or key vaults). Also, regularly review relying party configurations – ensure no outdated or insecure protocols are enabled that could be abused (e.g., older WS-Trust flows that allow weaker auth).

3. **Legacy Protocols:** As mentioned, disable or restrict legacy auth. This includes older LDAP binds (use LDAPS or modern auth if possible), NTLM in Windows environments (aim to use Kerberos or certificate auth), and any hard-coded passwords in scripts/integrations. Every legacy authentication that doesn't support modern policy is a potential hole.

4. **Conditional Access for Admin Protocols:** Some IAM systems allow you to enforce conditional access on things like PowerShell or SSH sessions (e.g., requiring MFA for an admin to open a remote PowerShell to Microsoft 365). Use those features. Essentially, wrap identity-based controls around even the IT management flows.

By closing these gaps, you reduce the ways attackers often move silently. For instance, without controls, an attacker who gets a foothold might create a new OAuth app in your tenant to persist access. Good practice is to lock down who can develop applications or at least monitor new app credentials (and enforce that they must be approved). Attack surface reduction is about eliminating unnecessary trust: if a legacy protocol or integration isn't needed, turn it off; if it is required, put it behind an auth method that you can monitor and control.

Monitor Identity Threats and Enable Identity Threat Detection and Response (ITDR)

Even with preventive controls, assume some attacks will slip through. Invest in Identity Threat Detection and Response (ITDR) capabilities - this is a relatively new category, but it essentially means applying threat detection specifically to identity systems and behavior. Some tips:

1. **Aggregate and Analyze Logs from Your IdP and AD:** Failed logins, MFA prompts, consent to applications, account lockouts, privilege changes - all are essential signals. Many IAM services now offer built-in anomaly detection (such as Entra ID Identity Protection and Okta ThreatInsight), which you should turn on. Additionally, feed logs to a SIEM and write correlation rules: e.g., alert if an inactive account suddenly logs in at an odd time or if a normally non-privileged user starts accessing admin pages.

2. **Protect the Identity Infrastructure:** Attacks such as the Golden Ticket (for AD) or Golden SAML (for federated IdPs) target the identity infrastructure itself. Use best practices to secure domain controllers (tiered admin model, no internet access, etc.) and IdP tenants (MFA for global admins, emergency break-glass accounts stored offline, etc.). Monitor for changes in identity configuration - such as new federation trusts or modified authentication methods - that could indicate an attacker backdooring the system (see Listing 2-3).

3. **User Behavior Analytics:** Over time, build a baseline of normal user behavior. If a user account suddenly downloads far more data than usual or accesses systems it never did before, that's a sign of potential compromise. Some XDR solutions or Cloud Access Security Brokers (CASBs) can do this. This crosses into data security, but because everything ties to identity, you often detect it via identity usage patterns.

4. **Threat Intelligence Integration:** If you receive intel about a campaign targeting your industry with specific techniques (e.g., MFA fatigue attacks), you might proactively adjust policies (like requiring number matching or limiting MFA prompts). Also, ingest threat feeds for IPs or device identifiers known to be malicious - these can bc plugged into conditional access or a SIEM.

Listing 2-3. Identity threat detections for SIEM/XDR

```
Newly registered OAuth client with broad privileges -
find events
where event_type == "app_registration"
and assigned_permissions contains_any ["Mail.ReadWrite","Directory.
ReadWrite.All"]

Impossible travel after successful MFA -
find signins
where distance_km(prev(location), location) > 5000
and minutes_between(prev(timestamp), timestamp) < 60
and mfa_result == "succeeded"

Excessive user consents to a single app -
find consents
summarize count() by app_id
order by count() desc
limit 10
```

By actively detecting and responding to identity-related threats, you can catch things early. For example, you might detect that an attacker who phished credentials is now trying to enroll their own device for that user's MFA (a tactic observed in some cases) – you could have an alert on multiple failed MFA enrollments or unusual MFA factor changes. An identity-first SOC mindset essentially means your security operations give as much focus to identity telemetry as they traditionally did to network or endpoint telemetry. It's often the identity clues that reveal an attack in progress (e.g., a login from a new IP address followed by the creation of a new inbox rule – a sign of a potential email breach).

User Awareness and Phishing Education

While identity security is not purely technical, user training remains a vital layer. Because identity attacks often start with social engineering, users should be educated about phishing, MFA fatigue, suspicious password reset requests, unexpected authentication prompts, and safe credential handling. They should know how to report suspicious login prompts or emails quickly. Many organizations run simulated phishing exercises to keep users alert, but these exercises should be designed to educate rather than simply penalize mistakes. The human element of identity security cannot be ignored. A user who understands the value of their credentials and how attackers manipulate trust becomes an additional line of defense. Conversely, no amount of advanced technology will help if users routinely approve authentication requests they did not initiate. Identity security awareness should therefore be included in the overall security training program.

Note Adopt number-matching for push MFA, rate-limit prompts, and educate users never to approve unexpected requests.

Summary of Best Practices

To recap, here are the key best practices for reducing attack surface via identity-first security:

1. **Centralize Identities**: Use one primary IdP or federated network to manage all user and service identities.

2. **Enforce MFA Everywhere**: Especially phishing-resistant methods for all users, including admins.
3. **Use Conditional Access**: Make access decisions context-aware; require compliant devices and low-risk signals for full access.
4. **Limit and Monitor Privileged Access**: Implement just-in-time admin access, separate accounts, and PAM solutions.
5. **Eliminate Unused Identities and Access**: Automate deprovisioning and run regular access reviews to remove orphan accounts and excess permissions.
6. **Secure Service Accounts and API Keys**: Rotate secrets, use managed identities or tokens, and restrict what they can do.
7. **Disable Legacy Authentication**: Require modern auth for everything so policies can be enforced and old vulnerabilities are closed.
8. **Constantly Monitor Identity Activity**: Aggregate logs, leverage identity threat detection tools, and hunt for abnormal usage.
9. **Prepare Incident Response for Identity Attacks**: Have playbooks for credential compromise, lost device, and stolen token scenarios (e.g., invalidate sessions enterprise-wide if needed).
10. **Educate Users**: On phishing, MFA fatigue, and good cyber hygiene (like not reusing passwords, recognizing unusual login prompts).

By following these practices, enterprises significantly reduce the "low-hanging fruit" that attackers often go after. The goal is an environment where it's hard for attackers to get in and, even if they do, hard for them to escalate or move around because identity controls trip them up at each turn. In an identity-as-perimeter world, you fortify that perimeter by both strengthening the gate (strong auth, adaptive checks) and narrowing the number of gates (unified identity and fewer redundant credentials) that need defending.

In the final sections, we will look at three special areas: securing workforce identities, consumer identities, and non-human identities. While much of the discussion so far has applied to workforce users, consumer IAM and non-human identities require equal attention, especially as digital services, automation, cloud-native workloads, and AI agents expand. The principles remain similar, but implementation differs. We will also tie together how these pieces form a cohesive identity-first architecture spanning hybrid and multi-cloud deployments.

Securing Human, Consumer, and Non-human Identities

Modern IAM must account not only for workforce users and consumers but also for a vast array of non-human identities. These include service accounts, application credentials, API tokens, container and VM identities, CI/CD pipeline identities, robotic process automation bots, AI agents, autonomous workflows, and other workload identities. In many enterprises, non-human identities now outnumber human users, and their growth is accelerating as automation, cloud-native architectures, and agentic AI become more common. Human, consumer, and non-human identities are all critical to secure, but the control patterns differ. This section explains how Zero Trust principles apply across these identity types while recognizing that workforce users, customers, service accounts, and AI-driven agents each require different governance and enforcement models.

Human Identities (Workforce Users)

Human identities are the users we interact with day to day: employees, contractors, and partners who log in to systems. Key considerations for securing these identities:

1. **Identity Proofing and Lifecycle:** Ensure robust processes for identity proofing when onboarding users (you don't want fraudulent or deactivated identities in your system). For the workforce, this often ties into HR: create accounts only for verified hires and terminate access promptly at offboarding. Consider periodic re-verification for long-term accounts (ensuring the person is still with the org and in good standing).

2. **Strong Authentication:** As hammered throughout, require MFA for human users. Also, encourage or mandate the use of passwordless methods where possible, which improve security and the user experience (e.g., Windows Hello for Business or phone-as-a-token methods). Phishing-resistant MFA for privileged users should be non-negotiable.

3. **User Education and Phishing Drills:** Humans can be tricked, so educate them to be the first line of defense. Teach not to approve unexpected MFA prompts (one defense against MFA fatigue attacks is simply awareness - users should know if a deluge of prompts happens, their password might be compromised, and they should report it). Provide clear procedures for reporting suspicious emails or login alerts.

4. **Least Privilege for Users:** Not every user needs local admin on their device or access to all data. Use role-based access control (RBAC) or attribute-based access control (ABAC) to ensure users only see what they need. This extends to things like network share permissions, SaaS app role assignments, etc. Overprivileged user accounts (such as an intern granted domain admin access) pose serious risks.

5. **Self-Service and User-Friendly Security:** Provide secure but user-friendly options like self-service password reset (with appropriate MFA) to reduce helpdesk calls and encourage good behavior (like not sticking with weak passwords or writing them down). Also use adaptive authentication to minimize friction - e.g., if a user's risk is low, let them in with SSO seamlessly; if risk is high, step up challenges. A good user experience means users won't try to bypass security and will adhere to policies.

6. **Monitoring and Anomaly Detection:** Watch user behaviors for signs of compromise. For example, if an employee account suddenly accesses a repository of data it has never touched before and starts downloading en masse, that could be an insider threat or an external compromise using that account. Having alerts or automated responses (like requiring re-auth) for such anomalies can catch attacks early.

7. **Privileged Users Special Case:** For highly privileged human users (admins of systems, executives with access to sensitive info), consider extra safeguards: dedicated admin workstations, hardware tokens for MFA, continuous monitoring of their accounts, and maybe limiting their access to business hours

unless explicitly extended. Executives are often targets of spear-phishing, so their accounts should be locked down (e.g., enforce that a CEO's mailbox can be accessed only from managed devices and require MFA). Also, tools like conditional access can enforce that privileged roles can only be assumed under certain conditions (e.g., the user must complete MFA again or be on an approved device).

In short, protecting human identities is about making the user the strongest link instead of the weakest: give them secure tools (SSO, easy MFA), educate them, and enforce policies that mitigate the impact if they slip up (like blocking the phished login at the second factor stage or not letting a single cred get too far). Humans will always be a bit unpredictable, so our systems must be resilient to human mistakes through layers of control.

Consumer Identities and CIAM

Consumer Identity and Access Management, often called CIAM, extends identity-first security to customers, members, patients, citizens, and other external users who interact with digital services. CIAM has different priorities from workforce IAM. Workforce IAM is usually optimized for employees, contractors, and privileged administrators within an enterprise operating model. CIAM must support large and often unpredictable user populations, self-service registration, consent management, account recovery, fraud prevention, privacy requirements, and a low-friction user experience. A customer who struggles to sign in may abandon a digital service, so CIAM must balance security and usability carefully.

Federation patterns also differ across workforce and consumer environments. In workforce scenarios, SAML and OIDC federation often connect an enterprise identity provider to SaaS platforms, cloud consoles, and internal applications. In consumer environments, OIDC and OAuth 2.0 are commonly used to support web, mobile, and API-based access. Social login, bring-your-own-identity models, customer-managed credentials, passkeys, and delegated authorization flows may also be used, depending on the business model. The key architectural principle is to select federation techniques that match the user population, risk level, privacy obligations, and application type.

CIAM should also be designed with fraud and digital trust in mind. Controls may include adaptive authentication, bot detection, account takeover protection, device fingerprinting, risk-based step-up authentication, verified email or phone enrollment, and clear consent and privacy flows. For high-risk transactions, such as changing payment details, accessing sensitive records, or initiating large transfers, CIAM should support transaction-level verification rather than relying only on login-time authentication. This ensures that customer identity protection becomes part of the digital trust model, not just a login mechanism.

Non-human, workload, and agentic identities refer to the credentials and identities used by software, devices, services, workloads, automation, and AI agents to authenticate and authorize actions. Examples include service accounts running on servers, application-to-API tokens, microservices authenticating within a service mesh, IoT devices identifying themselves to cloud services, CI/CD pipelines using deployment credentials, robotic process automation bots, and AI agents that invoke tools, retrieve data, or take actions on behalf of users or workflows. Securing these identities is equally vital because attackers target them to move laterally, persist in the environment, access sensitive data, or perform actions without direct human interaction. A leaked cloud API key, over-permissioned service principal, or poorly governed AI agent identity can create the same level of risk as a compromised privileged user account.

Key strategies for non-human, workload, and agentic identities:

1. **Avoid Shared Static Credentials:** Historically, organizations have used a single shared account (such as a Windows service account or database login) across multiple systems, often with a static password that rarely changes. This is dangerous; if one system is compromised, that credential opens all others. Instead, strive for unique identities for each service or component. Use separate accounts for each service, and apply the principle of least privilege to what each account can do.

Tip Prefer platform-issued identities (managed identities, instance roles) to eliminate embedded secrets and gain short-lived tokens by default.

---

2. **Use Modern Workload Identity Solutions:** Cloud providers and identity platforms offer features to manage non-human and workload identities without static secrets:

- In Azure, use **Managed Identities** for Azure resources so that VMs or Functions can get tokens to access other resources without storing credentials.
- In AWS, use **IAM Roles** for EC2 and other services (with Instance Profile) instead of embedding API keys. The AWS Security Token Service will provide temporary credentials that rotate.
- Leverage Kubernetes service accounts, workload identities, or service meshes (like Istio) that issue identities to pods using certificates.
- Use certificate-based authentication for services when possible (mutual TLS between services, for example, or client certs for devices).

These approaches eliminate the need to store secrets in config files or code, a common source of leaks (see Figure 2-4).

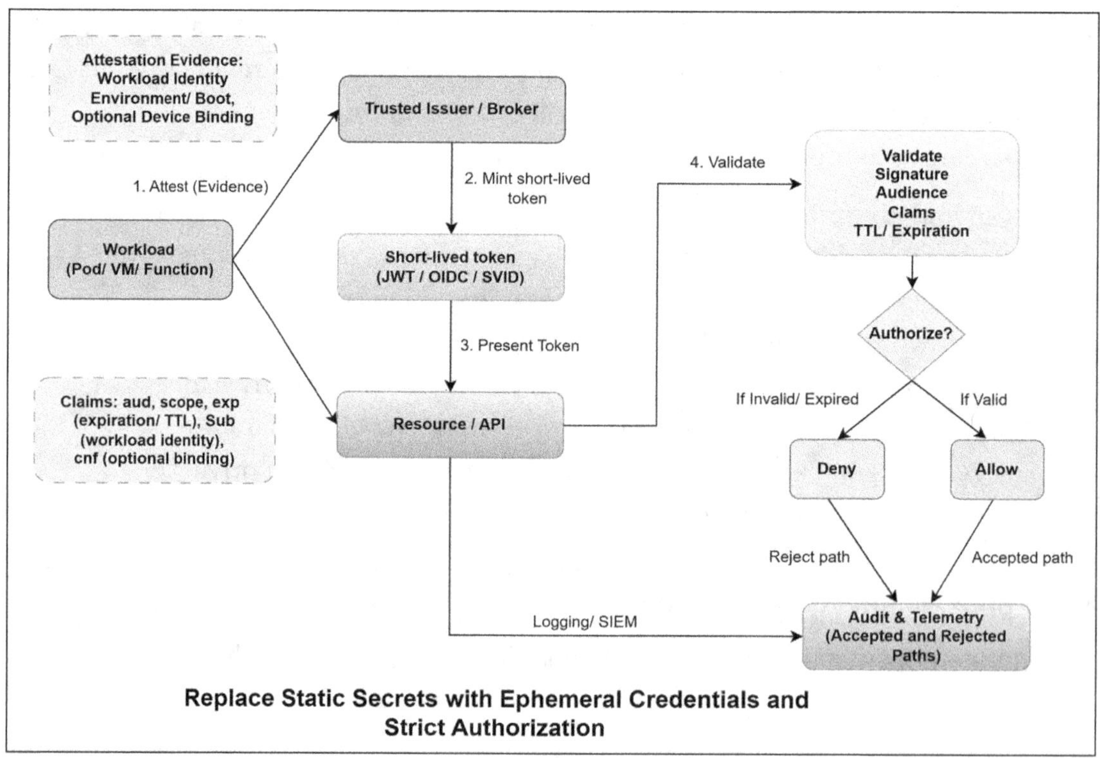

Figure 2-4. *Workload identity issuance flow*

3. **Secure Secret Storage and Rotation:** Wherever machine credentials still exist (API keys, certificates, encryption keys), store them in secure vaults (e.g., HashiCorp Vault, Azure Key Vault, AWS Secrets Manager) rather than on disk in plain text. Implement automated rotation of secrets, for instance, a database password an app uses can be rotated every 90 days (or even on every use, with dynamic secrets, as some vault solutions provide). Rotating credentials limits the window during which an attacker can misuse them if they are stolen.

4. **Non-human Privileged Access:** Just like users, machine accounts can have too many privileges. Audit what each service account can do. If a web application only needs read access to a database, don't grant it write access. Use cloud IAM policies to tightly scope what each app role can do in your cloud subscriptions. Remove unnecessary permissions from service accounts - e.g., a service account that runs a scheduled task might not need interactive login rights or network access beyond calling a specific API.

5. **Monitoring and Anomaly Detection for Non-human Identities:** Baseline normal behavior for service accounts and service principals. If a service account that usually only runs within one server is suddenly used to attempt login from another host, that's odd. If an API key that typically calls one API suddenly calls a different high-value API, investigate. Tools are emerging in the ITDR space to specifically monitor machine identity usage. Cloud provider logs can be beneficial – e.g., AWS CloudTrail to see every action a role performs. Set up alerts for unusual actions (like a service account creating new users, which it should never do).

6. **Lifecycle Management of Non-human Accounts:** It's easy to forget about service accounts, API credentials, and automation identities because no human complains when you turn them off - until something breaks. Keep an inventory of all service accounts/credentials, their owners, and their purposes. Periodically review them just like user accounts. Decommission those that are no longer needed (for instance, after retiring an application, did you also delete its service accounts and API keys?). Enforce credential expiration where possible (e.g., API keys that expire after a period if not renewed). This way, even if someone forgets an old script's credentials, it eventually becomes unusable.

Caution Every service principal must have a named owner, renewal date, and scope review. Disable accounts with no recent authentications.

7. **Zero Trust for APIs and Services:** Apply Zero Trust thinking to service communication. Just because Service A is in the same network or cluster as Service B, don't automatically trust it. Use mutual authentication (both sides verifying identity via certificates or tokens). Authorize each API call not just based on network location but on the calling service's identity and claims. Microsegmentation in networks can help – only allow the specific flows that are needed and require identity-based access. Essentially, treat service-to-service calls like user-to-service calls: challenge and verify each time. Initiatives like SPIFFE/SPIRE (for issuing identities in microservices) and cloud-native Zero Trust frameworks are worth exploring if you have a complex environment.
8. **DevOps and CI/CD Pipeline Security:** Non-human identities are heavily used in CI/CD (for compiling code, pushing artifacts, and deploying infrastructure). Secure your pipelines by limiting the scopes of pipeline access tokens, rotating them, and storing them in secure vaults. If using GitHub Actions or similar, use OIDC federation to the cloud so that short-lived tokens are minted per run instead of storing long-term cloud credentials. Essentially, ensure that compromise of your build server doesn't yield persistent cloud creds – use ephemeral federated tokens.
9. **Non-human Identity Governance:** Non-human identity governance is similar in principle to user governance, but it must operate at machine speed and cloud scale. If an organization has thousands of microservices, pipelines, service principals, certificates, secrets, API tokens, and AI agents, it must know who owns each identity, what it can access, when it was last used, and when it should expire. Who approves a service or agent having access to a secret? Who reviews whether an automation workflow

still needs production permissions? How are AI agents prevented from exceeding their intended scope? Governance processes should include ownership, lifecycle review, secret rotation, certificate renewal, permission recertification, and automated disablement of unused identities. Incorporating these controls prevents non-human identities from becoming unmanaged backdoors into the environment.

The bottom line is to bring non-human identities fully into the IAM and governance model. Workloads, services, automation, and AI agents should authenticate with strong methods, receive limited authorization, and be tracked and monitored like any other identity. The same Zero Trust principle applies: no workload or agent receives inherent trust simply because it operates inside the environment. A compromised server, pipeline, service account, or AI agent should not be allowed to communicate freely or access sensitive systems without explicit identity, authorization, and policy checks.

Architecture and Deployment Considerations in Hybrid/Multi-cloud Environments

Bringing it all together, how do you architect an identity-first security model across hybrid and multi-cloud environments? Many enterprises have a mix of on-premises AD, Azure services, AWS/GCP, and numerous SaaS providers. Achieving a unified, secure identity perimeter in such complexity is challenging but feasible with careful planning:

1. **Establish an Identity Hub:** As mentioned, choose a primary identity platform as your "hub." Many organizations use a cloud IdP (Entra ID or Okta, for example) as the hub because it's accessible everywhere and designed to integrate with both cloud and on-prem systems. Integrate on-prem AD via ADFS or cloud sync so that on-prem accounts become cloud identities. Integrate other clouds by federating them to the hub (AWS IAM Identity Center or SAML to Entra ID, etc.). Integrate SaaS apps via SSO. This hub then becomes the place to enforce conditional access and MFA consistently across the board.

Note Federate AWS/GCP consoles and SaaS to the same IdP so CA/MFA telemetry is centralized. Avoid separate standing accounts per cloud.

2. **Hybrid Join and Device Management:** Manage devices in hybrid mode - e.g., Windows machines hybrid-joined to AD and Entra ID - so that device compliance info is available to conditional access in the cloud, and also policy can be applied on-prem. Leverage tools like Microsoft Intune or alternative MDMs to enforce device compliance policies on all endpoints (including mobile, which might use different solutions). This bridges the gap between on-prem device trust and cloud identity trust.
3. **Network Still Matters - Enforce Identity at Network Layers:** Even though identity is the new perimeter, using network segmentation and microsegmentation in conjunction strengthens security. For instance, implement software-defined perimeters or Zero Trust Network Access (ZTNA) tools that require user authentication (via SSO) before establishing network connections to internal apps. Products from Zscaler, Palo Alto (Prisma), Cisco, etc., can integrate with your IdP such that the network tunnel setup itself is gated on identity and policy. This helps secure legacy apps that maybe can't do modern auth; you wrap them in an identity-aware access proxy.
4. **Policy Enforcement Points Placement:** Decide where PEPs will sit. Some options:
    - At the application layer (e.g., integrate identity libraries in the app to do authZ)
    - At gateway/proxy layer (an access proxy in front of apps or API gateway enforcing OAuth scopes)
    - At the endpoint (an agent on devices that controls access)

Likely a combination. For SaaS, the PEP is often the SaaS app itself, which honors SAML/OAuth tokens. For on-prem apps, you might put an NGINX with OIDC authentication in front as a PEP. For network access, a client agent and an edge gateway act as a PEP. Ensure all these PEPs connect back to the PDP (your identity provider or policy engine) for decisions.

5. **Multi-cloud Federations:** If you operate across multiple cloud accounts, consider using identity federation rather than separate accounts. For example, an engineer in AD wanting to use AWS assumes an IAM role via SAML SSO; they don't have a standing IAM user in AWS. This means AWS respects the central identity's policies (like if their account is disabled, they can't log in to AWS either), similarly for GCP or others. This reduces identity duplication and the risk of forgetting to turn off one copy. Some organizations also consider multi-home IdPs (e.g., running both Entra ID and Okta in parallel or one as a backup) - if you do, ensure they're synced and policies are aligned; otherwise, you create gaps.

6. **Resiliency and Fail-Safe:** If identity is the gate to everything, its availability is crucial. Plan for IdP outages or lockouts. Strategies include having break-glass accounts (with MFA) that can bypass SSO in emergencies or enabling cached credentials for key admin access if SSO is down. Monitor your identity system's health and have DR plans. For on-prem AD, have multiple domain controllers, etc.; for cloud IdPs, understand their SLA and any on-prem fallback (Entra ID has ADFS fallback if needed, etc.). Also, ensure logs are sent to off-IdP so an attacker who somehow compromises the IdP can't erase their traces from the logs.

Tip Monitor IdP SLOs; test tenant-wide sign-out, token revocation, and CAE. Store logs off-tenant to preserve forensic integrity.

---

7. **Costs and Licensing:** It's worth noting that some advanced features (adaptive policies, risk-based controls) may require premium tiers of IAM products. Plan budget accordingly; the investment is often justified by risk reduction. If using multiple products (e.g., Okta + a CASB + a PAM tool), ensure you're not paying for overlapping functionality and that they integrate well (e.g., a CASB can enforce device state from Intune, Okta can trigger session control in a CASB, etc.).

8. **Standards and Interoperability:** In a heterogeneous environment, favor standards (SAML, OIDC, SCIM for provisioning, FIDO for auth, etc.) so that components work together. Avoid proprietary lock-in that might limit one part of your environment. If you have a unique application that doesn't support modern auth, consider updating it or wrapping it (e.g., with an authentication proxy).

9. **Compliance and Data Sovereignty:** Be mindful of where identity data flows. In multi-national environments, sending all auth through a global cloud might raise compliance issues. Use features like conditional access to restrict data access by region, if needed. Or deploy separate tenants if data residency is required (but then manage the federation between them). This gets complex, but identity can be configured to comply with regulations (e.g., not syncing specific attributes to the cloud if not allowed).

The end-state architecture should look like a mesh of trust centered on identity. Users anywhere can authenticate to a central authority that enforces policy. Resources, whether on AWS, Azure, on-prem, or SaaS, all rely on the issued token or assertion to determine access. The network is configured to be open enough to allow this but closed enough to prevent unauthenticated access. Telemetry flows to a central SOC. And governance processes overlay it to keep it all clean (no excess access, no forgotten accounts).

Many organizations are at different stages of maturity on this journey. It's perfectly fine to progress iteratively: for example, start by integrating MFA and SSO across all major apps (a huge immediate win), then implement conditional access policies for critical scenarios, then introduce PAM for admins, then address non-human identities, and so forth. Zero Trust is a security strategy that improves security incrementally by closing gaps one at a time.

Summary and Key Takeaways

In today's perimeter-less environments, identity is the new perimeter – the primary control point that stands between attackers and your critical assets. A modern security architecture must therefore put identity at the center, verifying who (or what) is requesting access and whether they should be allowed access continuously. We explored how traditional perimeter defenses have given way to identity-focused strategies out of necessity: users and applications operate everywhere, and adversaries target identity systems as the path of least resistance.

Implementing an identity-first security model involves multiple layers and best practices, which we covered in depth:

1. **Federation and SSO***:* Evolved our ability to unify identities across systems, enabling central authentication and seamless single sign-on. Embrace these to collapse identity silos – they improve security by reducing password proliferation and enabling central monitoring.

2. **Multi-factor Authentication***:* A crucial defense against credential theft. Requiring MFA (preferably phishing-resistant methods) for all users dramatically lowers account compromise risk. Today, MFA should be ubiquitous – especially for privileged roles – and integrated by default in IAM solutions.

3. **Zero Trust Principles***:* "Never trust, always verify" means every access is explicitly authenticated, authorized with least privilege, and continuously validated. Zero Trust is a journey, but even steps like enforcing MFA and conditional policies embody its principles.

4. **Conditional Access and Adaptive Policies***:* Use the contextual signals of identity (user risk, device health, location, etc.) to adapt authentication requirements in real time. This provides security when needed and usability when risk is low, striking a balance. Conditional access policies are your "security brain" that decides who can access what under which conditions – implement them thoughtfully and test thoroughly.

5. **Identity-Focused Attack Surface Reduction***:* Centralize identities for visibility, enforce least privilege (for users and machines), eliminate legacy authentication, rotate secrets, and remove unused accounts. These hygiene practices close standard holes that attackers exploit. Many breaches have occurred because of orphaned accounts or credentials left floating around - don't let your organization be next.

6. **Privileged Access Management***:* Treat admin accounts with extra care (JIT access, monitoring, dedicated devices). Assume that attackers will target them, so put them in a "vault" of controls. The cost/effort to protect high-privilege identities is worth it to avoid a total breach.

7. **Human, Consumer, and Non-human Identities**: Apply Zero Trust principles across all identity types. Workforce users need strong MFA, user education, and lifecycle governance. Consumer identities need secure registration, privacy-aware consent, fraud controls, and low-friction authentication. Non-human identities, including service accounts, API credentials, workload identities, and AI agents, need strong authentication, scoped authorization, ownership, lifecycle review, and regular rotation or expiration. Do not neglect service accounts, API credentials, automation identities, or agentic workflows in your security planning.

8. **Architecture Considerations***:* Deploy an integrated identity control plane across on-prem and multi-cloud. Your identities and policies should transcend individual environments to ensure unified enforcement. Use tools and services that extend your policy enforcement to wherever your workloads and users are - whether through proxies, cloud-native integrations, or endpoint agents. Remember that the availability and performance of identity systems are critical: design for resiliency so that security doesn't become a single point of failure for productivity.

Finally, cultivating an identity-aware culture in both IT and users is key. This means security teams think in terms of identities (not just IPs or devices) when analyzing threats, and users recognize their personal role in safeguarding their identities (reporting phishing attempts, using MFA correctly, etc.).

By implementing the strategies outlined in this chapter - from the basics of MFA and SSO to advanced adaptive policies and machine identity management - organizations can significantly strengthen their security posture in an era where the network perimeter is diffuse and attackers relentlessly target identity systems. Identity truly becomes the new perimeter: a living, dynamic perimeter that surrounds each user and device, enforcing security wherever they go. When done right, identity-first security enables businesses to confidently embrace the cloud and mobility, knowing that protection follows the user and the data, not being confined to a firewall box.

In the following chapters, we will apply these identity-first and Zero Trust fundamentals to non-human, AI-driven, and autonomous environments, examining how to manage the growth of workload identities, service principals, automation credentials, and agentic AI identities. The foundation remains the same: strong, adaptive identity controls are a cornerstone of security across the modern technology landscape.

Key Takeaways

- The corporate network boundary is no longer the primary security boundary - identity is. Every access request should be authenticated and authorized based on identity, not network location.
- **Zero Trust** is an approach that embeds security at every access, continuously verifying identities and context. Its core tenets (verify explicitly, least privilege, assume breach, continuous validation) should guide your architecture.
- **Modern IAM technologies** like federation/SSO and MFA are essential building blocks. Use SSO to centralize identity control and MFA everywhere to thwart password-based attacks.
- **Conditional access policies** allow dynamic risk-based decisions, greatly enhancing security by adapting to threats in real time (e.g., blocking unusual login attempts, requiring MFA on risky conditions).
    - To reduce attack surface: consolidate and tightly manage identities (no unused or duplicate accounts), enforce least privilege on all accounts (human or machine), eliminate legacy auth and weak protocols, and monitor identity activity continuously for signs of attack.

- **Privileged accounts** deserve special handling (PAM) - they should be few in number, highly secured, and used only when needed.
  - Successful identity-first security in a hybrid/multi-cloud world requires architectural planning: a unified identity platform, integrated device management, and identity-aware proxies/gateways to cover all access scenarios. Aim for a single control plane for policy and visibility across your on-prem and cloud assets.
  - Ultimately, an **identity-centric security model** can enhance user experience (through SSO and intelligent authentication) while significantly improving security. It is a foundational element to enabling business agility securely - allowing users to work from anywhere and systems to be distributed, without increasing risk.
  - Transitioning to this model is a journey - start with quick wins like MFA and SSO adoption, then layer on conditional policies and gradually retire insecure legacy components. Continuously refine policies based on evolving threats (e.g., new phishing tactics). Security is not "set and forget," especially with identities, which are living, changing entities and must be managed as such.

By treating identity as the new perimeter, you take control away from attackers who try to exploit the gaps in traditional perimeters. Identities, when protected and managed well, can become the strongest defense, providing a flexible yet robust security layer across all your systems and data.

CHAPTER 3

Protecting Data in Motion, Use, and Storage

In an era of relentless cyber threats and strict compliance mandates, organizations must protect sensitive data throughout its lifecycle – whether it's in motion (transit), in use (actively processed), or in storage (at rest). CISOs, technology leaders, data owners, privacy teams, and security engineers face the challenge of safeguarding data across networks, cloud services, endpoints, and applications without unnecessarily slowing business productivity. This chapter provides a comprehensive guide to protecting data in all states, balancing strategic guidance with deep technical insight. We explore proven approaches (like encryption, data loss prevention, and access controls), vendor-neutral design patterns, and real-world implementations.

Multi-page case studies in healthcare, finance, education, and manufacturing illustrate how enterprises are defending data using modern solutions such as Microsoft Purview and Netskope – all while remaining vendor-neutral in principles. We also dive into technical configurations (sensitivity labels, DLP policies, CASB enforcement) and emerging trends shaping the future of data protection: Data Security Posture Management (DSPM), AI governance for sensitive data, and confidential computing for protecting data in use. Diagrams, tables, and examples are included to ensure clarity and practicality. By the end of this chapter, readers will have both high-level strategies and hands-on knowledge to implement robust data protection programs that secure information in motion, in use, and at rest.

Data Protection Across All States of Data

Data can reside in three primary states – at rest, in motion, and in use – and each state introduces unique risks and requires specific protections. Below is a quick overview of the data states and corresponding security mechanisms:

A. Gupta and S. Mittal, *Foundations of Modern Information Security*,
https://doi.org/10.1007/979-8-8688-2558-3_3

Data at Rest (Storage): Information stored on disk, databases, or backups. The chief risks are unauthorized access or theft of stored data (e.g., lost laptops, database breaches). Protection methods include encryption at rest (disk or file encryption), strong access controls, tokenization, and data governance policies.

Data in Motion (Transit): Information moving through networks (within the corporate network or over the internet). Risks include eavesdropping, man-in-the-middle attacks, and traffic interception. Protection methods include encryption in transit (TLS/SSL, VPNs), secure protocols, network DLP to monitor/block sensitive file transfers, and secure email gateways.

Data in Use (Active Memory/Processing): Information being processed in applications or residing in system memory/CPU. Risks here are more complex to mitigate - e.g., malware reading memory, rogue insiders capturing screenshots or processes. Protection methods include runtime memory encryption, hardware-based trusted execution environments, strict process isolation, and emerging techniques like confidential computing (discussed later).

While organizations focus on securing data in all three states, the cloud introduces a unique dynamic: security responsibilities are shared between the cloud provider and the customer. The Shared Responsibility Model clarifies who is responsible for what across cloud service types, Infrastructure-as-a-Service (IaaS), Platform-as-a-Service (PaaS), and Software-as-a-Service (SaaS) (see Figure 3-1).

Responsibility	On-premises	IaaS	PaaS	SaaS	FaaS
Data classification and accountability	Cloud Customer	Cloud Customer	Cloud Customer	Cloud Customer	Cloud Customer
Client and end-point protection	Cloud Customer	Cloud Customer	Cloud Customer	Cloud Customer / Cloud Provider	Cloud Customer / Cloud Provider
Identity and access management	Cloud Customer	Cloud Customer	Cloud Customer / Cloud Provider	Cloud Customer / Cloud Provider	Cloud Customer / Cloud Provider
Application-level controls	Cloud Customer	Cloud Customer	Cloud Customer / Cloud Provider	Cloud Customer / Cloud Provider	Cloud Customer / Cloud Provider
Network controls	Cloud Customer	Cloud Customer / Cloud Provider	Cloud Provider	Cloud Provider	Cloud Provider
Host infrastructure	Cloud Customer	Cloud Customer / Cloud Provider	Cloud Provider	Cloud Provider	Cloud Provider
Physical security	Cloud Customer	Cloud Provider	Cloud Provider	Cloud Provider	Cloud Provider

Cloud Customer Cloud Provider

***Figure 3-1.** Shared responsibility model for cloud data protection*

In IaaS, the provider secures the physical infrastructure (data centers, storage, and networking), while customers remain responsible for securing operating systems, applications, and data. In PaaS, the provider additionally secures the runtime and platform services, whereas customers manage their applications, configurations, and access controls. In SaaS, most operational security shifts to the provider, but customers still own identity management, data governance, and compliance enforcement.

Understanding this division is crucial: encrypting a database (data at rest) or using TLS (data in motion) must complement the provider's baseline controls, not replace them. Misconfigurations, weak identity practices, or neglected access reviews remain the customer's liability even in fully managed environments.

It's critical to understand that adequate data security requires layered controls across all three states. For example, encrypting a database (at rest) is not enough if someone can intercept the data as it is being queried in motion or scrape it from application memory while it is in use. Likewise, robust network encryption will not prevent an insider with authorized access from misusing data in an application. Thus, organizations should implement a holistic data protection strategy that classifies sensitive data and enforces appropriate controls no matter where the data resides or flows.

Core Strategies for Protecting Data in Motion, Use, and Storage

Protecting data throughout its lifecycle calls for a combination of policies, technologies, and user education. In the following, we outline core strategies and controls, many of which are enabled by enterprise data protection platforms:

1. **Data Classification and Labeling:** The foundation of data protection is knowing which data is sensitive and where it resides. Organizations should inventory and classify data using categories such as public, internal, confidential, and highly confidential. Data classification may be performed manually by users, automatically through content detection, or continuously through data discovery and posture management tools. Solutions such as Microsoft Purview Information Protection, DSPM platforms such as Cyera or Concentric AI, and similar tools can help identify sensitive content and apply sensitivity labels to documents, emails, repositories, and cloud data stores. Labels can persist with the data and enable policies such as encryption, watermarking, access restriction, and DLP enforcement. A unified classification scheme ensures consistency across storage, cloud apps, endpoints, and data platforms. For example, an engineering drawing labeled "Company Confidential" may trigger encryption and restricted access wherever it goes.

2. **Encryption and Key Management:** Encryption renders data unreadable without the proper keys, making it a critical control for all data states. **At rest**, full-disk or file-level encryption (e.g., BitLocker, Azure SQL TDE) protects against device theft or unauthorized access to the filesystem. **In motion**, protocols like HTTPS, TLS, IPsec, and SSH provide encryption for web traffic, VPNs, and remote management. **In use**, emerging memory encryption (e.g., Intel SGX, AMD SEV) and application-layer encryption keep data encrypted even during processing. Equally important is key management - keys must be protected (ideally in hardware security modules or cloud key vaults), and procedures such as key rotation and separation of duties should be in place. Vendor-neutral tip: Use open standards (AES-256, RSA, TLS 1.3) and interoperable key management (KMIP) to avoid lock-in.

Note Prefer modern suites (e.g., TLS 1.3 for transport, AES-256-GCM at rest). Use customer-managed keys for regulated workloads; rotate keys and segregate duties.

---

3. **Data Loss Prevention (DLP):** DLP technologies monitor and control the movement of sensitive data to prevent unauthorized disclosure. DLP can operate at multiple layers:

    a. **Endpoint DLP:** Runs on user devices to detect sensitive data in use (e.g., copied to USB drives, screenshots, clipboard) and enforce policies (block, warn, log). For example, a policy might block copying files tagged as "Confidential" to external drives.

    b. **Network DLP:** Inspects network traffic (emails, web uploads, cloud app traffic) for sensitive content signatures. It can block or encrypt emails with PII or prevent uploads of customer data to unsanctioned cloud storage.

    c. **Cloud DLP:** Integrated into cloud services or via Cloud Access Security Brokers (CASBs) to scan data stored in cloud apps (like OneDrive, Box) and apply policies. Modern DLP solutions often combine these into a unified policy framework (see Figure 3-2).

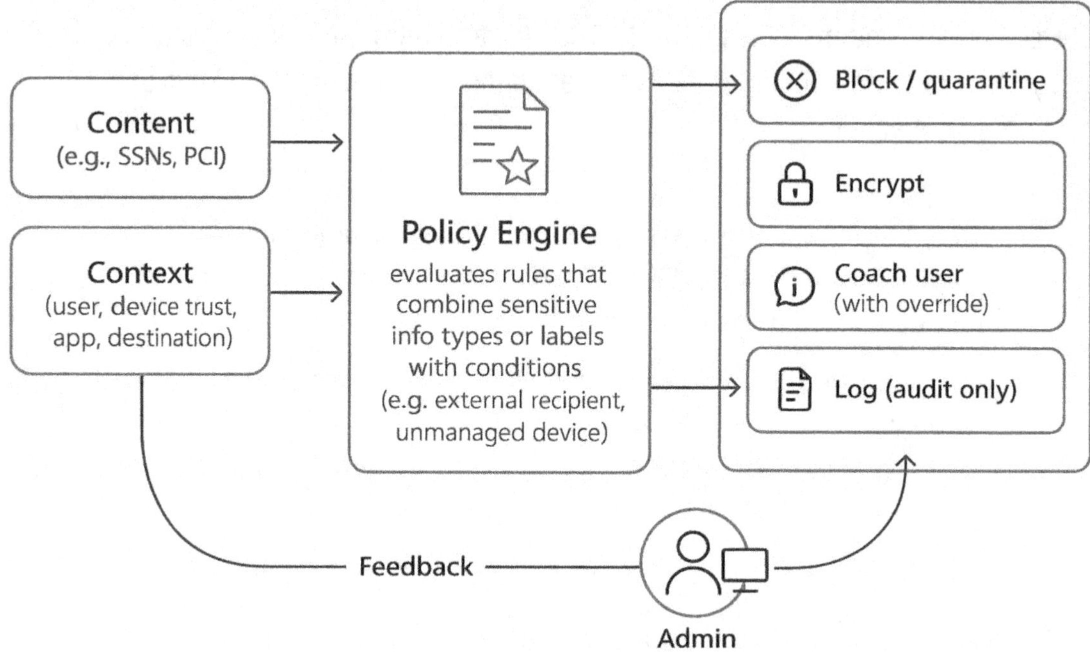

***Figure 3-2.** DLP policy enforcement flow*

4. **Access Control and Rights Management:** Limiting who can access data (and what they can do with it) is a fundamental security tenet. Strategies include

   a. **Identity and Access Management (IAM):** Strong authentication (MFA), role-based access control, and least privilege ensure only authorized users access data. For instance, use Microsoft Entra ID or another IAM to enforce that only HR personnel can open files labeled "HR-Private".

   b. **Rights Management/IRM:** Beyond the initial access, Information Rights Management can enforce restrictions on forwarded documents (e.g., preventing printing or adding watermarks). Sensitivity labels in Microsoft Purview, for example, can be configured to prevent printing or screenshots of highly confidential documents. This ensures that even if a user can read a file, they cannot easily copy or redistribute it in plain text form.

c. **Zero Trust Networking:** Rather than trusting any user or device by default, adopt a Zero Trust approach where every access to data is verified for legitimacy (user identity, device posture, location, etc.). Technologies like Netskope Zero Trust Engine enable granular policies based on user, device, app, and data context to determine whether a transaction is allowed.

5. **Monitoring and Analytics:** Continuous monitoring of data access and movement is key to detecting anomalies. Solutions often provide analytics and alerts (e.g., an unusual spike in a user's file downloads can trigger an Insider Risk alert). Integrated audit logs (like Microsoft Purview's Audit and Insider Risk modules) help trace data flows and spot potential breaches. Machine learning is increasingly used to baseline normal behavior and flag deviations (e.g., Netskope's use of LLMs for SaaS risk assessment and UEBA signals).

6. **Policies and User Training:** Technology alone isn't enough – organizational policies (acceptable use, data handling procedures) and user awareness are critical. Employees should be trained to classify and handle sensitive data (e.g., recognizing confidential information and using the tools provided to encrypt it). In many of our case studies, you'll see how culture and training were as important as tools. For example, at National Bank of Fujairah, extensive training (six sessions per month) accompanied the DLP rollout to ensure users understand how to use the new controls. Building a culture of "data care" turns employees into allies in protecting information.

Tip Start in audit/simulation mode to measure impact, then phase in blocking. Provide coaching messages and approved alternatives to reduce user workarounds.

With these fundamentals established, we now turn to detailed explorations of leading solutions and their implementation. The following sections offer technical deep-dives into two prominent (but vendor-neutral in principle) platforms – Microsoft Purview and Netskope – demonstrating how to configure data protection policies in practice. Following that, we will examine extended case studies in four industries, illustrating how the strategies above come together in real-world scenarios with measurable results. Finally, we discuss emerging trends that are reshaping data protection, including DSPM, AI governance, post-quantum readiness, and confidential computing.

Technical Deep-Dive: Implementing Data Protection Solutions

In this section, we provide practical guidance on deploying and configuring key data protection technologies. We focus on two comprehensive solutions as examples: Microsoft Purview (an integrated data governance and protection platform) and Netskope (a leading Cloud Access Security Broker and Security Service Edge platform). We also briefly mention other tools (Forcepoint, Broadcom/Symantec DLP, etc.) to maintain a vendor-neutral perspective. The goal is to illustrate concrete steps and design patterns for protecting data in motion, in use, and at rest:

Microsoft Purview: We will walk through setting up sensitivity labels, DLP policies, and leveraging its unified approach to protect data across Microsoft 365, endpoints, and cloud services.

Netskope: We will demonstrate how to enforce data-centric policies via a CASB, including real-time (inline) controls for data in motion and API-enabled scanning for data at rest in cloud apps, and how it integrates with other security layers.

Other Tools: We highlight comparable capabilities in other enterprise DLP suites (e.g., Forcepoint, Broadcom) and how organizations can choose between a unified and best-of-breed DLP strategy.

Microsoft Purview: Unified Data Protection via Sensitivity Labels and DLP

Microsoft Purview provides a unified platform for data discovery, classification, protection, and compliance. It spans information protection (labels and encryption), Data Loss Prevention, insider risk management, eDiscovery, and more – all integrated with Microsoft 365 cloud services and endpoint devices. Below, we focus on two core components for protecting data: sensitivity labels and unified DLP policies.

1. **Sensitivity Labeling and Persistent Protection:** Sensitivity labels in Purview allow you to classify data and optionally apply protection (encryption, watermarks, access restrictions) that stay resident with the file or email. Administrators define a taxonomy of labels (e.g., Public, General, Confidential, Highly Confidential) in the Purview compliance portal. Each label can have associated protection settings. For example: A "Confidential - Finance" label might encrypt the document and restrict access to only the Finance AD group, with watermarks indicating the user's name and timestamp. A "Public" label might have no protection, just a visual footer indicating the document is approved for public release.

Labels can be applied manually by users (e.g., selecting a label from the Office apps' toolbar) or automatically based on conditions (via auto-labeling policies). Purview includes built-in trainable classifiers and sensitive information types (over 300 predefined patterns for PII, credit card numbers, etc.) to detect sensitive content. For instance, Purview can auto-label a file as "Confidential" if it detects ten or more credit card numbers in it. These labels travel with the content; if the file is emailed or saved to OneDrive, the label and its protections remain in effect.

Configuration walkthrough: To set up sensitivity labels:

1) **Define Labels:** In the Purview portal, go to Information Protection ➤ Labels and create labels with appropriate names and descriptions (e.g., "Confidential - Internal"). Optionally, configure protection: encryption (choose who can access, whether it expires, etc.), content marking (headers/footers, watermarks), and endpoint settings (e.g., restrict offline access or printing).

2) **Publish Label Policies:** After creating labels, publish them to users or groups. This determines who sees the labels in their Office apps and which default label (if any) is applied. For example, you might auto-apply a "General" label to all new documents and allow users to escalate to Confidential as needed.

3) **Auto-Labeling Rules:** Define auto-labeling policies for SharePoint/OneDrive and Exchange if desired. For example, a rule: "If content contains > 5 bank account numbers (using built-in sensitive info type), apply label Confidential." Purview supports simulation modes to test auto-labeling rules before enforcement.

Once deployed, users will see labels in their Office apps. When a label with encryption is applied, the file is encrypted using Microsoft Purview Information Protection encryption and usage-rights controls. Only authorized users (per the label's policy) can open it. This persists even if the file is stolen - an attacker without access keys would see gibberish. Additionally, labels can serve as conditions in DLP policies (discussed next), effectively linking classification with enforcement. For example, you can create a DLP rule: "if a document is labeled Highly Confidential, block it from being shared externally." Purview's unified platform makes the label metadata available to DLP scanning engines.

1. **Unified DLP Policies Across Email, Cloud, and Endpoints:** A highlight of Microsoft Purview is its ability to define a single DLP policy that applies to multiple locations - Exchange email, SharePoint/OneDrive, Teams chats, and Windows endpoint devices. This unified DLP approach helps ensure consistent enforcement of data protection rules across the organization.

   Key capabilities of Purview DLP:

   1) **Pre-built Policy Templates:** Purview provides out-of-the-box templates for standard regulations (GDPR, HIPAA, PCI-DSS, etc.) and sensitive data types. For instance, a template for "U.S. Financial Data" will detect ABA routing numbers, SWIFT codes, account numbers, etc. Administrators can start with templates and customize actions.

   2) **Locations and Conditions:** When creating a DLP policy, you select the locations it will apply to. Options include Exchange (email), SharePoint sites, OneDrive accounts, Teams (chat/channel messages and files), Endpoint devices (Windows 10/11 and macOS endpoints onboarded via Intune or configuration), and even on-prem file shares via the **Purview scanner**. Conditions can be based on content (e.g., contains a credit card or matches a sensitivity label) and/or context (e.g., document is shared outside the organization, or user is accessing from an unmanaged device).

3) **Actions:** Purview DLP supports a variety of response actions when a policy match is found. For email, it can block sending, forward to the admin, or notify the user. For SharePoint/OneDrive, it can block external sharing or log the event. For Teams, it can prevent the message from being posted if it contains sensitive information. For endpoints, it can block or audit the attempted action (copy to USB, print, upload via browser, etc.). Administrators can choose to use "test mode" initially (policy only logs matches and user notifications but does not actually block) to gauge the impact before full enforcement.

4) **User Notifications and Overrides:** DLP can inform users in real-time via policy tips (e.g., a pop-up in Outlook saying "This email contains sensitive info; sending is blocked"). Admins can allow overrides (user justifies and proceeds) for specific policies – this can reduce frustration if a user has a valid business need while still logging the event. All events are logged to the Activity Explorer in the Microsoft Purview portal for review.

Purview's unified DLP means one policy can cover multiple channels. For example, a single rule "Block any outbound sharing of data labeled Highly Confidential outside the organization" could simultaneously prevent emails to external domains with such attachments, stop a user from uploading a labeled file to a personal OneDrive or USB drive, and block posting that file in a third-party app via Defender for Cloud Apps integration. This unified approach is more straightforward to manage than separate point solutions for each channel. A contrast might be a specialized tool that only handles email DLP – it would not catch, say, a user uploading a sensitive file via a web browser or chatting in Teams.

Example: Consider implementing a DLP policy for protecting customer PII. Using Purview (see Listing 3-1):

- Scope it to **All locations** (Exchange, SharePoint, OneDrive, Teams, Devices).

- Condition: Content contains **Sensitive Info Type = U.S. Social Security Number** (with instances >= 1, and perhaps confidence level high).

- Actions: If the destination is external (outside the tenant), then Block transfer. If internal, maybe Allow but Audit. Enable user notifications: e.g., "Sensitive data detected: SSNs are not allowed to be shared externally." Allow override with justification for internal false positives.

- In Endpoint, configure it to block copying such data to removable media or printing it.

- Test in simulation mode for a week, review logs (to adjust any false positives), and then activate enforcement.

Purview would then catch someone trying to email a spreadsheet containing SSNs or copying it to a USB drive – the user would get a pop-up, and the action would be stopped (assuming an external target or removable media). The incident would be logged in the DLP reports, including the sensitive information found and the rule that triggered it.

Purview's integration with Microsoft 365 is a significant strength: because it's built into Exchange Online, SharePoint, Teams, and related services, it can detect sensitive data before it leaves the Microsoft ecosystem. For example, if a user tries to share a labeled document via Teams, Purview intercepts it in real time. Moreover, because endpoint DLP is tied to Intune management, it can block actions on managed devices at the OS level (e.g., copying an account number to the clipboard to paste into Twitter can be blocked and logged).

Note For endpoint DLP, devices must be onboarded and licensed appropriately. Because Microsoft Purview capabilities vary by plan and compliance add-on, architects should confirm the current licensing matrix before finalizing the design.

Listing 3-1. Microsoft Purview unified DLP policy creation

```
# Connect to Microsoft Purview Compliance PowerShell
Connect-IPPSSession

# 1) Create a unified DLP policy for PII across M365 workloads
New-DlpCompliancePolicy -Name "PII - External Egress Protection" `
  -Comment "Blocks external sharing of SSNs/CCNs across Exchange,
  SharePoint, OneDrive, Teams, and devices." `
```

```
  -Mode Enable `
  -ExchangeLocation All -SharePointLocation All -OneDriveLocation All
  -TeamsLocation All

# 2) Block email/file egress if SSN is detected and the recipient/
destination is external
New-DlpComplianceRule -Name "Block external SSNs" `
  -Policy "PII - External Egress Protection" `
  -ContentContainsSensitiveInformation @(@{Name="U.S. Social Security
  Number (SSN)"; MinCount=1}) `
  -BlockAccess $true -BlockAccessScope All `
  -NotifyUser $true -NotifyUserType PolicyTip,Email `
  -GenerateIncidentReport $true -IncidentReportContent Sender,Recipients,
  Subject,MatchedContent `
  -StopRuleProcessing $true

# 3) For lower-volume matches, require M365 Message Encryption instead of
blocking
New-DlpComplianceRule -Name "Encrypt small SSN payloads" `
  -Policy "PII - External Egress Protection" `
  -ContentContainsSensitiveInformation @(@{Name="U.S. Social Security
  Number (SSN)"; MinCount=1; MaxCount=10}) `
  -ApplyOME $true `
  -NotifyUser $true -NotifyUserType PolicyTip,Email
```

Policy Management and Monitoring: Microsoft provides a unified DLP dashboard that aggregates alerts across cloud apps and devices. Security teams can investigate incidents using Activity Explorer (to see events like "User X attempted to upload file Y to dropbox.com, which was blocked due to the file containing sensitive info"). They can also leverage Microsoft Sentinel or Defender to correlate DLP events with other signals (e.g., an insider threat scenario combining DLP alerts + unusual login locations).

Note Leverage Activity Explorer and incident exports to a SIEM; tune high-noise rules weekly for the first 60–90 days.

Tip – Sensitivity Labels As DLP Conditions: A recent capability allows using sensitivity labels to match a condition in DLP. For instance, instead of inspecting content for a pattern, you say, "If item's label = Highly Confidential, treat it per this policy." This is powerful because it leverages the manual or automatic classification already done. This capability increasingly allows classification decisions to drive DLP enforcement across email, collaboration, cloud storage, endpoints, and other supported channels. Administrators should verify current platform support by workload before designing enforcement rules. It's an elegant way to tie together the classification and prevention aspects of data security in Purview.

Purview in Action – Summary: Microsoft Purview exemplifies a baked-in, platform-level approach to data protection by combining classification, security, and DLP into a single solution, reducing integration complexity. The advantages include a unified classification engine (the same sensitivity label travels from an email to an endpoint file), consistent user experience (users see one set of labels and receive similar DLP prompts across apps), and shared analytics (alerts feed into a single system, including Insider Risk Management and auditing). A real-world outcome of this approach is faster incident response and fewer gaps. For example, suppose an employee tries a workaround (like renaming a file or using a different channel). In that case, the unified DLP still applies as long as the content or label remains detectable.

From an implementation perspective, organizations often start with a few core labels and simple DLP policies, then gradually expand. A recommended rollout might be

1. **Discover**: Use content scan reports, data discovery tools, and activity logs to understand where sensitive data resides across email, collaboration platforms, endpoints, cloud storage, databases, and shared repositories. This step should identify high-risk data locations, unmanaged repositories, excessive sharing, and sensitive content that is not yet labeled or protected.

2. **Classify**: Create a simple sensitivity label taxonomy and publish it to the right users and groups. Start with a manageable set of labels, such as Public, Internal, Confidential, and Highly Confidential, before adding more specialized labels. Train users on when to apply labels and use automatic classification where appropriate. Validate licensing requirements early because advanced capabilities such as endpoint DLP, automatic classification,

insider risk management, communication compliance, and some advanced audit or governance features may require higher-tier licensing or compliance add-ons.

3. **Protect**: Enable protection controls based on the classification model. This may include encryption, watermarking, access restrictions, external sharing limits, rights management, and DLP enforcement. Begin with the highest-risk data types, such as regulated data, financial records, intellectual property, customer records, and highly confidential business documents.

4. **Test and Refine**: Run DLP and auto-labeling policies in audit, simulation, or test mode before full enforcement. Review false positives, business exceptions, user impact, and workflow disruption. Refine sensitive information types, thresholds, labels, and policy conditions before moving to blocking actions.

5. **Extend**: Expand protection beyond email and document repositories to endpoints, Teams or collaboration platforms, browsers, unmanaged devices, SaaS applications, and cloud storage. For endpoint DLP, ensure devices are properly onboarded and that user coaching messages are clear. Where third-party CASB or SSE tools are used, align their policies with the same classification and DLP model.

6. **Govern**: Establish ownership, approval workflows, exception handling, and periodic access reviews for sensitive data. Use governance tools to review oversharing, stale access, unlabeled repositories, orphaned data, and high-risk collaboration patterns. In multi-cloud or hybrid environments, coordinate Purview or equivalent platform capabilities with DSPM, IAM, CASB, and SIEM workflows.

7. **Monitor and Iterate**: Continuously monitor DLP alerts, audit events, user overrides, policy matches, and incident trends. Tune noisy policies during the first 60–90 days, then continue periodic reviews as business processes, data locations, regulations, and collaboration tools change. Feed meaningful incidents into the SIEM or security operations process so data protection becomes part of the broader detection and response program.

To conclude the Purview section: Microsoft Purview demonstrates how a **modern, cloud-powered platform** can protect data in motion, at rest, and in use in a unified way. It is particularly effective for organizations deeply in the Microsoft ecosystem. The principles learned here - classify once, enforce everywhere; balance blocking with user education; use context-aware policies - are vendor-neutral and can be applied with other toolsets as well.

Netskope: Cloud-Centric Data Protection via CASB and SSE

As organizations increasingly rely on cloud services and remote work, Cloud Access Security Brokers (CASBs) have become essential for protecting data in motion to and from cloud apps, as well as data stored within those apps. Netskope is a leading CASB and part of a broader Security Service Edge (SSE) platform. It provides visibility and control over data across SaaS, IaaS, and web traffic through a combination of inline policy enforcement and API-based scanning. In this section, we'll explore how Netskope can be configured to protect sensitive data in both real-time (inline) and asynchronous (API/at-rest) modes, how it integrates DLP and threat protection, and reference deployment design patterns.

1. **Architecture Overview**: Netskope operates through two main modes:

   a. **Inline Proxy (Real-Time Protection)**: Traffic from users to cloud services (or any web traffic) is steered through Netskope's cloud proxy (often via a lightweight endpoint agent or network routing). This allows Netskope to inspect data in motion in real time - e.g., a user uploading a file to Dropbox or typing a message in Slack - and enforce policies immediately (allow, block, coach user, etc.). Netskope's high-performance cloud infrastructure (NewEdge) with global data centers enables this with minimal latency.

   b. **API Integration (Out-of-Band Scanning)**: Netskope connects directly to cloud apps via APIs (using the apps' published APIs for third-party developers) to scan data at rest within those services. For example, Netskope can use the Microsoft 365 Graph API to enumerate files in OneDrive or emails in Exchange Online, identify sensitive content or exposure (such as an overly shared file), and then take action (such as quarantining the file or removing external shares). This mode doesn't require user traffic to be proxied; instead, it periodically checks cloud repositories for policy violations. It's excellent for covering scenarios like a user uploading data when off the VPN – the file might go to the cloud, but Netskope's API scan will catch it soon after and remediate if needed.

By combining these, Netskope can protect data at rest (through API scans of SaaS/IaaS) and data in transit (through inline). Inline covers sanctioned and unsanctioned app usage in real time, while API mode covers sanctioned app content comprehensively.

2. **Data Loss Prevention and Policy Control**: Netskope's DLP capabilities are rich and on par with enterprise DLP suites:

   a. It includes hundreds of predefined data identifiers and compliance templates (for PCI, PHI, PDPL, etc.). It supports advanced detection, such as file fingerprinting, exact data matching, regular expression patterns, OCR (optical character recognition for images), and even ML-based image classification. For instance, you could fingerprint your source code files; if any chunk of that code appears in an outgoing transfer (even partial or renamed), Netskope can recognize it and trigger a policy.

   b. Netskope also offers "Train Your Own Classifier (TYOC)" features using AI/ML, enabling organizations to train custom machine learning models on their unique data to identify sensitive content (beyond regexes) automatically.

3. **Policy Granularity**: A key differentiator of Netskope is context awareness. Policies can incorporate user, app (and even a specific instance of an app), action, data, device, location, risk score, etc. For example: "Allow Salesforce upload of customer data by sales reps on corporate devices but block the same on personal devices or unsanctioned CRM apps." Traditional security gateways might only block or allow an entire site; Netskope can enable the app with nuanced rules (maybe allow downloads but not uploads of sensitive files for specific roles).

a. **Coaching and User Feedback**: Netskope can provide user coaching messages when blocking an action (similar to M365 policy tips). For example, if a user tries to upload a file with client PII to their personal Google Drive, Netskope can block it and show a message: "Uploading company confidential data to personal cloud is not allowed. Your action has been blocked." This serves both as education and a deterrent.

Example Policy: Consider protecting confidential design documents in a manufacturing firm (which we'll revisit in the case study). A Netskope policy might be as follows: If a file upload is detected and the file content matches an engineering design blueprint (perhaps via file fingerprint or a regex for CAD file headers) and the destination is not an approved corporate app (e.g., user's personal Dropbox or any site categorized as "Personal Storage"), **block** the transfer. Additionally, if the destination is a corporate-approved app like Autodesk cloud and the user is outside the R&D group, then **alert** or **quarantine**. Simultaneously, schedule an API scan on the corporate OneDrive/SharePoint repositories to find any engineering blueprint files, and ensure they are correctly labeled and not shared externally. If any are found publicly exposed, remove external sharing and notify SecOps.

4. **CASB Deployment and Integration**: Deploying Netskope requires enabling traffic redirection for managed users:

a. **Endpoint Client**: Netskope offers a client agent (Netskope One Client) that can be installed on corporate endpoints. This agent can steer relevant traffic to the Netskope cloud. It's smart enough to differentiate personal vs. corporate app instances (like personal OneDrive vs. corporate OneDrive) and can apply policy selectively. The endpoint client also enables endpoint DLP features akin to those in Purview (e.g., controlling USB copy), although Netskope has historically focused more on network vectors.

b. **Network Routing**: Alternatively, or additionally, companies can route traffic via a proxy auto-config (PAC) file or secure web gateway settings to the Netskope cloud. Some use cases might route all HTTP/HTTPS through Netskope's Next-Gen Secure Web Gateway, which includes CASB functions. The New Edge infrastructure optimizes performance through many local POPs and direct peering with primary cloud services (Microsoft, Google, etc.).

c. **API Connections**: Admins will connect Netskope to apps like Microsoft 365, Google Workspace, Box, etc., by granting API access (OAuth or service account tokens). Netskope CASB then continuously monitors those apps for new content or configuration changes. For example, it can check if any SharePoint site is misconfigured to be public when it contains sensitive data.

   Example: Protecting Data in Microsoft 365 with Netskope: Even if an organization uses Microsoft's native protection, some opt for an additional layer like Netskope for cross-platform coverage or to manage a hybrid multi-cloud environment. Netskope provides deep visibility into M365 usage and can enforce granular policies. According to Netskope, it can uniquely combine API-enabled (out-of-band) and real-time controls to implement data protection in Microsoft 365. For instance, it can intercept and scan files being downloaded from OneDrive in real time (via an inline proxy) to prevent an unmanaged device from downloading sensitive files, complementing Microsoft's native policies. At the same time, it can use the Graph API to scan OneDrive and detect whether a user created a publicly shared link to a sensitive document - and automatically revoke that sharing or apply encryption.

5. **Integration with On-Prem and Other Security Tools**: Netskope can forward incidents to on-prem DLP or IRM systems if needed. For example, if content violates a policy, Netskope can ICAP redirect it to an on-prem DLP for deeper analysis (a pattern in

which cloud CASB and traditional DLP work together). However, many organizations find Netskope's built-in DLP sufficient and use it as the primary engine. Netskope also integrates with SIEMs and SOAR tools – alerts can go to Splunk or Sentinel for correlation. It supports standards such as STIX/TAXII for threat intelligence and includes a Cloud Exchange module for sharing events with other tools.

6. **Modern Use Cases – Shadow IT and AI**: One of the valuable features of Netskope is Shadow IT discovery – identifying cloud apps being used in the environment (through traffic analysis) and assessing their risk. Netskope's platform uses a Cloud Confidence Index (CCI) database with thousands of apps and even employs generative AI to analyze new apps' risk profiles. An admin might discover that users are using a new, previously unknown file-sharing app and decide to block uploads to it until it's vetted.

   CASB and SSE platforms are also evolving to govern the use of AI tools. For example, modern data protection platforms can inspect prompts and responses flowing to enterprise AI services, detect sensitive data, and apply policies such as block, warn, redact, or log. This is important because users may otherwise paste confidential data, source code, regulated information, or customer records into generative AI tools without realizing the downstream risk. This means Netskope can detect when someone tries to enter confidential data into ChatGPT and apply policies (block or redact) – extremely relevant given many enterprises' concerns about users leaking data to AI. In fact, with over 50 compliance templates and 3,000 data identifiers at its disposal, Netskope's DLP can be extended to AI application traffic to ensure, say, no GDPR or HIPAA data is sent to an AI model. We will cover AI governance more in Emerging Trends, but it's worth noting that CASB solutions are evolving to cover those scenarios.

7. **Outcome – Data Protection with Netskope**: By deploying Netskope, organizations gain uniform control over data across any cloud app or web destination. Real-world outcomes often include

    a. A substantial reduction in data leakage incidents. For example, one financial institution using Netskope and a strict cloud usage policy saw an 80% drop in incidents of sensitive data uploads to personal cloud storage in a quarter (hypothetical metric based on typical success criteria).

    b. Visibility into cloud data usage that was previously opaque – e.g., identifying hundreds of unsanctioned apps and either blocking them or coaching users toward approved alternatives.

    c. More granular safe enablement: Instead of outright blocking services like "Dropbox" entirely (which users may circumvent), the organization can allow Dropbox for basic usage but prevent uploads of corporate files or downloads of regulated data. This nuanced approach keeps productivity while protecting data.

    d. Improved compliance: By using Netskope's compliance templates, firms can quickly enforce policies for standards like PCI or GDPR across all cloud channels. For example, blocking any upload of credit card numbers to cloud apps that are not PCI-compliant.

    e. Insider threat mitigation: When combined with user/entity behavior analytics, Netskope can detect and stop patterns like a soon-to-depart employee attempting to mass-download client lists to personal storage (the platform note: departing employees upload 5× more data to personal instances in their last 30 days, and Netskope's controls specifically address that risk).

In summary, Netskope exemplifies a **cloud-first data protection strategy**. It ensures that whether data is traveling to a managed SaaS app, a personal app, or residing on cloud platforms, the organization's security policies apply. The technical deep dive here shows how to create those policies and leverage both inline and API methods to cover all bases. While we used Netskope as an example, other CASB/SSE solutions, such as Zscaler, Skyhigh Security, Microsoft Defender for Cloud Apps, Cisco Secure Access, and similar platforms, operate on similar principles, discovering cloud usage, using proxy/API controls, and integrating DLP. The key is to align the CASB policies with your data classification scheme and risk appetite.

Other Vendor Solutions (Forcepoint, Broadcom, etc.): It is worth noting that several established security vendors offer robust data protection suites with analogous capabilities:

1) **Forcepoint:** Forcepoint's DLP and SSE capabilities are known for policy depth, data classification, and fingerprinting technology. Their offerings now include cloud proxy and CASB features. A bank's case with Forcepoint DLP showed that with a phased rollout (monitor then block), they achieved full DLP enforcement with minimal business disruption. Forcepoint also emphasizes user education and has tools for behavioral analytics.

2) **Broadcom (Symantec) DLP:** A long-time leader in enterprise DLP, covering endpoints, network, and discovery. Broadcom Symantec DLP can be integrated with cloud security and CASB/SSE controls for broader cloud app coverage. Many large enterprises still use Symantec DLP for its proven detection capabilities and layer newer CASBs on top.

3) **Others: Digital Guardian (Fortra)** focuses on endpoint and IP protection in manufacturing and other sectors. Trend Micro and McAfee (Trellix) also have DLP components. There are also specialized solutions, such as GTB Technologies and Safetica, for specific markets.

4) **Unified vs. Specialized:** A crucial decision for CISOs is whether to go with a unified platform (like Microsoft Purview for M365 environments or a single vendor SSE stack) vs. best-of-breed components. A unified platform offers easier management and integration (e.g., one console, one agent), whereas best-of-breed might offer superior features in each area but requires integration. For example, combining Symantec DLP with Netskope CASB could yield powerful results but needs careful setup to avoid overlaps or gaps. Some organizations adopt a hybrid approach: using Microsoft's native DLP for Microsoft 365, but a third-party CASB for non-Microsoft cloud traffic. It's essential to ensure that policies and classifications are consistent across tools (e.g., import the same regular expression patterns or keyword dictionaries into both systems).

Tip Ensure PAC/agent steering excludes private apps that can't tolerate proxying; use app-instance awareness to differentiate corporate vs. personal SaaS.

In practice, many enterprises find that consolidation is beneficial, reducing the number of agents and consoles by leveraging a platform. This is reflected in trends like SSE (Secure Service Edge), where a single cloud service provides SWG, CASB, DLP, and more. Netskope, Zscaler, Microsoft Defender for Cloud Apps, and other SSE platforms are examples in that direction. Microsoft is also integrating DLP into its Defender suite. Regardless of the tool, the concepts of classification-driven policies, real-time control, and user engagement remain universal.

With the technical foundations set, we will now pivot to extended case studies. These will demonstrate how the strategies and tools described above manifest in real organizations - the challenges faced, the solutions designed (often using a combination of the above technologies), and the outcomes achieved. Each case study is multi-faceted and provides lessons for professionals seeking to protect data in motion, in use, and at rest in their own contexts.

Extended Case Studies: Protecting Data in Four Key Sectors

To ground our understanding, we present four in-depth case studies across the Healthcare, Finance, Education, and Manufacturing industries. Each case study will outline the organization's background, the data protection challenges encountered, the solutions and policies implemented (with a mix of vendor tools and best practices), and the measurable outcomes or lessons learned. These real-world examples show how the principles of data security are applied in practice - often using a combination of Microsoft Purview, Netskope, and other technologies, but always tailored to the specific business context and risks. (All company names are generalized for confidentiality, focusing on the substance of the scenario.)

Case Study 1: Healthcare – Safeguarding Patient Data and Enabling Cloud Mobility

Background: HealthyLife Health System is a regional healthcare provider operating several hospitals and clinics. They handle sensitive patient information (PHI) across electronic health record (EHR) systems, billing databases, and cloud collaboration tools. The organization was pursuing a "cloud-and-mobile-first" strategy to improve care delivery - doctors and nurses using tablets, cloud-based scheduling apps, and remote consultation platforms. HealthyLife also had to comply with healthcare regulations, such as HIPAA, and ensure patient data privacy. The IT environment included Microsoft 365 for email and file sharing, a cloud EHR portal, and various medical IoT devices.

Data Protection Challenge: Healthcare data is among the most sensitive - breaches can violate patient privacy and incur heavy fines. HealthyLife faced multiple challenges:

1) Clinicians were increasingly using personal mobile devices to access patient information on the go, increasing the risk of data leakage or unauthorized access.

2) The organization wanted to leverage cloud solutions (like cloud storage, telehealth apps) but needed to enforce HIPAA compliance (e.g., ensure Business Associate Agreements with any cloud service handling PHI, and prevent PHI from being uploaded to unvetted apps). Past incidents in the industry raised concern: research shows healthcare workers sometimes inadvertently upload patient files to personal cloud apps or AI transcription services. HealthyLife wanted to prevent such policy violations without inhibiting productivity.

3) They also needed to monitor internal privacy practices - e.g., staff accessing patient records they shouldn't (insider threat scenario) or sending unencrypted emails with PHI.

Solutions Implemented: HealthyLife adopted a combination of Microsoft Purview for internal data protection and Netskope for cloud usage control, achieving a balance between protecting data at rest in their systems and data in motion to external cloud services.

1) **Sensitivity Labels and Encryption**: They defined labels for patient data. EHR exports and reports were labeled "PHI – Confidential". Through Purview, these labels automatically applied encryption such that only authorized clinical staff could open the files (integration with Microsoft Entra ID groups for doctors, nurses, etc.). Emails containing patient data were labeled and automatically encrypted (using Microsoft Message Encryption) when sent outside, satisfying HIPAA encryption-at-transit requirements.

2) **DLP Policies (Internal):** HealthyLife configured Purview DLP with HIPAA templates to detect PHI (medical record numbers, patient names with diagnoses, etc.) in Exchange emails and Teams chats. For example, if a nurse tried to send a referral letter containing a patient's SSN or diagnosis via email to an external physician, DLP would trigger. The policy was "Warn if PHI is detected in an external email and require encryption or block if not an approved recipient." Initially, they ran this in test mode; results showed dozens of attempts per week, which allowed them to fine-tune the rules. Once enforced, accidental sending of unprotected PHI via email dropped dramatically.

3) **Cloud Usage Control (CASB):** HealthyLife deployed Netskope mainly for cloud app visibility and blocking of unsanctioned services. They discovered via Netskope that users were using consumer file-sharing apps (like personal Dropbox) to collaborate on research, which was risky. A policy was set to block uploads of any files containing PHI to personal cloud storage or to non-approved domains, using Netskope's DLP engine with a "PHI data identifier" (covering items such as health insurance numbers, ICD-10 codes, etc.). On sanctioned cloud apps (they had a BAA in place with Microsoft 365 and a secure medical imaging cloud), Netskope was set in allow mode but still monitored. Netskope's coaching messages were enabled, so if a doctor attempted to use a disallowed app, they'd get a prompt, "This action is not permitted – use our approved system for patient data." This measure alone significantly reduced risky behavior by raising awareness at the moment of action.

4) **Mobile Device Management and Conditional Access:** They extended data protection to mobile. Doctors' tablets and smartphones were enrolled in an MDM solution (Intune). Conditional Access policies ensured that only managed, compliant devices could access the EHR or open PHI-labeled files. For example, if a physician tried to open a patient report on a personal phone, access would be denied unless that phone was enrolled and met encryption/password requirements. This prevents the scenario of lost personal devices leaking data.

5) **Insider Monitoring:** Using Purview's Audit and Insider Risk Management, HealthyLife set up policies to flag unusual data access – e.g., if an employee looked up thousands of patient records unrelated to their unit or attempted to download bulk patient info. This was more of a detective control; indeed, in one case, it caught a receptionist snooping on medical records out of curiosity, leading to retraining and stricter role-based access to the EHR.

6) **Secure Collaboration Tools**: For external sharing with research partners or other hospitals, they implemented secure portals. When they had to email patient data, they used Purview's **"Encrypt-Only"** email option (users added a [Encrypt] tag to the subject or selected the label). Recipients then needed to authenticate to read it. This met compliance while allowing necessary flow.

HealthyLife's implementation leaned heavily on automation, automatically encrypting or blocking, rather than relying on staff to always remember. They also updated policies: clear guidelines that "No patient data should be copied to personal accounts or devices. Always use approved systems or the secure messaging app for sending PHI."

Measurable Outcomes: The outcomes were significant:

1) **Regulatory Compliance:** The measures kept HealthyLife in full compliance with HIPAA's technical safeguards (encryption, access control, audit controls). An audit by an external assessor found their controls for data in transit and at rest to be robust, with encryption and DLP preventing most avenues of accidental disclosure.

2) **Reduction in Incidents:** Within six months, the incidence of improper data sharing dropped by an estimated 70%. For example, before DLP, several emails per week with patient data went unencrypted; after, virtually zero went out without encryption or were outright blocked. Netskope's logs showed that attempts to use personal cloud for PHI stopped almost entirely after users encountered a few blocks and coaching messages (culture shift).

3) **Enablement of Cloud and Mobility:** Clinicians reported they could still do their job effectively with minimal disruption. They embraced the provided secure clinical mobile app, and the organization's cloud-first strategy continued. In fact, during the COVID-19 pandemic period, HealthyLife was able to expand telehealth services rapidly - thanks to these controls, doctors could safely consult from home without fear of data leakage (e.g., consultations happened over an approved, encrypted platform and any session data was stored in the secure cloud with DLP scanning the chat transcripts for compliance).

4) **Case in Point:** Apria Healthcare, a similar healthcare company, achieved success with a cloud-first security approach. By using cloud DLP and CASB, Apria protected sensitive patient data while enabling mobile access. This mirrors HealthyLife's outcome - improved patient outcomes and data security going hand in hand.

The HealthyLife case illustrates that in healthcare, data protection is a lifesaver in more ways than one: it protects patient privacy (a core trust issue), and it protects the organization from legal and financial harm. Key takeaways include the importance of encryption for PHI, strict control over cloud channels, and user-friendly, secure alternatives (if you block something, provide a sanctioned way to do it). The combination of Microsoft and Netskope technologies in this case was complementary - Microsoft's tools handled internal Microsoft ecosystem data well, while Netskope provided an umbrella over all cloud/web usage. Other healthcare providers may use different vendor combinations, but the layered controls and policy enforcement strategy remain consistent.

Case Study 2: Finance – Preventing Data Exfiltration and Ensuring Compliance in a Bank

Background: GlobalBank is a mid-sized international bank offering retail and corporate banking. Handling financial data (account numbers, transactions, personal client info) and operating under regulations like GLBA, PCI-DSS, and various privacy laws, data security is paramount. The bank has thousands of employees, as well as a significant number of contractors and partners who access data. In recent years, GlobalBank underwent a digital transformation, adopting cloud email and collaboration (Microsoft 365) to enable more remote work. They were aware that banks are prime targets for both external attacks and insider threats (fraud or IP theft), and they had seen industry examples of both.

Data Protection Challenge: GlobalBank's challenges included

1) **Regulatory Pressure:** They needed to comply with PCI DSS for credit card data, which mandates strict control and monitoring of PAN (Primary Account Numbers) storage and transmission. Similarly, GLBA requires safeguarding customer financial information.

2) **Insider Risk and Culture:** The bank's CISO recognized that a data protection program would fail without employee buy-in. Past attempts to lock down data faced resistance (front-line employees complained controls slowed them down). Business heads were wary that DLP blocking might disrupt critical workflows (e.g., sending data to regulators or customers). The challenge was to implement DLP "with a soft touch" initially and then ramp up.

3) **Complex Data Flows:** Bank data flows range from mainframe extracts to modern cloud apps. For example, customer reports generated from core banking had to be transferred to an analytics team; traders frequently exported data from systems to Excel for analysis. These legitimate flows risk leakage if not protected.

4) **Shadow IT and Personal Devices:** Though policy forbade using personal email or cloud for work, in practice, some managers were known to forward work docs to personal Gmail to work from home (a big compliance no-no). They also had high-privilege IT admins and developers who posed a risk if they extracted databases or code.

5) **Past Incidents:** They had a close call where an outgoing employee attempted to download an extensive client list and upload it to a personal Dropbox – caught after the fact by logs. This sets the stage for management to support a stronger solution.

Solutions Implemented: GlobalBank decided on a phased DLP rollout combined with strong stakeholder engagement. They chose a best-of-breed DLP solution (Forcepoint DLP) integrated with their existing secure web gateway and email security and later incorporated CASB (Netskope) for cloud-specific control. Their approach focused as much on process and people as technology:

Phase 1 – Visibility (Monitoring Mode): For the first six months, they ran DLP in monitor-only mode across the enterprise. They created policies to detect key data types, e.g., 16-digit card numbers (with a Luhn check) for PCI data, account balances or SWIFT codes for banking data, and keywords indicating confidential reports or insider information. If these were left via email, web upload, or USB copy, they were logged but not blocked. This proof-of-concept phase yielded invaluable data: surprisingly, they found fewer outright incidents than feared but did find "low awareness" issues (staff sending spreadsheets home to themselves, etc.). They also identified patterns (e.g., spikes at month-end when reports are compiled). This data helped them make the case to executives with concrete numbers and examples, shifting the focus from "DLP might disrupt us" to "Imagine the impact if those spreadsheets got leaked."

Phase 2 – Stakeholder Buy-In and Policy Refinement: They presented the monitoring results to C-level and business unit leaders. By showing actual incidents (anonymized) and how DLP could have prevented potential breaches, they gained strong top-down support. They formed a cross-departmental DLP committee to refine policies, decide on exceptions, and serve as DLP ambassadors. Notably, they involved the business early so that when blocking was later enabled, everyone was on board (including the CEO, whose data might be blocked too – leadership led by example).

Phase 3 – Gradual Enforcement and Training: After six months, with refined policies, they enabled data blocking on critical policies. For instance, any email with over 50 customer account numbers to an external address was now blocked (with a message to contact security for override if legitimate). They did the same for uploads: uploading customer PII to external websites (other than sanctioned ones) was blocked. For less critical channels or borderline cases, they used "user self-override with justification." If, say, an analyst needed to email a report with some sensitive info to a trusted external party, they could override by providing a business justification, which was logged for review. Simultaneously, the bank conducted mandatory training sessions – at least six per month, targeting different teams – to educate employees on working with DLP and data security. Even the CEO had to attend when one of his emails was blocked (to everyone's surprise, which underscored that no one is exempt – interestingly, that incident turned into a positive story, reinforcing the program).

Technical Specifics: Forcepoint DLP was configured with its fingerprinting module. They fingerprinted sensitive documents (like a file containing all high-net-worth clients) – ensuring that if that data appeared anywhere else, it would be flagged. They integrated DLP with their Secure Email Gateway and Web Proxy via ICAP, so that any data leaving those channels was scanned in real time. Endpoint DLP agents were deployed to critical users (wealth managers, executives) to protect offline vectors (USB, printing), which the bank aimed to reduce any way for security and sustainability. They also enforced that any reports exported from core systems were labeled and stored on encrypted drives.

CASB for Cloud: As they adopted Microsoft 365 and allowed OneDrive/SharePoint use, they extended DLP to the cloud. Netskope was layered to monitor cloud file sharing. A specific concern in finance is insider trading or leaks of financial results. So, they set up a policy: if any document containing words like "Earnings Preview" or financial results was attempted to be shared externally (via any channel, email, OneDrive link, etc.), it would be blocked and trigger an alert to compliance. This was like a virtual "insider trading prevention" system. They also used Netskope to control personal email usage: for managed devices, web access to Gmail was allowed, but file attachments were blocked if they contained certain data (Netskope could see that content).

Encryption and Rights Management: In cases where data had to be shared, they encouraged using IRM-protected files (e.g., using Azure Information Protection) so that even if files traveled, they remained encrypted. For instance, sensitive strategy documents were labeled "Confidential - Strategy," which automatically enabled encryption and allowed only internal access. If someone tried to forward that file outside, the recipient couldn't open it - DLP would also catch it, but it was defense-in-depth.

Data Posture and Cleanup: An often-overlooked part - GlobalBank also used their DLP findings to clean up excess data. They discovered many old spreadsheets with client info sitting in open file shares. This triggered a data minimization project: moving or deleting old data, reducing what could potentially leak. They integrated DLP with their data classification to tag files at rest and either archive or protect them.

Measurable Outcomes: GlobalBank's case is a strong success story in building a data protection program:

1) **Full DLP Deployment with Executive Support:** They became one of the few banks in their region to fully leverage DLP blocking with top-down support. The cultural change - from seeing security as a roadblock to a necessary safeguard - was evident. The CISO reported that after initial rollout, pushback from business units was minimal because those leaders had been part of shaping the policies.

2) **Incident Reduction and Response:** The bank achieved a 90% reduction in major data leakage events. In the first-year post-implementation, no incidents of unencrypted customer data leaving the bank's perimeter occurred (at least none that were detected and stopped). False positives, which can plague DLP, were significantly reduced through fingerprinting and policy tuning. One metric: false positive incidents dropped by ~75% after they implemented data fingerprinting for critical databases. This improved user trust in the system (few things annoy users more than being blocked for something they perceive as a mistake by the tool).

3) **Faster Compliance Audits:** When auditors came (internal or external), the bank could demonstrate concrete controls for GLBA and PCI. For PCI, they have shown that any credit card number in email or files is automatically detected and prevented from

leaving the network, thereby satisfying several PCI requirements. The audit results improved, and the bank avoided penalties. The Central Bank regulators were also impressed; one regulator commented that the bank's DLP incident reports and user training approach were becoming an industry benchmark (especially in a region where not many banks had turned on blocking).

4) **Ancillary Benefits:** They observed some side benefits. For instance, in line with sustainability, the DLP's reduction in printing sensitive docs led to reduced overall paper usage (since employees knew printing customer data could trigger DLP if someone tried to scan it or if the print logs were audited, they moved to digital sharing with protection). Also, the mandatory security training improved overall security hygiene, not just DLP awareness - phishing click rates went down concurrently (likely because people grew more cautious about data and, by extension, suspicious emails).

5) **Incident Response and Insider Threat:** On a couple of occasions, the DLP system directly thwarted malicious insiders. In one scenario, an IT staff member tried to compress a bunch of sensitive files and upload via an obscure web HTTP tool at 2 AM - Netskope's inline proxy caught it and blocked it, and an alert was generated. Investigations found the employee was planning to take data to a competitor; they were terminated, and legal action was pursued. **The confidence** in data protection grew - as one senior executive put it, "I sleep better at night knowing that even if someone tries to leak data, we have a net to catch them."

This case highlights the importance of phased implementation and user involvement. Technology was only half the battle; winning hearts and minds was the other. The bank's use of monitoring, demonstrating value, and enforcing carefully is a model approach. Also, their combination of solutions (traditional DLP, CASB, and encryption) provided layered coverage. Many financial institutions follow similar paths, sometimes using different products (e.g., some might use Symantec DLP or Microsoft's DLP). Regardless, key elements are the classification of sensitive data, careful rollout of controls, and continuous improvement.

Case Study 3: Education – Protecting Student Data and Research in a School District

Background: Citysville Public Schools (CPS) is a large K-12 school district with dozens of schools and over 80,000 students. In recent years, CPS undertook a massive tech initiative: issuing laptops to every student (1:1 device program), adopting cloud-based learning (Microsoft 365 and Google Workspace for Education), and moving many services online (grading systems, counseling communications, etc.). With students and teachers heavily using collaboration tools, CPS had to safeguard students' personally identifiable information (PII) (subject to laws like FERPA) and ensure a safe digital environment (prevent cyberbullying, inappropriate content sharing, etc.). The district's IT team is relatively small and faces not only typical data security but also the safety of minors online.

Data Protection Challenge: Education environments are uniquely challenging:

1) **Massive User Base of Young Users:** Students as young as 8 or 10 use email/Teams/Google Drive - they may inadvertently (or intentionally) share personal data or engage in risky behavior. Teachers and staff handle sensitive data, such as student grades, health information, and counseling records.

2) **Compliance Requirements:** FERPA (Family Educational Rights and Privacy Act) mandates protection of student educational records and controls on disclosure. Additionally, CIPA (Children's Internet Protection Act) requires filtering harmful content for minors and monitoring their online activities.

3) **Decentralized Environment:** Each school site had some autonomy, and thousands of devices roamed off campus, especially during remote learning phases. So, data could be anywhere - a student might download a class list to a home computer.

4) **Need for Unobtrusive Monitoring:** They needed to identify problems (like cyberbullying or a student sharing personal info publicly) without violating privacy or creating a perception of heavy surveillance. Privacy by design was necessary.

5) **Resource Constraints:** Unlike a corporation, the budget and IT manpower in public schools are limited. Solutions had to be cost-effective (leveraging existing Microsoft or Google capabilities, if possible) and not require a legion of analysts to review logs.

Solutions Implemented: CPS focused on leveraging Microsoft Purview's education-focused features and some third-party tools to address both data loss and student safety:

1) **Communication Compliance for Student Safety:** Microsoft 365 includes Communication Compliance policies (part of Purview), which CPS configured to detect signs of cyberbullying, harassment, or sharing of private info in student communications. For example, they set rules to flag when a student's email or Teams chat contained certain bullying keywords or profanity, combined with a student's name. Another rule detected if students tried to share home addresses or phone numbers in chats (to prevent them from doxxing themselves or others). These policies were privacy-protected; they pseudonymized usernames for reviewers and required dual-admin approval to investigate content, ensuring no one snooped on students without cause. This setup helped CPS identify several instances where a student was being harassed online; principals could intervene early - essentially preventing potentially worse outcomes (it even possibly saved a student from self-harm by catching severe harassment in chats).

2) **DLP for Sensitive Student Data:** CPS applied DLP policies for faculty and staff communications. They used Microsoft's built-in FERPA template (which might look for things like student ID numbers, names with words like IEP (Individualized Education Plan), etc.). If a teacher tried to email a spreadsheet of student test scores to a personal email address, the system would block it or warn them. Uploads of student PII to unauthorized cloud apps (like posting a list of students on a public forum) were also blocked. Since they had Google Workspace too, they enabled similar rules in Google's DLP for Gmail/Drive - focusing on Social Security Numbers (some older systems still used those as IDs), medical info, etc. Essentially, any document containing multiple students' personal data was tagged and restricted to internal use.

3) **Endpoint Management and Controls:** All student laptops were managed via Intune and had Windows 10 in S mode (restricting app installs) or Chromebooks with Google Admin controls. They enforced that devices use school cloud storage and locked down USB ports to prevent copying data to personal drives (a critical measure in case devices got lost or stolen, which happened a lot with kids). For staff devices, Intune policies prevented saving files locally unless they were encrypted; most were directed to use OneDrive, which was monitored.

4) **Incident Response Workflow:** Given limited staff, they set up automated alerts but also partnered with the district's counselors and security officers. For example, if Communication Compliance flagged a severe bullying message, it would alert a small group (IT plus a student safety officer). They would review and, if confirmed, escalate to the school's principal or counselor to handle the students involved. This multidisciplinary approach was critical: IT alone didn't discipline students, but it provided educators with the insight to act. On the data side, if a FERPA violation (e.g., a teacher accidentally shared a student's grades with another student's parent) was detected, the data privacy officer handled it, rectified it, and reported it if needed.

5) **Education and Policy:** They rolled out training for teachers about properly handling student data (e.g., do not use personal email for school data, always use the district's OneDrive or Google Drive, which are monitored). Students were introduced to digital citizenship lessons - part of which included not sharing personal info online and understanding that certain activities are monitored for their safety. They were transparent: students and parents were informed that "for your protection, communications on school platforms are monitored for bullying and self-harm indicators", aligning with many districts' approaches to comply with CIPA and maintaining trust.

6) **Use of Vendor-Neutral Tools:** In addition to Microsoft, CPS considered some education-specific DLP solutions, but Microsoft's suite was largely sufficient and included in their licensing. They used a web filtering appliance (Lightspeed Systems) for CIPA web filtering, which also included some DLP Lite features (e.g., blocking web forms if they detect SSN patterns, so someone can't accidentally post a student's SSN).

Measurable Outcomes

1) **Student Data Stays Protected:** Since deployment, CPS has had zero major FERPA breaches. For instance, they had a scare when a teacher mistakenly attached a file containing multiple students' information to an email to one parent. The system caught it and blocked it - avoiding an inadvertent FERPA violation that would have been distressing and potentially legally troublesome. The teacher was notified and realized the mistake; they were thankful the system had a safety net.

2) **Improved Cyber Safety Climate:** The proactive monitoring of student communications yielded notable improvements. Over the school year, they flagged and intervened in dozens of bullying or self-harm-related cases. According to district reports, the number of severe cyberbullying reports by students themselves dropped, possibly indicating that the toxic communications were mitigated early. One principal noted, "We're able to address issues before they spiral quietly. In a few cases, we likely prevented tragedy by catching cries for help in chats." This outcome, while not directly "data loss prevention" in the traditional sense, was a vital goal for the district.

3) **Efficient Use of Tech:** The district leveraged existing tools (thus saving cost). Microsoft Purview's education features (which are part of their A5 licenses) meant they didn't have to buy an expensive third-party DLP for staff email, a big plus given budget constraints. Automation was key: one IT security specialist could manage the alerts each morning, review them, and forward them to the appropriate school staff, which scaled well even for 80k students.

4) **Compliance Assurance:** During state audits or funding reviews, CPS could demonstrate compliance with privacy regulations. They showed their policies and anonymized Purview logs to auditors, proving that if any private student data was mishandled, there was a record and a mitigation. This gave regulators confidence and kept the district in good standing for grants that require data privacy assurances.

5) **Challenges and Adjustments:** It wasn't without hiccups. At first, some teachers complained that their routine emails (like sending a class list to a colleague) were being flagged. CPS fine-tuned the policies to reduce false positives (e.g., allowing internal sharing of certain data freely while focusing on external disclosures). They also improved training - after a semester, most staff knew how to work within the system (e.g., using secure internal methods rather than quick but insecure shortcuts).

This case study demonstrates that protecting data in an academic setting means not only preventing breaches but also ensuring a secure learning environment. The combination of DLP and communication monitoring served both purposes. A key takeaway is the emphasis on **privacy-by-design**: CPS used pseudonymization and role-based access controls for those monitoring student communications, showing respect for privacy even as they monitor. Also, involving educational stakeholders (counselors, principals) in the loop was vital - technology was an enabler, but human judgment was needed to handle incidents with care and in context.

Case Study 4: Manufacturing – Protecting Intellectual Property and Trade Secrets

Background: InnovateTech Manufacturing is a company that designs and produces high-tech components (imagine something like semiconductor equipment or automotive parts). Their competitive edge lies in proprietary design documents, CAD drawings, and process recipes. They operate globally, with R&D centers in the United States and Europe and manufacturing in Asia. Protecting intellectual property (IP) is mission critical. The industry has seen cases of corporate espionage and insider theft (competitors trying to poach designs, employees leaving to start rivals with stolen IP).

Moreover, specific contracts (with government/military clients) impose strict data security requirements (e.g., ITAR for defense-related tech, which requires controlled access to technical data).

Data Protection Challenge: InnovateTech's threat landscape includes

1) **Insider Threats:** Highly skilled engineers with access to crown jewels – if even one decides to steal data (perhaps to join a competitor or a startup in a country with weaker IP laws), years of R&D could be lost. In fact, a few years back, a well-known case in their industry involved an engineer stealing thousands of design files (via USB and encrypted archives) to benefit a foreign company. That cautionary tale prompted InnovateTech to act.

2) **External Espionage:** Nation-state or competitor hacking attempts are common. While perimeter security handles a lot of that, they wanted to ensure that even if someone breached the network, they couldn't easily exfiltrate sensitive data (hence internal DLP as a last line of defense).

3) **Balancing Collaboration:** Engineers need to collaborate, including with external partners or customers. For example, they might share some design aspects with a customer's engineering team for integration. They needed a secure way to do that, as outright blocking everything wasn't feasible for business.

4) **Manufacturing Sites:** On the factory floor, machines produce data (some of which might be sensitive, like yield metrics). Third-party service providers have access to some of that. They were concerned about data leaving via those channels as well (maybe not classic DLP since machines don't email, but via unauthorized USB or taking photos, etc.).

5) **Classification Complexity:** Unlike straightforward PII, their sensitive data wasn't easily identifiable by simple patterns. How do you tell a standard CAD drawing from a secret one via an algorithm? They needed to rely on classification (like letting engineers label critical projects) or fingerprinting known sensitive repositories.

Solutions Implemented: InnovateTech implemented a multi-faceted IP protection program blending technology and process:

1) **Data Classification and Labeling of IP:** The company identified its most sensitive data (crown jewels) - such as certain design databases, source code repositories, formula documents, etc. They implemented a classification scheme, e.g., "Public, Internal, Confidential, Secret, Top-Secret," with "Top-Secret" assigned only to a short list of projects. Engineers were trained to apply these labels (using an IRM tool or a simple document template) to new documents. They also used Microsoft Purview to scan and auto-label items residing in known sensitive SharePoint sites. The labeling is integrated with Azure Information Protection, which automatically encrypts anything marked as Secret or higher. So, if someone downloaded a Top-Secret PDF, it was encrypted and would only open for authorized users (and attempts to forward it would fail).

2) **Enterprise DLP Enforcement:** They deployed Symantec (Broadcom) DLP on endpoints and the network, as it was a solution they had used partially before. They enabled endpoint DLP agents on all R&D user laptops and workstations. These agents monitored for any file transfers of sensitive data types: they configured file fingerprinting for critical CAD drawings and BOM (Bill of Materials) spreadsheets. If an exact or even partial match of those files was detected, leaving them (via email, USB copy, uploading, printing, etc.) would block it. For content that wasn't fingerprinted, they used broader rules: e.g., any file created in the secure R&D network segment is tagged by the agent as "company-confidential" and cannot be moved to an unapproved location without justification. Email DLP ensured that emails with attachments containing technical drawings or keywords such as "proprietary" were either encrypted or blocked outside.

3) **Insider Threat Behavioral Analytics:** They paired DLP with an insider threat tool (like Splunk UEBA or Microsoft Insider Risk if using that). This looked for patterns like an employee who usually downloads 5 files a day suddenly downloads 5000 files in a week (a sign of data hoarding before leaving). Or someone accessing repositories they never did before at odd hours. When

such patterns arose, it would generate alerts for the security team to investigate - often correlating with DLP alerts (e.g., lots of downloads followed by attempts to copy to USB).

4) **Controlled Collaboration Platform:** Instead of free-for-all file sharing, InnovateTech invested in a secure collaboration portal for external sharing. Essentially, a hardened SharePoint/OneDrive instance with extra controls: external users had to go through multifactor auth, data was view-only or watermarked if needed, and DLP monitored what external parties did (with their consent in agreements). This meant that if engineers were required to share a design with a partner, they did so through this portal, where it could be tracked, and access could auto-expire after a project. The portal prevented the file from being downloaded in many cases (view in browser only), mitigating the risk of further distribution.

5) **Policy on Personal Devices and Printing:** InnovateTech enforced that no work on sensitive projects could be done on personal devices - only company devices, which were monitored. They also severely restricted the printing of sensitive documents. Printers in R&D required badge release (so you had to come swipe your ID to get the printout, preventing forgotten papers) and watermarked every print with the user's name, date, and "Confidential". DLP agents also logged attempts to print a sensitive document on an unauthorized printer (or print to PDF).

6) **Response Plan:** In case an incident was detected (like an employee actually tried to exfiltrate data), they had an IR plan. For example, when an engineer was caught uploading encrypted .rar files of drawings to a personal cloud (which happened once, possibly as a test of the system by the employee), DLP blocked it. Security immediately isolated the machine, interviewed the employee, and ultimately terminated that person (zero tolerance for intentional IP theft). Legal was involved to assess if any data had actually been left (it hadn't, thanks to the block). This response sent a clear message across the company.

Measurable Outcomes

1) **No Major IP Leaks Detected:** Since the program launch, InnovateTech has had no confirmed incidents of IP theft or leaks. It's possible that the controls themselves deterred attempts – employees knew monitoring was in place. There were a handful of "near-misses" where DLP caught unusual activity: for instance, an engineer about to resign attempted to copy some files, which was quickly stopped and handled. Leadership and customers' confidence in their IP security grew; in fact, during contract negotiations, they could assert and demonstrate their robust data protection, which helped secure a partnership with a cautious government client that required strict IP handling.

2) **Cultural Shift to Security by Default:** Initially, some R&D staff found the controls cumbersome ("Why do I need to label everything? Why can't I just email this home to work on?"). Over time – aided by periodic security training and seeing competitors suffer breaches in the news – they embraced it. Engineers took pride in protecting their designs. The ease of use improved, too: classification became part of template documents, and many controls were behind the scenes (transparent encryption). When asked, a senior engineer said, "At first I thought it was overkill, but now I get it – our designs are our crown jewels. I'd be devastated if one leaked. The tools are just part of our workflow now."

3) **Reduced Data Hoarding and Cleanup:** A surprising positive outcome – knowing that old sensitive files shouldn't linger, they cleaned up or archived a lot of stale data. Data that wasn't needed was securely deleted or moved to a vault. This reduced the amount of sensitive material floating around (which in turn reduces DLP noise and risk). They used DSPM-like scanning to identify repositories of sensitive info and did access reviews (ensuring only those who need it have access).

4) **Meeting Compliance/Contractual Obligations:** For the defense-related projects, InnovateTech complied with ITAR by controlling access to those project files (only US persons, etc.) and monitoring every transfer. The DLP and classification system helped implement those controls and log evidence. They passed several customer security audits, during which auditors specifically probed how they prevent IP exfiltration. InnovateTech could show audit logs, demo DLP triggers, and describe how even printing is controlled - the auditors gave high marks.

5) **Incident Response Speed:** In the one or two insider incidents, the time from detection to action was minutes. For example, in the scenario of attempted exfiltration via an encrypted .rar file, the SOC received the DLP alert in real time, correlated it with anomalous behavior (large file assembly), and within 30 minutes suspended the employee's network access and initiated an investigation. This fast reaction likely prevented any attempt at re-exfiltration by other means. Compare this to the GE case in the news, where an engineer encrypted files over the course of weeks before being caught - InnovateTech's layered monitoring aimed to detect such patterns earlier.

This manufacturing case underscores the criticality of IP protection and the lengths companies go to achieve it. It also illustrates the use of multiple techniques: classification, encryption, DLP, user monitoring, and strict policy enforcement. One notable aspect is how user education and acceptance were fostered - something often overlooked in IP protection programs that focus too much on tech and not enough on the people. The case also shows the evolving threat: it's not just about someone emailing a file; it can be as subtle as encryption misuse or steganography (as in the case of the GE engineer who hid files in an image to exfiltrate). To combat this, InnovateTech's approach had to be adaptive (like blocking unauthorized encryption tools and monitoring anomalies).

In conclusion, across these four case studies, healthcare, finance, education, and manufacturing, we have seen common threads:

1) The need to **classify what is sensitive** (be it PHI, financial data, student data, or trade secrets)

2) The use of **technological controls (encryption, DLP, CASB, monitoring)** to enforce policies

The importance of **user training and policy buy-in** to ensure controls are effective and sustainable. Measurable improvements in security posture, often translating to compliance success, incident reduction, and even saving lives or core business value in some cases.

Next, we turn our attention to the future: with the threat landscape constantly evolving and technology advancing, what emerging trends will influence how we protect data in motion, in use, and at rest? The final section explores Data Security Posture Management, the impact of AI (and how to govern it), and confidential computing – all poised to reshape data security over the next phase of enterprise data protection.

Emerging Trends and Future Directions in Data Protection

Organizations must continually prepare for new challenges and technologies that are reshaping data protection. This section discusses three major emerging areas: Data Security Posture Management (DSPM), AI governance and control of sensitive data in AI/LLM usage, and confidential computing and privacy-enhancing computation. Each of these trends addresses gaps or new requirements in protecting data in motion, use, and storage – and together they herald a more intelligent, automated, and secure data security paradigm for the future.

Data Security Posture Management (DSPM)

With data sprawled across on-premises and multi-cloud environments, keeping track of where sensitive data is, who has access to it, how it's used, and its security posture has become extremely difficult. Data Security Posture Management (DSPM) is a response to this challenge. Coined in the early 2020s and now becoming a core part of modern data security programs, DSPM refers to a set of tools and practices that give organizations a holistic, continuous view of their data security posture.

In essence, DSPM platforms discover and catalog data across the environment (databases, file stores, cloud buckets, SaaS apps), classify data sensitivity, identify vulnerabilities or policy violations (such as misconfigurations or overexposed data), and recommend or automate remediation. Think of it as an extension of Cloud Security Posture Management (CSPM), but focusing on the data itself rather than just infrastructure.

Key characteristics and capabilities of DSPM include

1) **Comprehensive Visibility:** DSPM tools automatically scan both cloud and on-prem repositories to find sensitive data wherever it lives. For example, it might find that an AWS S3 bucket contains files with customer PII or that a developer copied a production database to an unsecured cloud instance. Shadow data – unknown or forgotten data stores – are uncovered (a big deal, since "you can't protect what you can't see" and lots of sensitive info sits in forgotten corners).

2) **Contextual Risk Assessment:** It's not just finding data, but assessing its security posture: Who/what can access it? Is it encrypted? Is it in a location that violates policy (like sensitive data in a publicly accessible share)? Are there anomalous access patterns? For example, a DSPM might flag that a database containing credit card numbers is accessible by too many internal accounts or that an employee uploaded a file containing PHI to a personal OneDrive.

3) **Integration with DLP and IAM:** DSPM does not replace DLP or IAM, but augments them by giving security teams better visibility into where sensitive data resides, who can access it, and whether the surrounding controls are appropriate. It can feed data locations discovered into DLP solutions so policies cover the right repositories, and it can integrate with IAM or identity governance tools to help remove stale or excessive access. Figure 3-3 illustrates this integration stack, showing how DSPM connects data discovery, classification, access analysis, DLP enforcement, identity governance, and security operations into a broader data protection model.

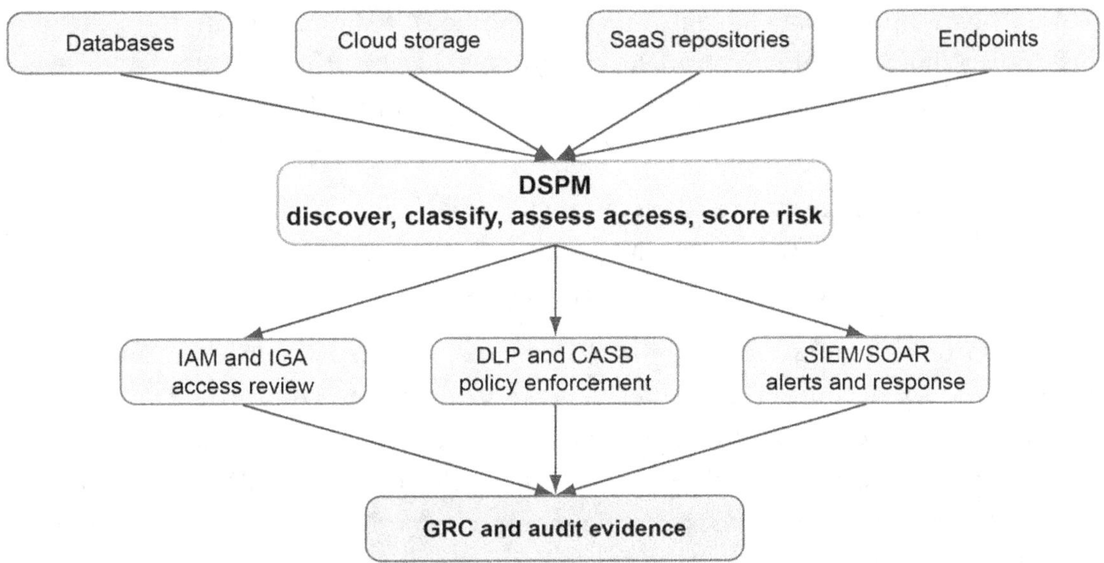

Figure 3-3. *DSPM integration stack*

4) **Automated Remediation and Response:** Advanced DSPM solutions can orchestrate fixes. For instance, if they find a sensitive file in an open AWS S3 bucket, they could automatically apply an ACL to restrict access or trigger an encryption of that bucket. Or if a sensitive data store is not encrypted, they alert or, if possible, enable encryption. This reduces the window of exposure.

5) **Use Cases:** According to analysts, common DSPM use cases include

   i. Finding stale or unused data (and then possibly deleting or archiving it to reduce risk and costs).

   ii. Detecting shadow IT data stores – e.g., a marketing team using a third-party cloud app to collect user info without security's knowledge.

   iii. Monitoring data flows to AI/ML: Interestingly, with AI, companies worry about what data is being fed into models. DSPM can help track whether sensitive data is being used to train models or sent to external AI APIs without authorization.

iv. Mapping data lineages and flows: Some DSPM tools visualize how data moves through your systems (like from a prod DB to analytics copy to a report), which helps identify where controls are needed.

v. Incident response acceleration: If a breach happens, DSPM can quickly show what sensitive data was in the affected resource, saving a ton of time in impact analysis.

Why is DSPM gaining attention now? The explosion of data, multi-cloud adoption, and remote work all contributed to data being more distributed than ever. Traditional DLP might not detect a misconfigured database or a data lake copy on its own, whereas CSPM focuses on cloud config rather than data content. DSPM fills that gap by continuously scanning for data risks at the source. Gartner placed it in the hype cycle, indicating it's an emerging must-have for data-centric security management.

Examples of DSPM in action: Suppose an organization has dozens of AWS accounts and Azure subscriptions. A DSPM tool (such as those from startups like Cyera and Dig Security or from established companies like Palo Alto after acquisitions) is deployed. It discovers

1. A forgotten AWS S3 bucket from 2018 containing a CSV of customer records (PII) that was left publicly readable – immediate red flag. The tool alerts and auto-blocks public access.

2. Several Azure SQL databases are not encrypted (TDE off), containing HR data – it suggests enabling encryption and tighter network controls.

3. It finds that certain sensitive files that should only be on SharePoint are also sitting in a developer's personal cloud storage – indicating a potential policy violation that DLP missed. Now, SecOps can investigate how that got there (maybe a DLP gap or an intentional act).

4. The DSPM risk dashboard gives an overall score and trending, which the CISO can use to report improvements. Over six months, they say they reduced "high-risk data locations" by 60% by cleaning up, encrypting, or restricting access, as guided by the DSPM findings.

One might ask, couldn't we do this manually? Possibly, but at cloud scale with ephemeral resources, manual audits fail. DSPM's continuous nature is key - new data stores are scanned immediately upon appearance, closing windows of exposure.

Another integration: DSPM with data loss prevention - some vendors pitch that DSPM can drive DLP policies. For instance, if DSPM finds sensitive data in a certain SaaS app, you'd want your CASB/DLP to start monitoring that app or apply policies. Or DSPM might label data, which DLP then uses (like automatically tagging all discovered "Customer Data" which then triggers a DLP rule on egress).

In summary, DSPM is like having a data security guardian that watches over all your data repositories in the cloud and on-prem, shining light into dark corners. It complements DLP (which watches data in motion) by continuously monitoring data at rest and in use in applications. DSPM is increasingly becoming part of comprehensive data protection platforms. Organizations are advised to incorporate DSPM practices - even if initially via existing tools or manual processes - to ensure sensitive data is not left unmanaged. If the previous case studies identified "unknown unknowns" (such as the school district finding files containing student data in open shares), DSPM aims to systematically root them out.

AI Governance and Sensitive Data in AI/LLMs

The rise of generative AI and large language models (LLMs) in enterprise settings has introduced new data security concerns. On the one hand, AI tools, such as ChatGPT, Microsoft 365 Copilot, Google Gemini, Claude, enterprise AI assistants, or custom LLMs, offer productivity leaps, summarizing documents, writing code, and analyzing data. On the other hand, they pose a risk of data leakage: users might input confidential information into an AI prompt, or an AI might generate outputs that inadvertently contain sensitive data from training data. Additionally, AI systems themselves need protection against malicious input (prompt injection) and misuse.

Many organizations are now asking: How do we enable AI for employees while preventing it from becoming a data leakage vector? Governance in this context means policies, controls, and risk management specifically for AI usage:

1) **Preventing Unauthorized Data Exposure to AI:** A considerable risk is employees pasting confidential text into a public AI chatbot (like the infamous case of a Samsung engineer pasting proprietary code into ChatGPT, which then could become part of OpenAI's training data). To address this:

i. Many companies implemented usage policies: e.g., "Do not input any customer PII or company confidential info into external AI tools." Some outright-banned tools, like ChatGPT, are being kept out of work systems until solutions mature.

ii. More constructively, some provided enterprise-sanctioned AI: e.g., ChatGPT Enterprise (which promises not to use your data for training and offers an admin console) or hosted LLMs internally that have data isolation. Microsoft's Copilot, for example, is designed so that prompts and responses stay within the tenant and are not used to train the foundation model.

iii. Tools like Netskope (as mentioned earlier) and others have extended DLP to AI prompts. For example, an AI proxy or CASB can detect if someone is about to submit what appears to be source code or a client's name to ChatGPT and block or redact it.

2) **Mitigating AI Model Data Memorization:** Research has shown that large models can sometimes regurgitate parts of their training data, especially if that data was unique (like some person's SSN or a confidential paragraph). If a company fine-tunes an internal model on its data, it must ensure that the model doesn't output raw, sensitive records. Approaches here include

i. **Differential Privacy Techniques During Training**: Adding noise so the model learns patterns but not specifics.

ii. **Prompt Filtering and Output Filtering:** Ensuring that if a prompt tries to get the model to spill sensitive info (like "List all customer emails in the training set"), the model either refuses or the system filters that response.

iii. **Data Minimization for Training:** Only train AI on data that is approved and scrubbed of direct identifiers unless absolutely needed. Some companies generate synthetic data for AI training to avoid using sensitive real data.

3) **AI-Specific Security Measures:** LLMs introduce novel threats like prompt injection (where an attacker's input can trick the AI into ignoring safety instructions and perhaps revealing information or performing unauthorized actions). Vendors and researchers have begun addressing these with

    i. Input sanitization and user role separation in prompts (so a user can't override system-level instructions).

    ii. Monitoring AI outputs for policy violations (e.g., if an AI is asked to produce some sensitive content, does it comply with policy?).

    iii. **AI Usage Logs**: Logging AI prompts and responses for audit (with privacy considerations) so that any incident can be traced. Microsoft, for instance, logs Copilot interactions and ensures they align with compliance commitments.

4) **Regulatory Compliance for AI:** Globally, regulations are emerging (the EU's AI Act, for example) that will require transparency about data used in AI and risk management for AI outputs. Companies are starting AI governance committees that include legal, compliance, and security to ensure they use AI responsibly. One example: if an AI helps generate customer communications, who verifies they don't inadvertently include someone else's data? Some orgs require human review of AI output that contains any facts derived from internal data.

Practical steps many organizations are taking:

1) Provide an **Enterprise AI Platform**: e.g., a company might deploy Azure OpenAI in their own cloud, so any prompts stay in their environment (with **"no training on your data"** guarantee). This way, employees have a safe AI to use, reducing the temptation to use random online ones.

2) Use **AI Gateway/Proxy** Solutions: Startups and cloud security companies have created "AI gateways" that route all AI API calls through a control point to apply DLP and policies (similar to how Web Secure Gateways work). Netskope's ChatGPT integration is one example.

3) **Train Employees**: Like with phishing, now there's training on "Think before you prompt." Highlight real-life mishaps (Samsung, Apple, banks blocking ChatGPT) to illustrate the risk. Many CISOs issue guidelines (e.g., "You may use AI for general tasks, but do not input source code or sensitive schematics. Summarize without identifiers," etc.).

4) **AI Ethics and Bias**: While not directly causing data loss, governance includes ensuring AI doesn't produce biased or toxic content. Some companies have implemented filters so that if an AI output includes certain sensitive categories (race, health info), it gets reviewed. This overlaps with data protection when dealing with personal data (e.g., ensuring that AI decisions about people are fair and that their data isn't mishandled).

To illustrate, consider a customer service department integrating an AI assistant. Governance measures might include

1) The AI (like MS Copilot) is configured not to use any customer data for model training.

2) It respects M365's underlying permissions - i.e., it only shows data the user asking already has access to (so one employee can't prompt it to reveal another department's confidential files).

3) Copilot has protections to block insertion of protected data in responses if the user lacks rights (Microsoft mentions it has content filtering for harmful or sensitive content).

4) All usage is logged; if an employee tried to abuse it (like using search prompts to gather restricted info), that's auditable.

As AI becomes embedded in everyday workflows, AI governance frameworks are becoming as necessary as cloud security and data protection frameworks. Organizations should define which AI tools are approved, what data may be used in prompts, how outputs are reviewed, how AI activity is logged, and how exceptions are approved. Enterprise AI platforms increasingly provide administrative controls for usage monitoring, data boundaries, prompt and response logging, and source restrictions. These controls are especially important for sensitive repositories, regulated data, and workflows where AI-generated output may influence business decisions or customer communications.

In summary, AI governance and data protection are about extending our policies to a new kind of "user" (the AI) and new workflows. We must ensure AI is used responsibly: it should not become an inadvertent mole siphoning out data, nor a source of false or biased decisions due to poor training data. Security teams should collaborate with data science teams to implement these controls. The paradox is that we want AI to be robust (trained on rich data) but safe (not exposing that data). Solutions like enterprise LLMs, hybrid processing (where sensitive data is processed in a secure enclave by the AI, see confidential computing next), and robust user training are key to resolving that paradox.

Confidential Computing and Privacy-Enhancing Computation

One of the historically toughest areas of data protection is securing data in use – i.e., while it is being processed in memory or by applications. Traditional encryption protects data at rest and in transit, but once decrypted for use, it can be exposed (to a malicious OS, a hypervisor, an insider with memory access, etc.). Confidential computing has emerged to address this gap by leveraging hardware-based trusted execution environments (TEEs) that keep data encrypted throughout processing.

The core idea: perform computation in an isolated, secure enclave so that neither system administrators nor cloud providers can see the data or code within it. For example, imagine analyzing encrypted healthcare data in the cloud. Usually, you'd have to decrypt it to process. Still, with confidential VMs or enclaves, you can keep it encrypted in memory, and only the enclave (which is heavily isolated) has the keys to decrypt inside itself.

Key aspects of confidential computing:

1) **Hardware-Enforced Isolation:** Modern CPUs (Intel, AMD, ARM) offer TEEs like **Intel SGX/TDX**, **AMD SEV**, etc. These create secure enclaves in memory. The data and code inside are encrypted in memory and decrypted only within the CPU, so other processes, the OS, or the hypervisor can't access them. Also, enclaves can provide remote attestation – a remote party can verify that an enclave is genuine and running expected code before sending it sensitive data.

2) **Cloud Adoption:** Cloud providers now have confidential computing offerings (e.g., Azure Confidential VMs, AWS Nitro Enclaves, Google Confidential VMs). They allow customers to run workloads such that even the cloud provider's admins can't peek into them. This is big for industries like finance and healthcare, which are hesitant to move to the cloud due to concerns about data exposure.

3) **Use Cases**

   i. **Multi-party Computation**: Two companies want to collaborate on data (e.g., train a joint AI model) without exposing their raw data to each other. They can each put their data into a confidential computing environment that merges it for analysis, but neither party sees the other's raw input – the enclave protects it while still computing joint results.

   ii. **Secure SaaS**: If you use a SaaS service with confidential computing, your data might be processed in an enclave that even the SaaS provider can't access. Microsoft, for instance, was exploring confidential computing for things like SQL databases (so Microsoft can't see the plain text in their cloud).

   iii. **Regulated Workloads**: Government or defense workloads requiring top secrecy can run in cloud enclaves safely.

   iv. **Cryptographic Key Management**: Hosting a Certificate Authority or key management service in an enclave so that keys are never exposed, even in memory outside. As organizations prepare for the post-quantum transition, certificate infrastructure also deserves attention. Many current public key infrastructure designs still rely on RSA or elliptic curve algorithms for digital signatures, certificate chains, TLS authentication, code signing, and device identity. These algorithms remain widely used today, but they are considered quantum-vulnerable in the long term. A future-ready key management strategy should therefore include certificate inventory, crypto-agility planning, renewal process review, and readiness for post-quantum or hybrid certificate models as standards and vendor support mature.

4) **Privacy-Enhancing Computation (PEC) Techniques:** Confidential computing is one, but there are others often mentioned:

    i. **Fully Homomorphic Encryption (FHE):** Allows computations on encrypted data without decrypting it at all. For example, you could add two encrypted numbers and get an encrypted result that, when decrypted, equals the sum of the plaintext numbers. This is like the holy grail of privacy – the server never sees any data in clear. The downside: FHE is extremely slow (though improving). It's currently feasible for limited operations but not for widespread, complex-task production use due to performance constraints.

    ii. **Secure Multi-party Computation (SMPC):** Splits data among multiple parties (often as encrypted shares) who compute a function together such that no one sees the complete data. Only the final result is revealed to certain parties. Useful for, say, calculating industry benchmarks from private data of competitors without exposing individual companies' data.

    iii. **Differential Privacy:** A bit different – it allows gathering insights from datasets (like statistical queries) while adding noise to ensure individual entries (like a person's data) can't be deduced. Companies like Apple and Uber use it, and even the US Census Bureau, to release valuable data without compromising individual privacy.

    iv. **Zero-Knowledge Proofs (ZKP):** Cryptographic proofs that allow one to prove something (like "I am over 18" or "This transaction is valid") without revealing the underlying data (like your birthdate or the transaction details). ZKPs are big in blockchain and ID verification contexts.

These PEC techniques often complement each other. For instance, one could use differential privacy on outputs of a confidential computing process to safely share aggregated results.

The **impact on data protection**: Confidential computing directly addresses data in use, which was often the weak link. It essentially extends encryption across all three states:

Data is encrypted at rest. Data is transmitted into an enclave, encrypted, and, within the enclave, decrypted but protected by hardware.

After processing, the results can be encrypted again for output. A diagram of the **three states of data protection** highlights this (see Figure 3-4) – where confidential computing fills the "data in use" gap.

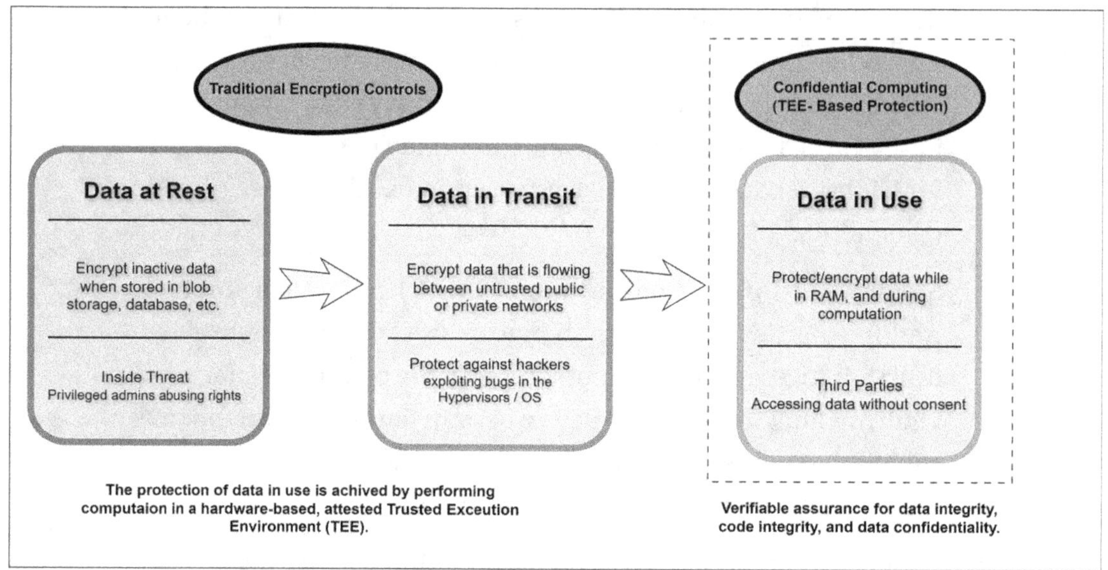

Figure 3-4. *Confidential computing encrypts data in use*

Consider a scenario: a bank wants to use a cloud machine learning service to detect fraud on encrypted transaction data (because they don't want to expose real transactions to the cloud provider). They could use FHE to allow the model to score transactions without decrypting (some research has done ML inference on homomorphically encrypted data). If that's too slow, a practical approach is to use an Azure confidential VM: the ML model runs in an enclave; encrypted data is sent to it; it decrypts within the enclave, processes, and sends back results (which can be encrypted). The cloud provider (Azure) cannot see the data or model internals – they only see an encrypted blob going in and out. This reduces the trust needed in the cloud. Azure provides attestation that the VM is indeed an enclave running the intended model (so the bank knows it's not a spoofed environment).

We see early adoption: e.g., healthcare consortia using enclaves to jointly analyze patient data across hospitals without exposing patient privacy. Central database and analytics platforms are adding support (SQL Server Always Encrypted with secure enclaves, confidential Kubernetes for processing sensitive data). According to industry updates, 2024 saw many new products and standardization efforts around confidential computing. The Confidential Computing Consortium (CCC) fosters these standards.

Note TEEs reduce exposure for data in use but do not replace DLP or access governance. Monitor for side-channel mitigations and attest enclaves before use.

Challenges: It's not a silver bullet. Side-channel attacks on TEEs have been demonstrated (e.g., exploiting CPU power patterns or memory access patterns to glean secrets). Vendors continually patch and improve, but it's an arms race. Also, using these techs often requires changes to applications. Homomorphic encryption is computationally heavy (latencies 1000× normal in some cases, though that's improving with better algorithms and hardware acceleration). Multi-party computation can be network-heavy. So, organizations must choose the right tool for the job:

1) Use TEEs for general-purpose and complex processing with manageable overhead.

2) Use FHE or ZKP for very sensitive cases or where data can't be revealed at all (accepting the performance cost).

3) Combine with traditional controls – e.g., confidential computing doesn't negate the need for DLP; you still wouldn't want, say, someone to take a screenshot of enclave output.

Nevertheless, confidential computing enhances cloud trust: companies hesitant to move sensitive workloads to the cloud now have an option to do so with minimal trust (even if the cloud is breached at the host level, enclave data remains safe). It also opens up new collaborative analytics that were not possible before due to privacy concerns.

Privacy-enhancing computation and confidential computing are likely to play significant roles in sectors such as finance (e.g., privacy-preserving financial analytics), healthcare (e.g., sharing research on patient data without violating privacy), and AI (e.g., privacy-preserving model training across organizations). Gartner and others predict adoption will grow steadily as hardware support becomes ubiquitous and as regulatory frameworks encourage their use (the EU's data strategy mentions encouraging the use of PETs – Privacy-Enhancing Tech – for data sharing).

Note Data residency ≠ compliance by itself. Document lawful bases, transfer mechanisms, and third-party BAAs/DPAs alongside region pinning.

In summary, these emerging trends - DSPM, AI governance, and confidential computing - indicate a future where

1) We know where our data is always and its risk (DSPM)
2) We harness AI but with control and oversight to protect data (turning a potential threat into a managed tool)
3) We can compute data without exposing it, significantly reducing breach impact and enabling new secure collaborations (confidential computing and related crypto techniques)

The combination of these with traditional methods will define the next phase of data protection. Organizations should start exploring and piloting these technologies now, for instance, integrating DSPM into their security operations to uncover unknown risks; establishing an AI use policy and, if appropriate, deploying a secure AI sandbox; and trying out a confidential computing service for a sensitive application to become familiar with its benefits and constraints.

Conclusion

Protecting data in motion, use, and storage is a constantly evolving challenge. We've expanded this chapter to illustrate not only the foundational practices (classification, DLP, encryption, access control) but also to delve deep into how real organizations apply them and how new developments will enhance our defenses. A few closing thoughts and best practices for readers (CISOs, IT managers, engineers):

Adopt a Data-Centric Mindset: Focus on the data itself, know it, classify it, and track it. As echoed by numerous case studies and DSPM's emergence, visibility into data is paramount. Build inventories of sensitive data and continuously update them.

Defense in Depth with Integration: Use multiple layers of protection that reinforce each other. For example, in Microsoft Purview, we saw classification feeding DLP, and in Netskope, we saw inline and API controls combined. Ensure your tools communicate with each other (e.g., CASB alerts go to the SIEM, DLP labels go to IRM, etc.). An integrated, unified policy approach reduces gaps and simplifies management.

Customize to Context (One Size Doesn't Fit All): Each industry and company has unique needs. A school district will employ different policies than a bank. Use templates as starting points, but involve business stakeholders to tailor policies and thresholds so that security is practical and workable. The success stories often involved phased rollouts and stakeholder engagement (recall GlobalBank's approach to win buy-in before enforcement).

User Awareness and Culture: Technology fails if people circumvent it or resent it. Invest in user training, not just on "how," but also on "why." When employees understand the stakes (e.g., how a data breach could cost jobs or hurt clients), they are more likely to cooperate. Encourage a culture where protecting data is everyone's responsibility, akin to a safety culture in manufacturing.

Keep an Eye on the Future: Start exploring emerging solutions such as DSPM, confidential computing, AI governance controls, and post-quantum readiness early. For instance, consider a pilot with a confidential VM for a sensitive application, or try out a DSPM tool on a subset of cloud resources to understand where sensitive data is exposed. Begin building a cryptographic inventory that identifies where encryption, digital certificates, TLS, VPNs, code signing, device identity, and key management depend on RSA or elliptic curve cryptography. This inventory becomes the foundation for crypto-agility, certificate modernization, and future migration to post-quantum or hybrid cryptographic approaches. Experimentation now can provide a competitive edge and readiness for future compliance. Also, actively shape AI usage policies in your organization. AI adoption should not happen in a governance vacuum.

Vendor Neutrality and Zero Trust: While we discussed specific vendors (Microsoft, Netskope, etc.) for illustration, remember the principles are vendor-agnostic. Aim for **zero trust data security** – never assume data is safe just because it's inside a perimeter. Authenticate and authorize every access, inspect and log data movements, and minimize data exposure at all times.

Metrics and Continuous Improvement: Establish metrics such as the number of incidents, time to detect/respond, and the amount of sensitive data in unsecured locations. The case studies presented outcomes (e.g., a 70% reduction in breaches and a 100% compliance audit success rate). Use similar metrics internally to track progress and justify investment. Data protection is not a one-time project but an ongoing process of improvement.

Finally, protecting data is fundamentally about maintaining trust – trust with customers that their information is safe, trust with partners that IP is guarded, and trust with employees that the tools they use won't put them or the company in jeopardy. By implementing the strategies, technologies, and best practices detailed in this chapter, organizations can substantially mitigate the risk of data loss or misuse, thereby preserving that trust and upholding their obligations in an increasingly data-driven world. The combination of well-chosen solutions (such as Microsoft Purview, Netskope, and others) with sound policy and forward-looking adoption of emerging technologies will equip organizations to face current and emerging data security challenges with confidence.

CHAPTER 4

Cloud Security Architectures for Hybrid Enterprises

In today's cloud-driven world, organizations are leveraging combinations of Infrastructure-as-a-Service, Platform-as-a-Service, Software-as-a-Service, and on-premises systems to form hybrid and multi-cloud environments. With this flexibility comes significant security responsibility. Cloud incidents continue to be driven less by a failure of the underlying cloud provider and more by customer-side issues such as misconfiguration, weak identity controls, excessive permissions, exposed storage, poor monitoring, and unclear operational ownership. These patterns make cloud security architecture a business-critical discipline rather than a collection of provider-specific settings. This chapter provides a comprehensive guide to building adaptable, resilient cloud security architectures for hybrid enterprises, spanning on-premises environments, IaaS, PaaS, and SaaS in a vendor-neutral way. We revisit the shared responsibility model, explore reference frameworks that apply across providers, and examine cloud-native security controls such as logging, segmentation, encryption, key management, and post-quantum readiness.

Shared Responsibility Revisited: Cloud Security in Hybrid Environments

Cloud security is founded on the principle of shared responsibility between the cloud provider and the customer. In a hybrid enterprise (mixing on-prem and cloud), this model becomes even more critical to understand and implement correctly. Simply

A. Gupta and S. Mittal, *Foundations of Modern Information Security*,
https://doi.org/10.1007/979-8-8688-2558-3_4

put, cloud providers are responsible for the security of the cloud (the underlying cloud infrastructure), while customers are responsible for security in the cloud (their workloads, applications, and data). However, this division varies by service model and is often misunderstood, leading to dangerous gaps. "Shared" responsibility does not mean anything is automatically handled – it means both sides must clearly own their parts, or else "everyone assumes someone else is taking care of the problem," as one expert wryly noted. In practice, if you don't explicitly secure something in your cloud stack, it likely isn't being secured by anyone. Therefore, it's vital to delineate responsibilities across IaaS, PaaS, SaaS, and on-prem components.

Responsibility by Service Model

The balance of provider vs. customer security duties shifts depending on the cloud service model. With IaaS (e.g., AWS EC2, Azure Virtual Machines), you gain flexibility but also bear the most responsibility. The provider secures the physical data centers, network, and virtualization layer, but everything above the hypervisor is the customer's job – securing the OS, applications, data, network configuration, identity management, etc. Move to PaaS (e.g., Azure App Service, Google App Engine) and the provider takes on more – they manage the OS, runtime, and platform security, so you can focus mainly on your application code, configurations, and data. In SaaS (e.g., Microsoft 365, Salesforce), the provider handles almost the entire stack (infrastructure, runtime, application), leaving you with a much narrower scope: primarily user access, account management, data governance, and configuring service-specific security settings.

It's important to internalize that no matter the deployment model, you always retain responsibility for critical assets like your data and identities. For example, in a SaaS email service, the provider keeps the servers patched and physically secure, but you must set strong access policies, manage user identities, configure retention and encryption options, and monitor for suspicious logins or data leakage. As the US Cybersecurity and Infrastructure Security Agency (CISA) emphasizes, even when using FedRAMP-authorized SaaS, agencies "must understand where their responsibilities end and the CSP's begin," ensuring they handle things like incident response, log management, identity and access control, and configuration management for their usage of the service. Neglecting these duties just because the app is "in the cloud" can be a costly mistake.

On-Premises and Hybrid Considerations

In a hybrid architecture, you have on-prem systems (where you control everything) interacting with cloud services (shared model). This means your overall security architecture will blend different responsibility regimes. A helpful mindset is to treat on-premises like your private cloud - you own all layers (network, hardware, OS, etc.) - and treat each cloud service according to its model. For instance, if you integrate an on-prem database with an ERP SaaS, you must secure the database completely (patching, network firewall, backups, etc.) while also properly configuring and monitoring the ERP SaaS (managing accounts, applying available security settings, and reviewing logs). A clear definition of responsibilities and handoffs is essential so nothing "falls through the cracks." Many breaches occur when organizations assume the provider is handling something that, in reality, the provider considers to be the customer's job. One infamous example was a major cloud storage breach caused by a misconfigured S3 bucket - the cloud provider (Amazon) provides the tools for securing buckets, but it was the customer's responsibility to use them (by setting proper access controls). Such misconfigurations persist as a top threat because exposed storage, weak identity governance, excessive permissions, and poor monitoring remain recurring causes of cloud incidents.

To avoid ambiguity, document the division of security tasks for each system in your hybrid cloud. Cloud providers publish their shared responsibility documentation - for example, AWS's and Azure's guides both emphasize that customers always own data protection, identities, and client-side security. You can use these as a starting point. Then, internally, create matrices or RACI charts to map out who secures what in your environment. Include not just IT teams but also clarify provider responsibilities and any third parties (e.g., a managed service provider or cloud broker, if you use one). Some organizations formalize this in cloud security governance policies or in contracts with the providers. Clarity here is not only good practice but often a compliance requirement as well (for instance, regulators expect you to understand and manage your cloud security obligations, not assume the vendor handles everything).

The Shared Responsibility "Gap" Problem

Without careful management, the shared model can leave gaps - areas that both the customer and provider assume the other is covering. A classic example is data backups in IaaS. The cloud provider ensures the underlying storage hardware is reliable (and perhaps offers optional backup services), but typically the customer is responsible for implementing backups of their virtual machines or databases. If the customer assumes "the data is in the cloud, so it's automatically backed up," that data may not be recoverable after, say, an accidental deletion or ransomware attack. Similarly, in PaaS, a provider might manage the OS security, but if you don't configure your application properly (e.g., leaving an API open), it's a gap. Minding these gaps requires a combination of cloud provider tools and third-party solutions. For instance, enabling versioning and backup features for storage services, using cloud-native security services (like AWS GuardDuty or Microsoft Defender for Cloud) to cover areas you might miss, and employing configuration management to enforce security baselines.

A common lesson from cloud security incidents is that shared responsibility can become a shared responsibility gap unless the customer actively assigns, verifies, and monitors ownership. To counter this, treat shared responsibilities as joint responsibilities - both you and the provider have roles. For example, while a cloud provider might offer DDoS protection at the network level, you should still architect your applications for resilience (using rate limiting, failover, etc.). Regularly review cloud service documentation to identify which security controls are your duty. One useful approach is to leverage frameworks or checklists from independent organizations. The Center for Internet Security (CIS) publishes a "Shared Responsibility Matrix" and CIS Benchmarks mapping that show, for each major cloud (AWS, Azure, GCP), which party is responsible for each security control area. Adopting such guidelines can help ensure you're covering your side of the bargain. In addition, cloud provider trust programs (like Azure Well-Architected or AWS Well-Architected Framework) include security pillars that basically guide you through your responsibilities, so make use of those design reviews.

In summary, revisiting and truly internalizing the shared responsibility model is step one in any hybrid cloud security architecture. It sets the stage for everything else: you know what you must protect vs. what the provider handles. With that foundation, you can then build out the proper controls in each domain. The rest of this chapter assumes that you, the cloud consumer, are proactively taking charge of all the security areas under your purview - because if you don't, it's very likely no one else will, and the result could be a preventable breach. Now, with the "who protects what" clarified, we turn to designing the overall security architecture in a way that is vendor-neutral and adaptable across a hybrid, multi-cloud enterprise.

Vendor-Neutral Cloud Security Reference Models

Designing a robust security architecture for hybrid enterprises can be daunting, given the plethora of vendor-specific services and terminology. To avoid getting locked into one vendor's mindset (or missing critical elements when spanning multiple platforms), it's wise to use vendor-neutral reference models as guides. A security reference architecture is essentially a blueprint or framework that outlines security domains, components, and controls in a generic way, so you can then map your specific technologies (whether AWS, Azure, GCP, or on-prem tools) onto it. The goal is to ensure completeness and consistency in your security design - covering all bases - regardless of which cloud or technology is in use.

Several industry-standard models and frameworks can help here:

- **NIST Cloud Security Reference Architecture:** The National Institute of Standards and Technology (NIST) provides a high-level Cloud Computing Reference Architecture (SP 500-292) that identifies key roles (Cloud Consumer, Provider, Broker, Auditor, Carrier) and the major functional components of cloud environments. While a bit dated (2011) and not security-specific, it offers a baseline vocabulary. Building on that, NIST and others have published cloud security architectures that map security controls to these roles and layers (e.g., NIST SP 800-144 and others outline considerations for security in cloud). The core insight from NIST is to explicitly define all the actors and components in the cloud ecosystem - not just your organization and the provider, but also third-party brokers or auditors, network carriers, etc., that might be in play. For a hybrid enterprise, you may effectively play multiple roles (you are the Cloud Consumer; you might also operate as a Cloud Provider if offering a service to others, etc.). Using NIST's reference model helps ensure you've identified who is responsible for what (tying back to shared responsibility) and what technical components (identity management, networking, monitoring, etc.) must exist in the architecture.

- **Cloud Security Alliance (CSA) Enterprise Architecture and Cloud Controls Matrix:** The CSA, a global not-for-profit, has developed comprehensive vendor-neutral frameworks for cloud security. Their Enterprise Architecture (EA) is a methodology and set of tools to help security architects map cloud security capabilities to business needs in a neutral way. It defines security domains (such as identity and access management, data protection, etc.) and provides reference models that cloud providers and consumers can align with. CSA's Cloud Controls Matrix (CCM) is another resource - a detailed control framework mapping security controls to cloud-specific implementations. When designing your architecture, you can use the CCM as a checklist to ensure all necessary controls (from governance to technical safeguards) are addressed, regardless of platform. Notably, CSA's approach is inclusive of all cloud vendors and even offers a certification (CCSK) that is vendor-neutral, underscoring the importance of abstract principles over product-specifics. In practice, you might use CSA's reference model to say, "Okay, for identity federation - that's a required component; in AWS, we'll use IAM with AWS IAM Identity Center, in Azure, we'll use Microsoft Entra ID, etc., but the architecture always has an IdM component."
- **Security Architecture Frameworks (SABSA, OSA, etc.):** Classic security architecture methodologies like SABSA (Sherwood Applied Business Security Architecture) or the Open Security Architecture (OSA) provide structured approaches to building security architectures that align with business objectives and risk management, independent of technology. SABSA, for instance, encourages developing architectures through multiple layers (contextual, conceptual, logical, etc.), ensuring you address everything from business drivers down to technical controls. This can be very useful in a hybrid cloud context: at the contextual level, you define business requirements for security (e.g., "protect customer data across all environments under GDPR"); at conceptual/logical levels, you define how (e.g., "we need encryption of data at rest and in transit, multi-factor auth for all users, continuous monitoring, etc."), and only at the physical layer do you pick specific solutions ("we will

use AWS KMS for encryption keys, Entra ID for identity, Splunk Cloud for SIEM," and so on). By separating the "what" and "why" from the "how," SABSA helps maintain vendor neutrality and adaptability - if you change a technology later (say, swap Splunk for a different SIEM), your overall architecture and principles remain intact.

- **Zero Trust Architecture (ZTA):** Zero Trust is more of a philosophy/design principle than a reference model, but it has become a cornerstone of modern security architectures, especially for hybrid environments. The idea is "never trust, always verify" - every access request is continuously authenticated and authorized, regardless of network location. The US government (via NIST SP 800-207 and CISA guidelines) has been strongly encouraging Zero Trust adoption. For a hybrid enterprise, adopting a Zero Trust reference model ensures you build consistent identity-centric security across on-prem and cloud. This includes components like identity providers, secure access brokers, network micro-segmentation, device trust, and continuous monitoring (all of which can be mapped to vendor-specific services later). CISA's Cloud Security Technical Reference Architecture specifically calls out Zero Trust as a key model and provides a maturity model for agencies to implement it. By using Zero Trust principles as a guiding reference, you inherently remain vendor-neutral because Zero Trust is outcome-focused (e.g., verify user with MFA, verify device health, limit access to least privilege, log everything). Whether you achieve that with Entra ID + Conditional Access, or Okta + Zscaler, or AWS IAM + custom solutions, the model still applies. Figure 4-1 illustrates a vendor-neutral hybrid cloud Zero Trust architecture in which identity, policy, access enforcement, segmentation, and centralized monitoring work together across users, partners, workloads, SaaS platforms, cloud services, and on-premises systems.

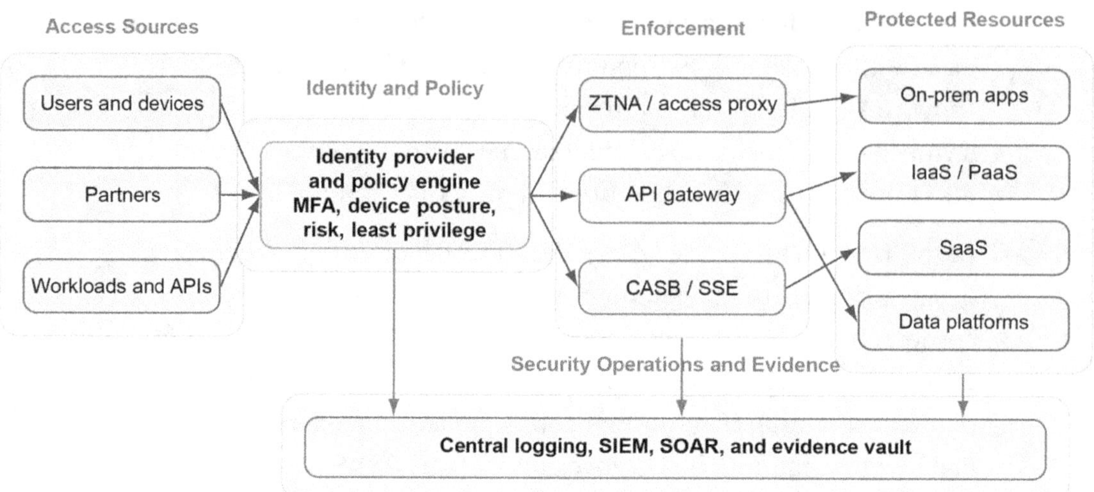

Figure 4-1. *Conceptual Zero Trust security architecture. Every access request in the hybrid environment (whether from a corporate user, a partner, or an application/API call) is treated as untrusted until verified. The architecture includes an identity provider (for strong authentication and SSO), context-aware policy engines to evaluate device posture and user context, and segmented application environments. Even within the cloud network, microsegmentation (illustrated by separated zones and firewalls) ensures that a compromise in one segment (e.g., a compromised VM in the development VPC) does not easily propagate to another (e.g., the production database). This vendor-neutral model can be implemented with various products, but the principle remains the same: authenticate and authorize everywhere, enforce least privilege, and assume breach by containing blast radius*

- **Multi-cloud Security Reference Architecture:** If your hybrid enterprise spans multiple public clouds (AWS, Azure, GCP, etc.), it is useful to create a multi-cloud security architecture that abstracts common services. For example, TechVision Research (as described by security architect Gunnar Peterson) developed a reference architecture for multi-cloud security that is "business-centric, product-neutral," providing diagrams that can be adapted to any environment. This reference model maps security processes (like incident response, threat intel, risk assessment) and security technology capabilities (like IAM, CASB, encryption, network security, monitoring) across hybrid multi-cloud IT stacks. One insight from Peterson's work is mapping controls to well-known frameworks like the NIST Cybersecurity Framework 2.0, which organizes cybersecurity outcomes across six core functions: Govern, Identify, Protect, Detect, Respond, and Recover. In a hybrid and multi-cloud architecture, the added Govern function is especially important because it connects cloud security design to risk ownership, policy, accountability, supply chain expectations, and executive-level prioritization. This helps ensure that security capabilities are not only deployed across each cloud and on-premises environment, but are also governed consistently across the enterprise. Such a model also highlights integration points - e.g., how your on-prem SIEM should ingest logs from all clouds or how your identity governance process must encompass accounts in every SaaS. By using a multi-cloud reference, you can avoid duplicating effort or leaving gaps when each cloud is managed in a silo. It encourages a "single pane of glass" approach for security management wherever feasible (we will touch on centralized logging/monitoring later as a key enabler).

In practice, building your own security architecture likely means taking elements of these reference models and tailoring them. A good approach is to start with a layered view: business layer (requirements, regulations, risk appetite), architectural layer (domains like network, app, data security, IAM, SecOps), and technology layer (specific products/services in each domain per environment). Using vendor-neutral references ensures you consider all necessary domains. For example, you might ensure you have solutions for Identity and Access Management, Threat Prevention (Network security, WAFs), Data Protection (encryption, DLP), Security Monitoring and Incident Response, Endpoint/Device Security, Application Security (code scanning, etc.), and Governance/Risk/Compliance. Each of those broad areas would be part of a reference model. The CSA or NIST frameworks would remind you to include, say, a Cloud Audit function (who audits configurations) or a Cloud Broker function (if you have an intermediary managing multi-cloud connectivity). If any of those pieces are missing in your plan, the reference model helps flag them.

It's also advisable to remain compliance-aware but not compliance-driven. Use models like ISO 27001, NIST 800-53, or PCI DSS as benchmarks to check your architecture. Many compliance controls map to technical architecture requirements (e.g., PCI requires network segmentation of cardholder data - so your architecture must have that capability). The CSA CCM, for instance, maps controls to regulations. A vendor-neutral architecture that meets these mapped controls will ease your burden when proving compliance later.

Lastly, keep the architecture adaptable. One of the goals stated for this chapter is building resilient, adaptable security architectures. Being vendor-neutral contributes to adaptability – you can swap out components as needed (e.g., change an EDR tool or move workloads from Azure to AWS) without redesigning from scratch, because your model defines the function needed, not a specific product. Embracing infrastructure-as-code and automation (to be discussed) also makes the architecture more nimble. In a hybrid enterprise, change is constant – acquisitions lead to new clouds, developers spin up new SaaS apps, etc. A solid reference architecture acts like a compass: no matter how the landscape changes, you have guiding principles and a target state to align to. Many organizations establish a Cloud Security Center of Excellence or architecture review board to maintain this model and evaluate new tech against it ("Does this new CI/CD tool integrate with our logging and IAM per our reference architecture?"). In summary, use vendor-neutral frameworks as the skeleton of your security architecture – this ensures nothing important is overlooked and that you maintain consistency across disparate technology stacks.

With our reference blueprint in mind, we can now delve into specific cloud-native security controls and design patterns that make a hybrid architecture secure and resilient. We'll cover logging/monitoring, network segmentation, and encryption/key management – three foundational pillars of cloud security – and illustrate how to implement them in a vendor-neutral yet effective way, with examples from major providers (AWS, Azure, GCP) and considerations for on-prem integration.

Cloud-Native Logging and Monitoring in Hybrid Clouds

"If you don't log it, you can't secure it." Effective logging and monitoring are the eyes and ears of a cloud security architecture. In hybrid enterprises, logging must span on-prem systems, cloud infrastructure, and SaaS applications to provide a unified view of security events. Designing a cloud-native logging architecture means leveraging cloud providers' native logging capabilities, but also aggregating and correlating logs centrally (potentially using third-party tools) to monitor the entire hybrid environment. The goal is to achieve timely detection of threats, facilitate incident response, and meet compliance requirements for audit and forensics.

Challenges of Distributed Logging

In a hybrid multi-cloud setup, logs are generated in many formats and locations: firewall logs and syslogs on-prem, AWS CloudTrail and VPC Flow Logs in AWS, Azure Activity Logs and Diagnostics logs in Azure, GCP Cloud Logging for Google Cloud, plus application logs, OS logs, and SaaS audit logs (like Microsoft 365 unified audit log). Without planning, you end up with silos of log data that are hard to use collectively. According to cloud experts, diverse logging habits inhibit effective use of logs to diagnose problems or detect attacks. Thus, centralizing or integrating logs is critical. This doesn't necessarily mean one giant log repository (though many organizations do funnel logs into a SIEM or data lake), but it means having a strategy where you can search and analyze all relevant logs from one place or platform.

Best Practices for Centralized Logging

Let's break down a few best practices (adapted from industry guidance):

- **Define Clear Logging Goals and Requirements:** First, determine what you need logs for – e.g., security incident detection, performance monitoring, compliance reporting – and the scope (real-time vs. periodic analysis). For example, if real-time intrusion detection is a goal, you'll require streaming ingestion of certain logs into a SIEM with correlation rules or an XDR (Extended Detection and Response) platform. The approach may differ by environment type: In a single public cloud, you might rely heavily on that provider's native tools (CloudWatch/CloudTrail, Azure Monitor, etc.). In a hybrid cloud, you might extend on-premises logging practices into the cloud (e.g., forwarding cloud logs to your on-prem Splunk or Security Operations Center). In a multi-cloud scenario, you may deploy a cloud-neutral log aggregation solution or service that pulls from all clouds. Knowing these goals informs the architecture.
- **Aggregate and Centralize Logs Thoughtfully:** A common objective is a "single pane of glass" for logging and monitoring. This can be achieved by centralizing logs in a cloud-based analytics platform or a self-hosted system. Many organizations choose a dominant platform – e.g., they collect all logs into an ELK (Elasticsearch/

Logstash/Kibana) stack, or a commercial SIEM like Splunk, or a cloud-native solution like Microsoft Sentinel– and then integrate others. A TechTarget tip suggests it's often easiest to adopt the logging framework of your primary cloud provider and ingest other logs into it. For instance, if most systems are in AWS, you might centralize in CloudWatch Logs and use AWS's OpenSearch Service to analyze while piping Azure/GCP logs into AWS via connectors. Alternatively, use a neutral third-party service (Datadog, Splunk Cloud, etc.) that has integrations for all sources. The key is that all critical logs end up in one place (or at least are queryable together), so attackers can't hide in the seams between systems.

- **Separate and Structure Log Data:** It's useful to distinguish different categories of logs. Application logs vs. resource logs should be handled somewhat separately. Application-level logs (from your software, services) contain business context (e.g., a user transaction, an error in code) and often are best parsed by APM (Application Performance Monitoring) tools or custom analysis. Resource or infrastructure logs (system events, network flows, cloud API calls) relate to the environment's health and security. While centralizing, don't blindly mix everything; instead, tag or index logs by source/type so you can isolate issues to the application or infrastructure layer. Also, enforce structure: use JSON or other structured log formats where possible, making it easier to parse and search.

- **Log Only What Matters (and Retain Properly):** With cloud scalability, it's tempting to log everything, but this can become unwieldy and expensive. Best practice is to know what to log and for how long. Focus on logs that have security or operational value. For security, this typically means: authentication logs, access control logs, changes to configurations, network connection logs, critical system errors, and any application events that indicate transactions (especially in financial or sensitive systems). Omit superfluous information or highly verbose debug logs unless needed. Also set retention periods appropriate for your needs and compliance – many regulations (like PCI DSS or government policies such as US OMB M-21-31) require certain logs to be kept for many months or years for forensic purposes. Cloud providers allow configuring retention on log storage - e.g., keep 13 months of CloudTrail, archive older logs to cheaper storage. Regularly review your logging levels; turn down noisy logs that never get used, to save cost and improve signal-to-noise ratio. Caution: Ensure PII (Personally Identifiable Information) is not inadvertently logged in plain text (e.g., don't log full credit card numbers in application logs). Sanitizing logs is part of compliance and good hygiene.

- **Secure Your Logging Pipeline:** Logs themselves contain sensitive info and provide a blueprint of your system - if an attacker can tamper with or read your logs, that's a problem. Implement strong security on log storage and transmission. This includes access controls for log systems, encryption of logs in transit and at rest, and often network isolation (e.g., only the log agents and SIEM can talk to the log repository). As one guide notes, treat every log portal or agent as a potential attack surface. Many organizations use a dedicated logging account or project (especially in multi-account AWS setups via AWS Organizations or in Azure management groups) so that logs are written to an account that normal users cannot access or delete. Also consider enabling features like CloudTrail log file validation (which uses hashes to detect tampering of AWS logs) and ensuring only append access (prevent deletion) where possible. Monitoring your logging is another meta-control - alerts if logging stops or if log volume drops unexpectedly (could indicate an attacker trying to cover tracks) are very useful.
- **Use Cloud-Native Logging Services:** Cloud providers offer a suite of logging and monitoring tools out-of-the-box, which you should enable and use as part of cloud-native security. For example:
- **AWS:** CloudTrail for API activity logging (essential for auditing who did what in your AWS accounts), CloudWatch Logs for collecting application and system logs, VPC Flow Logs for network traffic metadata, AWS Config for tracking configuration changes, and Amazon GuardDuty which analyzes logs (CloudTrail, DNS logs, VPC flows) for threats. AWS also offers CloudWatch Alarms and EventBridge for real-time alerts on certain log patterns.

- **Azure:** Azure Monitor is an umbrella for logging and monitoring. It includes Azure Activity Logs (subscription-level events), Diagnostic Logs for resources (e.g., an Azure Storage account logging read/write access), Log Analytics workspace to aggregate and query logs with Kusto Query Language (KQL), and services like Microsoft Defender for Cloud that analyze logs for threats. Azure also has Microsoft Sentinel, a cloud-native SIEM that can ingest logs from Azure, on-prem, AWS, etc., for threat detection.
- **GCP:** Google Cloud Observability services provide Cloud Logging which can ingest logs from all Google services and even on-prem (via agents) and Cloud Monitoring for metrics and alerting. Google's Chronicle and Security Command Center can play the SIEM/analytics role.
- **SaaS Logs:** Many SaaS applications (e.g., Salesforce, Microsoft 365, ServiceNow) provide audit logs and APIs for retrieval. Consider using Cloud Access Security Brokers (CASBs) or SaaS Security Posture Management tools that centralize SaaS logging and alert on suspicious events (like abnormal file downloads from a cloud drive).

Each provider's tools can often be extended to ingest external logs as well. For instance, AWS CloudWatch can pull logs from on-prem servers via the CloudWatch agent; Azure Monitor can collect syslog or performance data from on-prem via the Log Analytics agent; GCP's Logging can receive custom log entries via API. Leverage these capabilities to bring off-cloud logs into the cloud for central analysis, or vice versa (stream cloud logs to your on-prem SIEM).

- **Implement Log Analytics and Alerting:** Collecting logs is not enough; you need to analyze them for patterns that indicate security issues or performance problems. Use a combination of dashboards, queries, and alerts. For example, set up alerts for
  - Multiple failed login attempts (possible brute force attack)
  - Use of deactivated API keys or accounts
  - Unexpected spikes in outbound network traffic (could be data exfiltration)

- Changes to critical security groups or firewall rules
- New resources created in a region you don't use (could indicate compromise)

Modern cloud SIEM tools often come with built-in detection rules (Microsoft Sentinel, for instance, has templates for Azure and AWS anomalies). Even without a SIEM, simpler services like Amazon GuardDuty and Microsoft Defender for Cloud use threat intel and machine learning to monitor logs for known attack behaviors (like someone using stolen credentials – GuardDuty might flag an anomalous IP address making API calls). Enable these services; they are part of cloud-native security and greatly enhance visibility.

- **Visualization and Reporting:** Humans make better sense of visual data. Create visualizations of key log data to help operations teams spot issues. For example, a dashboard showing the number of blocked firewall events over time, by source location, could reveal an ongoing attack from a certain geography. Or a graph of CPU usage vs. number of user logins could show a suspicious correlation. As one survey noted, companies underutilize their logs partly because searching raw text is tedious – effective visualizations increase log usage. Many cloud tools provide this (e.g., CloudWatch dashboards, Azure dashboards, Kibana for Elasticsearch, etc.). Use them for both real-time monitoring (NOC/SOC dashboards) and periodic reviews (weekly security metrics reports).

To illustrate a practical logging setup, consider an AWS-centric hybrid logging architecture: On-prem servers run the CloudWatch agent to send system logs to AWS. In AWS, CloudTrail is enabled in all accounts and regions (with one "organization trail" consolidating events) – see code example below. VPC Flow Logs and other service logs (S3 access logs, Lambda logs, etc.) all send to a central CloudWatch Logs group or an S3 archive. An AWS Lambda function or Kinesis Data Firehose can then forward these logs to an external SIEM (if desired) or to an Amazon OpenSearch Service cluster for analysis. Similarly, Azure logs from the Azure footprint can be exported via Event Hubs into that SIEM, unifying everything. The key is not the specific tools but that every event of interest is captured and accessible.

Configuration Example: Enabling an Organization-Wide CloudTrail in AWS

In an AWS Organization, you can configure a CloudTrail that records all management events across all member accounts, delivering logs to a central S3 bucket (ideally in a log archive account). Below is a snippet using Terraform (infrastructure-as-code) to set this up. The Terraform configuration for this organization-wide CloudTrail setup is provided in Listing 4-1.

Listing 4-1. Organization-wide AWS CloudTrail configuration (Terraform)

```
# AWS CloudTrail for all accounts in an Organization
resource "aws_cloudtrail" "org_trail" {
  name                     = "OrgSecurityTrail"
  s3_bucket_name           = aws_s3_bucket.log_bucket.id
  # Bucket to store logs
  include_global_service_events = true
  is_multi_region_trail         = true
  organization_enabled          = true
  # Enable for all org accounts
  retention_period              = 90
  # Retain logs for 90 days (can archive older separately)
  enable_log_file_validation    = true
  # Ensure integrity of log files

  event_selector {
    read_write_type           = "All"
    include_management_events = true
    include_data_events       = false
    # (Optionally, could log data events like S3 object access)
  }
}
```

This code creates a multi-region trail named "OrgSecurityTrail" that captures management events (API calls) across all AWS accounts in the organization, storing them in a versioned S3 bucket with validation enabled. Such a trail ensures that any user's actions (creation of VMs, changes to security groups, etc.) are centrally logged. In a hybrid scenario, you would complement this by also collecting logs from other clouds. For instance, Azure's equivalent would be setting up Azure Monitor Diagnostics to send Activity Log and Sign-In logs to a Log Analytics workspace and possibly exporting those to the SIEM.

Unified Monitoring: Logging is closely tied to monitoring/metrics. While logs are discrete event records, monitoring involves tracking system health indicators (CPU, memory, application response times) and can generate logs (alerts) itself. A cloud security architecture should integrate monitoring for availability/performance with security monitoring, since sometimes a performance anomaly is a sign of a security issue (e.g., a sudden CPU spike on a server could indicate crypto-mining malware). Cloud-native services like Amazon CloudWatch, Azure Monitor, and GCP Monitoring provide metrics and can often be used to detect incidents (e.g., CloudWatch can alarm on sudden outbound network throughput increase, which might complement your log-based alerts). Use these tools to set threshold alarms and automated responses (e.g., auto-isolate an instance if it exceeds certain behavior, using automation scripts).

Finally, consider compliance and retention. Many industries require that logs be stored in a tamper-evident manner for a certain time. Using immutable storage (write-once) or vaulting logs to cold storage can help meet this. AWS has S3 Object Lock (WORM storage) which can be used on the log bucket to prevent deletion for a period. Azure has immutable storage for Blob containers as well. Ensure these are in place for critical audit logs.

By implementing these logging and monitoring practices, your hybrid cloud gets a nervous system - capable of sensing incidents anywhere and helping you respond. Logging, of course, goes hand-in-hand with the next topics: a lot of what you'll monitor are network activities and access to data. So, having set up visibility, we now discuss how to architect the network (segmentation strategy) to minimize damage from intrusions and how to protect data through encryption and key management.

Cloud Network Segmentation and Micro-segmentation

In traditional on-prem networks, network segmentation - dividing the network into zones or segments with controlled communication between them - has long been a key security strategy. In a hybrid cloud environment, segmentation becomes both more complex and more important. You must extend network segmentation principles across on-premises and multiple cloud networks and often implement even finer-grained segmentation (so-called micro-segmentation) within cloud virtual networks and application clusters. The goal is to limit the attack surface and contain potential breaches by preventing unnecessary connectivity, thereby reducing lateral movement opportunities for attackers.

Segmentation Basics

A classic segmented architecture will have tiers or zones such as external (untrusted) ➤ DMZ ➤ internal network ➤ restricted network. Each zone is isolated by firewalls or access controls that only allow the minimal required traffic. In an enterprise, you might segment by business function or sensitivity - e.g., a segment for Finance systems, one for HR, one for public-facing web servers, one for development/test environments, etc. Users or services in one segment cannot directly access another unless explicitly permitted. The same concept applies in the cloud: cloud providers have constructs like virtual private clouds (VPCs) or virtual networks (VNet) which act as isolated network segments. You can create multiple VPCs (or VNets) for different purposes and control connectivity between them (via routers, gateways, firewall appliances, or cloud-native firewall services). Even within a VPC, you use subnetting and security groups (or network security groups) to segment at a more granular level (e.g., separate subnets for web tier, app tier, DB tier, each with its own access rules).

Hybrid Network Architecture: Use of a Cloud DMZ

In a hybrid scenario, typically you connect your on-prem network to your cloud environment using either a VPN or a private circuit (like Azure ExpressRoute or AWS Direct Connect). It's recommended to insert a DMZ or perimeter network in the cloud as the entry point. For example, when extending a network to Azure, Microsoft suggests implementing a perimeter network (DMZ) between on-prem and the Azure virtual network, with all inbound/outbound traffic passing through a cloud firewall. Figure 4-2 shows such an architecture.

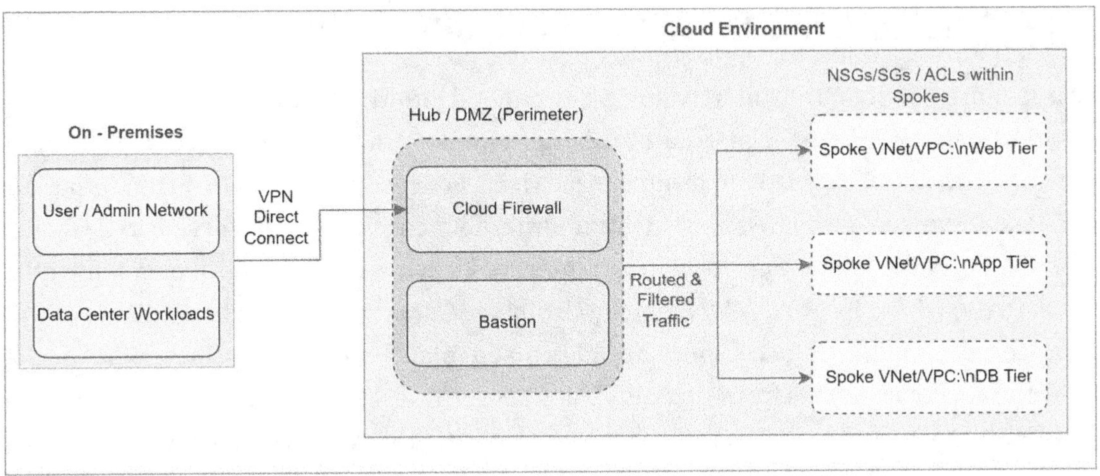

Figure 4-2. *Secure hybrid network with Cloud DMZ. This reference architecture (from Microsoft) extends an on-premises network into Azure while inserting a DMZ in the cloud. The on-prem network connects via VPN/ExpressRoute to an Azure Virtual Network. In Azure, a hub VNet acts as the DMZ/perimeter: it contains an Azure Firewall instance (managed cloud firewall) in a dedicated subnet, plus an Azure Bastion host for secure remote management of VMs. All traffic between on-prem and Azure (inbound or outbound) is funneled through the Azure Firewall, which applies central rules (e.g., DNAT, threat filtering). The hub then routes traffic to spoke VNets which contain the actual application subnets/ VMs (e.g., a web VNet and a database VNet). Network security groups (NSGs) are applied to subnets or NICs within those spokes to further restrict traffic (for instance, only allow the web subnet to talk to the DB subnet on port 3306). This setup isolates the cloud resources and ensures that even if on-prem is breached, the cloud has its own security barrier (and vice versa).*

There are analogous patterns in AWS (using a Transit Gateway or hub VPC with AWS Network Firewall or third-party firewall appliances in it) and in GCP (using Shared VPCs and firewall rules). The key is to treat cloud networks as an extension of your enterprise network, with equivalent (or stronger) segmentation and perimeter controls. Many organizations establish a "hub-and-spoke" topology: one central network hub in the cloud that connects to on-prem and to multiple isolated spokes/VPCs for different applications or business units, with firewalling in between. This limits direct on-prem to cloud East-West traffic and localizes potential breaches. For example, if a developer machine on-prem gets infected, and tries to scan cloud resources, the cloud firewall in the hub can detect and block unusual ports or volumes, whereas if the cloud were flat and fully open to on-prem, the attacker might reach deep into cloud subnets.

Segmentation Within Cloud Environments

It's not enough to just firewall between on-prem and cloud; within each cloud environment, implement segmentation similar to on-prem network zones. Use virtual networks and subnets to isolate groups of services. For instance, in AWS, you might place database servers in a private subnet with no Internet access and web servers in a DMZ subnet that is allowed to receive from the Internet via a load balancer but only allowed to talk to the DB on its port. AWS Security Groups (SGs) act as stateful firewalls on each instance/container interface - they should be used to allow only necessary traffic (e.g., the web SG allows ingress from the load balancer on TCP 443, and egress to the DB SG on TCP 3306, while the DB SG only allows ingress from the web SG on 3306). In Azure, network security groups serve a similar function at subnet or NIC level, combined with user-defined routes and Azure Firewall for more complex rules. GCP has a hierarchical firewall model plus VPC Service Controls to create service-level segments.

Micro-segmentation

Traditional segmentation might be segmented by application or environment. Microsegmentation takes it further by isolating at the level of individual hosts or workloads, often using software-defined policies. For example, in a Kubernetes cluster, you might use Kubernetes Network Policies to ensure that even within the cluster's flat network, pods from one app can't talk to pods of another app. In cloud VMs, you might deploy host-based firewalls or an agent-based microsegmentation solution (like Illumio, Cisco Tetration, or native OS firewalls) to enforce that only certain processes or services communicate. The principle of least privilege should apply to network connectivity as well: if two components don't need to talk, they should be completely separated at the network level. This significantly limits lateral movement if one component is compromised. For example, if an attacker gets a foothold on a web server in the cloud, strong microsegmentation would prevent them from accessing, say, an HR system on that same cloud environment, because there are simply no allowed network paths between them.

Identity-Aware Segmentation

One challenge in cloud is that IP addresses are dynamic and infrastructure is ephemeral. Traditional network ACLs based on IP ranges might not be sufficient. Modern cloud segmentation often leverages identity and tags. For example, an AWS Security Group can reference another Security Group by ID (rather than IP) to allow traffic - effectively saying "web servers can talk to DB servers" without caring about their IPs. Some advanced setups use application identity - e.g., in Zero Trust networks, each service is mutually authenticated with certificates or IAM roles, so even if the network connectivity is open, illegitimate connections won't be authorized at the application layer. This is part of a concept called software-defined perimeters or Zero Trust Network Access (ZTNA), where the network is essentially dark except for authenticated flows. As a practical tip: use cloud metadata (like tags, instance roles, Kubernetes service accounts) to drive segmentation policy. AWS has ways to do IAM-based networking (for instance, AWS PrivateLink exposes services internally without opening broad network routes). GCP's BeyondCorp (the model for Zero Trust) and products like Palo Alto Prisma Cloud or Azure's workload identities attempt to unify identity with network control.

Steps to Implement Segmentation in Hybrid Environments

1. **Assess and Plan Segments**: Start by analyzing your business and applications to define logical segments. A network and security team should work with business owners to categorize systems: e.g., public-facing systems, internal sensitive systems, partner accessible systems, development/testing, etc., mapping roughly to high/medium/low trust zones. Also consider regulatory boundaries: e.g., segment systems subject to PCI DSS (cardholder data) into their own enclave that has the required controls.
   In hybrid mode, decide which parts go on-prem vs. cloud - sometimes segmentation involves deciding that particularly sensitive data stays on a private cloud and only less sensitive workloads go to public cloud (a form of macro-segmentation for compliance).

2. **Align with Business and Gain Support**: Segmentation can inconvenience some users (by design, it restricts free access). So it's crucial to get management buy-in and user awareness. For example, if implementing a new network policy that developers in the lab subnet can no longer directly RDP into production servers (because those are now isolated), explain the rationale and provide alternative secure methods (like going through Bastion host with proper approvals). Early communication avoids later pushback that can undermine segmentation (e.g., someone might be tempted to create an "allow all" rule if they feel blocked unfairly – a big no-no).

3. **Design the Segmentation Architecture**: Draw out what your hybrid network will look like – including on-prem segments, cloud VPCs/VNets, connectivity between them, and any intermediate security layers (firewalls, gateways). For instance, you might design: On-prem network has VLANs A, B, C. There's a firewall between A and B, etc. On the cloud side, have VPC1 for public web, VPC2 for internal apps, VPC3 for shared services, etc., each with its own subnets. Then determine how these connect: maybe VPC2 has a private link to on-prem VLAN B but not to VLAN A. Possibly use a multi-cloud networking software or SD-WAN to manage connectivity so that each segment's connectivity is controlled. Some enterprises implement a "Zero Trust network architecture" bridging on-prem and cloud, where all connectivity between segments (even on-prem to on-prem or cloud to on-prem) goes through a policy engine.

4. **Select Technologies for Enforcement**: Utilize the tried-and-true network controls to enforce segments. Traditional enterprise firewalls (physical or virtual) can be deployed at key junctions (e.g., a firewall appliance in AWS controlling traffic between VPCs or cloud-native firewalls as shown in the Azure example). Security groups and access control lists (ACLs) are built-in and should be systematically used on every subnet/port. In a hybrid cloud, next-gen firewalls that work across on-prem and cloud can simplify management – for instance, Palo Alto or Fortinet have virtual

firewall instances that run in AWS/Azure and can be managed in tandem with on-prem devices, using consistent policies. Software-defined networking (SDN) solutions or cloud provider network managers (like AWS Transit Gateway, Azure Virtual WAN) can help create logically isolated segments at scale. Consider using overlay networks or segmentation at the host level for cloud workloads: e.g., a service mesh like Istio for containers can enforce which microservices can talk (this is identity-based segmentation at Layer7). There are also cloud provider offerings such as AWS Security Hub or Azure Firewall Manager to centrally manage rules across accounts and regions - useful for consistency.

5. **Implement Gradually and Test**: Don't flip the switch on a highly segmented policy without testing. A phased approach is best. For example, you might first implement monitoring-only (log what would be blocked), then move to a restrictive stance. Use cloud tools to simulate or log network flows. Many cloud firewalls have a "dry run" or audit mode. A/B test by applying new NSGs to a dev environment first. Penetration testing or at least connectivity testing is crucial after segmentation - ensure that intended communications still work (users can reach what they need) but forbidden ones are truly blocked. Verify, for instance, that a test VM in a segmented zone cannot ping or connect to another zone's machines. Also test fail-safes: e.g., if the central firewall fails, does traffic default to blocked (it should).

6. **Continuous Monitoring and Adjustment**: After deployment, continuously monitor network logs and alerts to gauge the effectiveness. If you see repeated blocked attempts from a certain segment to another and they're legitimate business needs, you might adjust the policy (with proper review). Conversely, monitor if any allowed traffic might be a misconfiguration - e.g., an NSG rule accidentally left too open. Also watch for any segmentation bypass attempts - an attacker might try to exploit a misconfigured VPN or a cloud routing rule to jump segments. Regular audits of firewall and security group rules are necessary. As one article noted, look at the reporting capabilities of your segmentation tools

to satisfy auditors that the network restrictions meet standards like PCI or HIPAA, where needed. Over time, consider more advanced segmentation if new needs arise (for instance, if you adopt a multi-cloud container platform, you'll need segmentation at that layer too).

A concrete example of micro-segmentation in practice: Kubernetes Network Policy. Suppose you have a Kubernetes cluster in the cloud running multiple apps (e.g., a front-end and a back-end microservice). By default, within a cluster, any pod can talk to any pod. But you want to restrict back-end pods to only accept traffic from front-end pods on a certain port. You can apply a NetworkPolicy YAML such as the following shown in Listing 4-2.

Listing 4-2. Kubernetes NetworkPolicy to allow front-end-to-back-end traffic

```
kind: NetworkPolicy
apiVersion: networking.k8s.io/v1
metadata:
  name: allow-frontend-to-backend
  namespace: prod-app
spec:
  podSelector:
    matchLabels:
      role: backend
  ingress:
  - from:
      - podSelector:
          matchLabels:
            role: frontend
    ports:
      - protocol: TCP
        port: 8080
```

This policy ensures pods labeled "role=backend" only accept connections on TCP 8080 from pods labeled "role=frontend" in the prod-app namespace, effectively microsegmenting at the service role level. Similar policies could isolate by environment (namespace) or restrict egress (prevent backend from calling the Internet, for instance).

For IaaS VM segmentation, Listing 4-3 provides an example of an AWS Security Group in JSON that allows MySQL traffic from a specific application server group.

Listing 4-3. Example AWS security group allowing MySQL from app servers (JSON)

```
{ "GroupName": "db-sg", "Description": "DB SG allowing MySQL from
app servers", "VpcId": "vpc-0123456789abcdef0", "IpPermissions": [ {
"IpProtocol": "tcp", "FromPort": 3306, "ToPort": 3306, "UserIdGroupPairs":
[ { "GroupId": "sg-0abcde12345f67890", "Description": "Allow app server
SG" } ] } ]
}
```

The above security group (in JSON form) allows inbound TCP 3306 only from another Security Group with ID sg-0abcde... (which would be the app servers' SG). No other traffic is allowed (implicitly denied). This is an AWS-specific way to do microsegmentation by resource identity rather than IP. The equivalent in Azure would be an NSG rule referencing a service tag or application security group and, in GCP, a VPC firewall rule with target tags.

Beyond Network: Segment Identities and Access Too – It's worth noting that network segmentation should be complemented by identity segmentation. This means ensuring that cloud IAM roles/accounts are scoped per application/segment as well. For example, developers of one application shouldn't have credentials that let them access another app's environment. In AWS, you might have separate accounts or at least separate IAM roles per segment; in Azure, separate resource groups with role-based access control limiting who can even see those resources. This way, even if the network is segmented, you also prevent human error (someone deploying a resource in the wrong segment, etc.).

Multi-cloud Segmentation: If you operate in multiple public clouds, achieving consistent segmentation is tough because each cloud has its own constructs and capabilities. Some solutions include the following:

- Using abstraction/overlay tools (e.g., Cisco Cloud ACI or VMware NSX can overlay a single segmentation policy across clouds).
- Ensure each cloud's implementation meets a baseline (e.g., all sensitive workloads, regardless of cloud, must be in a subnet with no internet gateway and behind a firewall).

- Central management through cloud security posture management tools which can at least alert if, say, a GCP firewall rule becomes too open compared to your baseline.

Be mindful of how segments interconnect across clouds. For instance, if you have an app where part lives in AWS and part in Azure, you might have a direct cloud-cloud network connection. Secure that tunnel and treat it like any other untrusted network route - possibly through a secure broker or SD-WAN that enforces firewall policies between the clouds.

In summary, segmentation is about risk containment. A well-segmented hybrid architecture ensures that even if one server or one section of your environment is compromised, the damage is limited. Attackers cannot easily leap to other systems because of network choke points and access restrictions. The continued investment in segmentation, microsegmentation, and Zero Trust Network Access reflects a broader recognition that hybrid cloud security depends on limiting blast radius and controlling lateral movement. With thoughtful design and modern cloud networking tools, you can implement segmentation that is as good or better than your traditional data center - often with more granularity. Combined with strong identity management (tying back to Zero Trust) and logging (to catch any policy violations), network segmentation becomes a powerful defense-in-depth technique for the cloud.

Having covered securing the "pipes" and connectivity, we now focus on securing the data itself - through encryption and effective key management.

Data Encryption and Key Management in Hybrid Cloud

Data is the crown jewel of most enterprises, and protecting it is a paramount concern in cloud security architecture. Encryption is one of the most important controls for protecting data confidentiality - ensuring that even if other defenses fail, stolen data remains unreadable to unauthorized parties. In hybrid cloud architectures, data may reside in various forms: files in cloud storage, records in databases, data lakes spanning on-prem and cloud, or data traversing networks between your sites and the cloud. A robust strategy includes encryption for data at rest, data in transit, and proper key management, all implemented in a way that's consistent and vendor-neutral across the environments.

Cloud-Native Encryption Capabilities

The good news is that major cloud providers have built-in support for encryption in many services:

- **AWS:** In AWS, services like S3, EBS volumes, RDS databases, etc., can be encrypted at rest with a click, often using AWS Key Management Service (KMS) under the hood. AWS KMS allows you to create customer master keys and either let AWS manage them or bring your own keys to import. AWS also supports hardware security modules (CloudHSM) for more control.
- **Azure:** In Azure, data at rest in Azure Storage, SQL Database, etc., can be encrypted using Azure Key Vault-managed keys. Azure calls this Azure Storage Service Encryption, Transparent Data Encryption for SQL, etc., with the option for customer-managed keys in Key Vault. Azure also offers dedicated HSMs and even bring-your-own-key scenarios (e.g., Azure Key Vault Managed HSM, which you control).
- **GCP:** In GCP, most storage services are encrypted by default. Google Cloud KMS can manage keys for services like Cloud Storage, BigQuery, etc., and they have Customer-Managed Encryption Keys (CMEK) options and even Customer-Supplied Encryption Keys (CSEK) for some services if you want to supply keys per API call.

Importantly, encryption at rest is now commonly enabled by default in many cloud services. However, the critical distinction is who controls the keys and who can decrypt. By default (provider-managed encryption), the cloud provider manages the encryption keys – the data is encrypted on disk, but the provider has the means to decrypt if needed to service your requests. For stronger security or compliance, customers often choose to manage keys themselves (e.g., via a KMS where you can revoke or rotate keys and where the provider's access is limited).

Shared Responsibility for Encryption

Encryption is a shared domain – the provider offers the feature, but the customer must use it properly. For example, AWS will not encrypt your S3 bucket unless you enable it or have a policy requiring it. So it's the customer's job to ensure encryption is turned on wherever possible (and mandated via governance – e.g., preventative guardrails that block creating unencrypted resources). Cloud providers meet you halfway by providing easy toggles and sometimes automatic encryption of new resources (for instance, since 2023, AWS encrypts all new EBS volumes by default). But checking and maintaining encryption settings is part of your security architecture duties (often automated via CSPM tools or infrastructure-as-code with encryption settings enabled by design).

Encrypting Data in Transit

This refers to using protocols like HTTPS/TLS for data moving between clients and the cloud or between cloud components. Cloud providers again offer help – e.g., AWS and Azure both have certificate management services, and by default, their services (like AWS API Gateway, Azure Front Door) require TLS for connections. On internal networks (within a VPC or between data centers), you might use VPN encryption (IPSec tunnels) or service mesh MTLS (mutual TLS) between services. In a hybrid cloud, any connection that goes over a public network (like from on-prem to cloud over the internet) should be encrypted (via VPN or SSL). Even private lines should use encryption if data is sensitive, because insiders or misconfigurations could expose traffic.

Key Management Challenges

The crux of encryption is not the algorithms (clouds use industry-standard AES-256, etc.), but rather managing the keys. In a hybrid enterprise, you might have multiple key management systems:

- An on-prem hardware security module (HSM) or key management system (KMS) that you've used historically.
- AWS KMS, Azure Key Vault, and Google KMS in each respective cloud, each with their own keys.
- Keys for SaaS applications (some SaaS allow you to supply keys or control encryption – e.g., Salesforce Shield or client-side encryption for Google Workspace/Microsoft 365 where you hold keys).

It's important to decide on a strategy: centralize vs. federate. Some organizations try to centralize key management, using one solution to manage keys across clouds – for example, using an on-prem HSM to generate and store keys, and then importing those into cloud KMS (Bring Your Own Key), or using APIs to distribute keys as needed. There are vendors (e.g., Thales, HashiCorp Vault, Fortanix) that provide multi-cloud key management or "bring your own KMS" where a single key authority serves all environments. This can simplify compliance (one place to do key rotation, one audit trail).

Others use the cloud-native KMS in each cloud but apply consistent policies (like keys must be rotated every 90 days, keys must be protected by HSMs, etc.). This is still vendor-neutral in concept, but implementation-wise, you'd have separate systems (one per cloud). What's crucial is that you maintain control of keys and limit provider access as much as feasible for sensitive data. That's where concepts like BYOK and HYOK come in.

Let's clarify those terms (Bring/Hold/Control Your Own Key), as they capture different levels of key control:

- **Provider-Managed Keys:** (Not BYOK) The default is where the cloud provider creates and manages keys for you. For example, AWS S3 managed encryption keys (SSE-S3) or Azure Storage Service Encryption with Microsoft-managed keys. Easiest, but you as a customer have the least control - you typically can't see or directly rotate those keys (it's abstracted).

- **BYOK (Bring Your Own Key):** You generate the key (often on-prem or in your HSM) and then upload it to the cloud's KMS to use. The cloud provider's KMS then uses that key to encrypt/decrypt data, but ideally never exposes the raw key to anyone (stored securely in KMS). Benefit: You have more control - you could decide to revoke or delete the key from the KMS, rendering the provider unable to decrypt the data (though caches or data already decrypted could still be an issue). Challenge: You must securely create, transfer, and manage the lifecycle of that key (back it up, rotate it by re-uploading new ones, etc.). If you lose it, the cloud can't help you recover your data. BYOK is supported in AWS KMS, Azure Key Vault, GCP KMS, and even many SaaS (e.g., you can bring keys for a Microsoft 365 customer key). It's a popular approach to balance control and convenience.

- **CYOK (Control Your Own Key):** This is a term used to denote when you keep the key material under your control such that the cloud provider never sees it in plain text, even though encryption happens in the cloud. One way to do this is by using a cloud HSM that you control. For instance, AWS CloudHSM or Azure Dedicated HSM - these give you a module in the cloud only you can access; your applications use it for crypto operations, but AWS/Azure themselves don't have the admin credentials. Another approach is using enclaves or secure enclaves (like AWS Nitro Enclaves) to process data with your key without exposing the key. CYOK overlaps with BYOK in many cases, but implies extra assurance that the key is never in the provider's domain in clear. Microsoft's Double Key Encryption (in M365, one key with Microsoft, one key with you required to decrypt) is an example - you control one key completely (on-prem), so Microsoft alone can't read the data. The Cryptomathic reference describes CYOK as keys that may be stored in a customer-controlled HSM or enclave, such that the provider only sees wrapped keys.
- **HYOK (Hold Your Own Key):** The most extreme - you never give the cloud provider the key at all. This usually means you encrypt the data yourself before uploading to the cloud and decrypt it after downloading, so the cloud is only ever storing ciphertext. Or the cloud app calls out to your on-prem key manager each time it needs to decrypt (some systems allow an API call to your KMS for each operation). HYOK provides maximum security (and is sometimes mandated by regulations for top-secret data), but it's difficult to use with many cloud services because the cloud can't operate on encrypted data easily. A pure HYOK example: using client-side encryption for files stored in Box or Google Drive, where an agent on your side encrypts files with a key only you know before sending to the cloud - the cloud just sees random blobs. Microsoft 365 had a HYOK mode for certain apps (where your key in Azure RMS never left on-prem HSM, used for viewing documents but with severe limitations). HYOK is typically used only for a subset of data that is so sensitive that even processing it in the cloud with cloud-managed keys is considered a risk. It's like an evolution of the old "encrypt

your database before putting it in cloud storage" idea – great for confidentiality, but you lose functionality like searching or processing that data in the cloud easily.

Most organizations will use a combination: for most data, provider-managed or BYOK is sufficient; for highly sensitive or regulated data, you might use HYOK or keep it on-prem. The choice should be guided by risk and compliance. For instance, if using cloud for healthcare data under HIPAA, you might use BYOK to ensure you can revoke access if needed (say, if you terminate the cloud contract, you revoke keys so the data is safe). If dealing with European personal data and worried about government subpoenas to cloud providers, HYOK or at least CYOK might be considered to prevent provider access (since under the CLOUD Act, US providers might be compelled to hand over data – if they don't have the keys, the data remains safe).

Key Management Implementation Tips

- **Use KMS Where Possible:** Cloud KMS services are reliable and integrate with other services (automatic key rotation options, audit logging of key usage). They greatly reduce the chances of mistakes in cryptography (e.g., using a strong random KEK to wrap data keys, storing keys securely). So, for most applications, use them instead of rolling your own crypto. But configure them to meet your needs (customer-managed keys, proper IAM on who can use the keys, etc.). For example, restrict key usage via policy: AWS KMS allows key policies that can require MFA for deletion or can restrict that a key can only be used if certain conditions (like coming from a certain service or account).
- **Manage Keys' Lifecycle: Have processes for key rotation (e.g., rotate keys** annually or if a key custodian leaves), key revocation (in case of suspected compromise, you might want to disable a key immediately), and key backup (for any on-prem or external keys, ensure you have secure backups – losing a key = losing data permanently). In KMSs, rotation is often automated (you can set an AWS KMS key to auto-rotate yearly), but note that rotation usually means the old key is still needed to decrypt old data, so you end up with key versions. Plan how far back you keep old keys and how you re-encrypt data with new keys if needed.

- **Post-Quantum Encryption Risk and Crypto-Agility:** A modern hybrid cloud encryption strategy should also account for post-quantum cryptography risk. Most current enterprise encryption architectures still depend heavily on public key algorithms such as RSA and elliptic curve cryptography for key exchange, certificates, TLS, VPNs, code signing, identity federation, and secure administrative access. These algorithms remain practical today, but they are considered quantum-vulnerable because a sufficiently capable future quantum computer could break the mathematical assumptions behind them. This creates a long-term risk for sensitive data that must remain confidential for many years. The most immediate concern is the "harvest now, decrypt later" threat. In this scenario, an adversary captures encrypted traffic or stored encrypted data today and waits until future quantum capabilities make decryption feasible. This is especially relevant for hybrid enterprises that transmit regulated, financial, health, intellectual property, government, or critical infrastructure data across cloud, SaaS, and on-premises environments. Even if the organization is not ready to deploy post-quantum cryptography everywhere, it should begin identifying where quantum-vulnerable cryptography is used and which data flows require long-term confidentiality. NIST's post-quantum cryptography standardization work provides a practical direction for this transition. The first finalized NIST standards include ML-KEM for key establishment and ML-DSA and SLH-DSA for digital signatures. For cloud security architects, this does not mean replacing every encryption control immediately. It means building crypto-agility into the architecture so algorithms, certificates, protocols, and key management patterns can be changed without redesigning the full environment. In hybrid cloud environments, post-quantum readiness should begin with a cryptographic inventory. Security teams should identify TLS endpoints, VPNs, API gateways, service meshes, certificate authorities, SSH access paths, code signing systems, secrets management tools, HSMs, KMS integrations, and SaaS encryption dependencies. This inventory should show which systems rely on RSA or ECC, which systems are externally exposed, which protect long-lived sensitive data, and which vendors have a road map for PQC or hybrid classical/PQC support. A practical migration strategy should prioritize the highest-risk areas first: externally exposed TLS services, VPN and remote access paths, privileged administrative access, long-retention data flows, software and firmware signing, and cloud-to-on-prem connectivity. The key architectural goal is not only stronger algorithms, but operational flexibility. A resilient encryption architecture should allow the organization to rotate keys, replace algorithms, update certificates, and adopt PQC-capable services with limited disruption.

- **Harmonize Encryption Across Environments:** Ensure that when data moves from on-prem to cloud or between clouds, it doesn't lose encryption. For instance, an on-prem database backup file – if it's unencrypted on-prem and you upload to S3, now it's in the cloud unencrypted unless you rely on S3's server-side encryption or you encrypted it before uploading. A better approach: have standard tools so that any data leaving a trusted zone is encrypted either at the file level (e.g., using PGP or AES before transfer) or by using secure transfer channels and storage encryption on arrival. Many companies adopt a policy: "All sensitive data stored in the cloud must be encrypted with at least AES-256 and keys stored in the specified KMS." Implement technical controls to enforce this (CSPM tools can detect unencrypted storage and raise alerts or auto-remediate by enabling encryption).
- **Consider "Encryption in Use" for Highly Sensitive Scenarios:** A burgeoning area is encrypting data while it's being processed (so even the cloud compute that processes it can't see it). Fully homomorphic encryption is still impractical for general use, but technologies like confidential computing are emerging – using secure enclaves (Intel SGX, AMD SEV, etc.) where data is decrypted only in a guarded CPU enclave. Azure Confidential Compute, AWS Nitro Enclaves, and GCP Confidential VMs are examples. If your use case demands that level of privacy (e.g., you want to run analytics on encrypted data), you might explore these. They often integrate with key management such that the decryption key is only released to the enclave after it's verified.

- **Encrypt Backups and Exports:** Don't forget that data tends to leak via backups, data exports, or analytic copies. Your security architecture should cover those as well. Ensure backup tools (whether on-prem or cloud) support encryption. For example, if you use Azure Backup or AWS Backup, configure them to store backups encrypted with your keys. If you dump a database to a file to transfer, encrypt that dump. This is part of making encryption pervasive.
- **Compliance Considerations:** Different regions have different crypto requirements. In the United States, FIPS 140-2 compliance might be needed for government workloads – ensure your cloud KMS is FIPS-validated (AWS KMS and Azure Key Vault offer FIPS modes). In Europe, some countries may require keys to be stored in EU data centers or by EU entities – consider using regional cloud KMS instances or external key management in that region. Some regulators (like financial authorities) might mandate BYOK or keys escrowed with a neutral party. Keep abreast of your industry's rules. For multi-tenant SaaS you consume, ask the provider about their encryption – if possible, choose SaaS that offer customer-managed keys for an extra layer of control.

To illustrate how one might enforce encryption via code, Listing 4-4 provides a Terraform example for AWS S3 object storage.

Listing 4-4. Enforcing default server-side encryption for an S3 bucket (Terraform)

```
resource "aws_s3_bucket" "secure_bucket" {
  bucket = "my-secure-data-bucket"
  acl    = "private"

  server_side_encryption_configuration {
    rule {
      apply_server_side_encryption_by_default {
        kms_master_key_id = aws_kms_key.my_key.arn  # use customer-
        managed KMS CMK
        sse_algorithm     = "aws:kms"
      }
```

```
    }
  }

  versioning {
    enabled = true
  }

  # (Other bucket configs like logging)
}
```

This ensures all objects uploaded are encrypted with a specific KMS key (which you control), rather than the default. If someone tries to put an object without encryption, S3 will encrypt it with that KMS key by default. You could also add a Bucket Policy denying any PutObject that doesn't have the encryption flag, as a safety net. Similarly, for an Azure Storage account via ARM template or CLI, you'd specify encryption is enabled and perhaps use a customer-managed key from Azure Key Vault. Most cloud services have similar hooks.

Beyond just encryption, data protection includes things like Data Loss Prevention (DLP) and data classification. It's wise to integrate those into your architecture too: for instance, use cloud DLP services (Azure Information Protection, Google Cloud DLP, etc.) to scan and alert if sensitive data appears in logs or in places it shouldn't (like PII showing up in a public bucket). Some organizations use classification labels on data and enforce that via encryption keys (e.g., a "Top Secret" label might mean the data must be encrypted with a specific key that has very restricted access).

One more note on regional considerations (focus USA with some global examples, as requested): In the United States, regulations like HIPAA for health data, CJIS for criminal justice, or FedRAMP for government all heavily emphasize encryption (often requiring it for data in transit and at rest with specific key management rules). For example, FedRAMP moderate requires customer-controlled encryption for certain data and key escrow procedures. In the EU, GDPR doesn't mandate encryption explicitly but strongly implies it as a safeguard for personal data (and encryption can reduce notification requirements if data is lost but encrypted). Many EU firms now look to hold their own keys (HYOK) to prevent US cloud providers from accessing EU personal data, aligning with the idea of "digital sovereignty." In APAC, countries like Australia (APRA regulations) and Singapore (MAS TRM) also expect robust encryption for cloud usage. For instance, Singapore's MAS guidelines say encryption of sensitive data in external cloud is a must, and keys should ideally be customer-managed. These regional nuances typically reinforce the practices we've described: control your keys, encrypt sensitive data everywhere, and manage cryptographic access rights diligently.

In summary, encryption and key management in a hybrid cloud should give you assurance that even if an attacker bypasses network defenses or compromises a cloud provider's systems, they still cannot read your critical data. Achieving that means using cloud-native encryption features (so you're not reinventing crypto), choosing the right level of key control (provider-managed vs. BYOK vs. HYOK) for each dataset based on sensitivity, and integrating key management into your overall security operations (with policies for rotation, segregation of duties – e.g., key admins vs. system admins – and monitoring of key usage). A well-architected approach might involve a centralized key management dashboard or team that oversees keys across on-prem and cloud, with strong policies in place (like dual control to approve key access, audit trails for every decrypt operation in KMS).

Conclusion: Building Resilient and Adaptable Cloud Security Architecture

Bringing it all together, a cloud security architecture for hybrid enterprises must be comprehensive, layered, and flexible. We revisited the shared responsibility model to clarify the division of duties – a foundational step so that your architecture covers all customer-responsible aspects (which, as we saw, is most of the stack in IaaS and significant even in SaaS). We highlighted using vendor-neutral reference models and frameworks to ensure your architecture design doesn't miss any critical domain and can span multiple cloud platforms. Adopting principles from frameworks like CSA or Zero Trust helps maintain a consistent posture even as technologies underneath change.

In the latter sections, we drilled into three key technical pillars:

- **Logging/Monitoring:** The importance of centralizing and standardizing logging across hybrid environments can't be overstated. A unified logging strategy, leveraging cloud-native tools (CloudTrail, Azure Monitor, etc.) combined with centralized analysis (like a SIEM or observability platform), will significantly improve detection and response. This also makes the architecture adaptable – new services plugged into the environment must adhere to the logging standard (e.g., any new app must send logs to X system). Logging is your early warning system and audit trail rolled into one.

- **Network Segmentation:** By designing your network with multiple layers of segmentation (perimeter DMZs, internal subnets, microsegments) and leveraging both traditional firewalls and cloud security groups, you reduce the blast radius of any incident and meet the principle of least privilege at the network level. We saw how Azure's reference architecture implements a DMZ in the cloud to isolate on-prem from cloud internal traffic and how microsegmentation can isolate even services within the same zone from each other unless needed. A segmented architecture is inherently more resilient - an attack in one segment can be quarantined and eradicated without automatically compromising the whole enterprise. It's adaptable in that you can create new segments for new projects or integrate another company's network via defined peering points, rather than making a flat network and hoping for the best.
- **Encryption/Key Management:** Encrypting data everywhere - and crucially, managing the keys wisely - is like the last line of defense. Even if an attacker gets to your data storage, strong encryption means they get gibberish. We elaborated on how cloud providers offer encryption features and how you can maintain control via BYOK or HYOK approaches. A hybrid cloud architecture should include a cohesive key management policy, possibly a centralized KMS or at least federated ones with consistent policy, so that whether data sits in a database on-prem or a storage bucket in AWS, it's protected under encryption that you control. This also gives you adaptability - you can move data from on-prem to cloud or between clouds, and as long as your encryption and key regime moves with it (or is applied to it), the data remains secure. We also touched on emerging tech like confidential computing which could become part of future reference architectures for sensitive workloads.

Resilience in architecture is not just about withstanding failures or outages (though that's important too - building redundancy, multi-region, etc., which is more on the availability side). In the context of security, resilience means the ability to prevent breaches and to limit damage if one occurs and to recover quickly. The architecture we've described achieves that:

1. Preventive controls (like segmentation, least privilege, MFA on access, encryption, etc.) reduce the likelihood of incidents.
2. Detective controls (logging, monitoring alerts) ensure that if something happens, you know about it fast.
3. Containment controls (like network isolation, automated responses such as quarantining a compromised VM) limit impact.
4. Recovery and adaptation are aided by having infrastructure-as-code and automated processes - for instance, if a breach forces you to rebuild environments or rotate all credentials, doing so programmatically is far quicker than manual.

Adaptability is key for hybrid enterprises because technology and threat landscapes evolve. A vendor-neutral approach insulates your security from specific tools - if tomorrow you switch cloud provider or a new logging service emerges, you can plug it in under the same overarching architecture. The reference models ensure you always include core functions (IAM, logging, etc.), even as implementations shift. Cloud-native services continue to advance, including AI-assisted security analytics, posture management, and integrated Zero Trust access capabilities. An adaptable architecture can incorporate those improvements without a complete redesign. It's built on principles, not products.

One should also not forget the human and process aspects: A solid architecture goes hand in hand with operational processes (incident response playbooks, change management to ensure configurations remain secure, continuous training of staff on cloud security). For example, DevSecOps practices should be embraced - embed security in the development pipeline so that misconfigurations or vulnerabilities are caught early (shift-left approach). A resilient architecture makes heavy use of automation to enforce policies (e.g., using policy-as-code so that developers cannot launch an open security group or unencrypted database because the pipeline will fail such builds). This reduces the strain on humans and lowers error rates.

Finally, let's briefly consider an example scenario to illustrate the architecture in action: Imagine a hybrid retail enterprise with an ecommerce platform. They have on-prem systems (for inventory and legacy ERP) and use AWS for customer-facing web apps and Azure for analytics and Microsoft 365 for email. The security architecture we propose would have shared responsibility clarity – the company uses AWS Well-Architected and Microsoft cloud Security Benchmarks to ensure they configure each cloud service securely and know their duties. They implement a vendor-neutral identity federation, linking on-prem AD with Entra ID, so a single set of strong authentication controls (with MFA) applies to admins and users across environments (Zero Trust principle: authenticate everywhere). They set up centralized logging where AWS CloudTrail logs, Azure logs, and on-prem syslogs all flow into a Splunk Cloud instance – their SOC can query any event from a single console and has alerts set (e.g., alert if an admin account is created in AWS or if someone modifies an Azure NSG rule). The network is segmented: on-prem connects to AWS via VPN into a restricted VPC; within AWS, prod and dev are separate VPCs; production VPC has public subnets for the web servers and private for databases, with network ACLs and security groups locking down traffic (plus an AWS Web Application Firewall on the front door). Azure analytics runs in its own VNet with no open inbound access; data from AWS to Azure goes through an encrypted connection and lands in a secure storage account. All databases (on-prem Oracle, AWS RDS, Azure SQL) are encrypted at rest with keys from a central HSM the company controls (BYOK model on cloud side) – meaning if needed, they could revoke keys to prevent data access. They schedule key rotations annually and have an auditable process for it. During operations, if a web server in AWS gets compromised via some zero-day exploit, the abnormal behavior (scanning internal DB subnet, strange API calls) is caught by GuardDuty and by Microsoft Sentinel (which ingests VPC flow logs). An alert triggers, and the response automation isolates that server (security group locked down via SSM automation). The encryption ensures that even if the attacker got some data from the DB, it's cipher text (they'd also need the KMS key which they don't have because the key requires a token that only the app with a proper IAM role can use). Meanwhile, incident responders analyze logs to confirm the scope and use the segmented architecture to their advantage – they see the attacker couldn't move to Azure analytics or on-prem because those networks aren't directly reachable from the compromised VPC without going through firewalls (which logged and blocked the attempts). They clean up, patch the exploit, and improve WAF rules to prevent reoccurrence. Business impact was minimal – thanks to the resilient architecture.

This illustrative scenario underscores the value of what we covered: defense in depth across identity, network, data, and monitoring. Each layer had controls that either prevented or limited the attack.

As a final note, cloud security is a continuous journey. The architecture we build must evolve as threats do. But by adhering to strong foundational principles – clarity of responsibility, least privilege, assume breach, encryption everywhere, and continuous verification – and by using the plethora of cloud-native security features in a coherent, orchestrated way, hybrid enterprises can achieve a security posture that is even stronger than traditional IT. In fact, many security advantages come with cloud: built-in high availability, automated patching options, massive logging scalability, and intelligent services that on-prem might lack. A well-architected hybrid security design capitalizes on these advantages while mitigating the new risks.

In conclusion, designing cloud security architectures for hybrid enterprises requires a holistic approach: technology architecture, processes, and people must all align to protect assets across diverse environments. By following the guidance in this chapter – revisiting shared responsibility, using vendor-neutral models, and implementing cloud-native logging, segmentation, and encryption – organizations can build adaptable, resilient architectures that inspire confidence as they pursue digital transformation in the cloud era. The cloud need not be a Wild West of insecurity; with proper architecture, it can be a fortress that dynamically extends and contracts with your business, all the while keeping your crown jewels safe and sound.

CHAPTER 5

Navigating AI and Quantum-Era Threats

Emerging technologies in artificial intelligence (AI) and quantum computing are rapidly redefining the cybersecurity landscape. These innovations bring immense benefits, but they also introduce unprecedented threats that challenge traditional defenses. Malicious deepfakes, autonomous malware, and looming quantum-powered attacks are no longer science fiction – they are part of a new frontier of risks that organizations must confront. Meanwhile, governance and policy frameworks struggle to keep pace with the speed of technological change, creating gaps in our collective security. In this chapter, we explore how AI-driven threats and quantum-era risks are shaping the future of cybersecurity. We delve into AI-driven threat modeling, the rise of deepfakes, the potential catastrophe of cryptographic failure in a quantum age, and the urgent need for quantum-resistant cryptography. Throughout, we emphasize the importance of forward-looking governance principles and highlight tooling gaps that must be addressed to secure our digital world. Together, these topics underscore a pivotal theme: to navigate this new era of threats, we must proactively blend technology, strategy, and policy in equal measure.

AI-Driven Threat Modeling in the Modern Era

AI has become a double-edged sword in cybersecurity – it empowers defenders with new tools for threat modeling and detection, even as attackers weaponize AI to craft more potent attacks. Threat modeling, the practice of identifying and analyzing potential attack scenarios, is being transformed by AI on multiple fronts. On one hand, AI augments defenders by automating and scaling the threat modeling process; on the other, AI expands the threat surface with novel attack techniques that legacy threat models never accounted for. In this section, we examine how threat modeling is evolving in the age of AI, including both the use of AI to improve defensive modeling and the need to model threats *to* AI systems themselves.

A. Gupta and S. Mittal, *Foundations of Modern Information Security*,
https://doi.org/10.1007/979-8-8688-2558-3_5

AI As a Co-pilot for Threat Modeling

Organizations are beginning to leverage AI to assist human experts in mapping out threats. By ingesting vast amounts of security knowledge and system design data, AI-driven tools can help generate threat models faster and flag risks that might be overlooked by humans alone. For example, a large financial institution recently deployed an internal *AI Threat Modeling Co-pilot* to aid its engineers. Early results demonstrated a significant boost in efficiency – the AI co-pilot reduced the time needed to produce threat models by roughly 20% while also uncovering on average several new potential attack scenarios that human modelers hadn't considered. Such gains come from AI's ability to rapidly cross-reference known attack patterns with a system's architecture and suggest relevant threats and mitigations. By democratizing expertise, AI can make "secure by design" principles more accessible, guiding developers and architects through security best practices early in the software development lifecycle. In essence, AI is acting as a force multiplier for defenders: expediting risk assessments, suggesting security controls, and continuously learning from expert feedback to improve its recommendations.

New Threats in an AI-Enabled World

At the same time, the threat landscape is being reshaped by adversaries wielding AI. Attackers are using AI to increase the scale, sophistication, and personalization of phishing, malware development, reconnaissance, and social engineering. Phishing emails that once contained obvious language errors can now be generated by advanced language models to be fluent, personalized, and context-aware. Recent threat reporting shows a sharp increase in phishing campaigns that bear the hallmarks of generative AI, making them harder for users and basic email filters to identify. Attackers have also used black-market or unrestricted AI tools to help draft spear-phishing messages, create malicious code, and accelerate reconnaissance. Beyond phishing, AI can support polymorphic malware, evasive scripts, and rapid exploit development. Threat modeling must therefore account for AI-enabled attack capabilities, including scenarios such as AI-assisted phishing, AI-generated voice instructions, automated vulnerability discovery, and malicious manipulation of AI-enabled workflows.

Modeling Threats to AI Systems

In addition to using AI as a tool, many organizations now deploy AI systems at the core of their business - from machine learning models making financial decisions to AI engines in autonomous vehicles or critical infrastructure. These AI systems themselves introduce new categories of risk that traditional threat modeling doesn't fully cover. AI threat modeling focuses on identifying how AI algorithms and data pipelines could be attacked or could fail in dangerous ways. Unlike conventional software, AI systems can behave unpredictably or degrade under malicious influence. Key threats include *adversarial inputs* (where an attacker subtly alters an input - like a pixel pattern in an image or a phrasing of a query - to mislead the AI into a wrong decision), *data poisoning* (tainting the training data so that the AI learns incorrect or harmful behavior), *model theft or inversion* (stealing an AI model's knowledge or extracting sensitive data from it), and *model misuse or misalignment* (where an AI might pursue objectives in unintended, unsafe ways). For example, a facial recognition system could be tricked by specially crafted glasses that cause it to misidentify an intruder as an authorized user, or a large language model in a customer service chatbot could be manipulated via cleverly worded prompts to reveal confidential information (so-called "prompt injection" attacks). Threat modeling for AI must account for these possibilities. Security teams are developing new frameworks and checklists - often extending classic models like STRIDE or adopting AI-specific ones such as MITRE's ATLAS knowledge base - to systematically analyze how an AI could be attacked at each stage of its lifecycle, from training to deployment. This might involve questions like: How could someone tamper with the training data? What if the AI is fed inputs outside its normal parameters? How do we handle the AI "hallucinating" false information in a critical context?

Human Oversight and AI Governance in Threat Modeling

While AI can automate and enhance threat modeling, experts caution that it is not a silver bullet. Human oversight remains vital. AI-generated threat analyses need review to ensure they are realistic and contextually valid, as AI may lack the intuition or business context that human security architects have. Moreover, giving AI systems autonomy in defensive tasks (such as automatically fixing code or blocking threats) demands safeguards - an overzealous AI might disrupt systems or miss subtle issues. Hence, leading organizations are pairing AI tools with *human-in-the-loop* processes: the AI does the heavy lifting of scanning systems and suggesting threats, but humans validate and refine the threat model, especially for high-risk decisions. Additionally, there is a focus on AI governance within cybersecurity functions: establishing clear rules for how AI will be used in security operations, how its decisions will be logged and explained, and how to prevent the AI itself from becoming an attack vector (e.g., ensuring an AI co-pilot cannot execute code or changes without approval, to avoid a scenario where an attacker tricks the AI into doing harm). This blend of AI-driven automation with human judgment and strong governance yields the best outcomes – accelerating defenses without sacrificing control. As we move forward, AI-driven threat modeling will be an indispensable part of cybersecurity strategy. Organizations that harness AI for security must also be prepared to defend *against* AI-enhanced threats, making this a continuously evolving chess match between attackers and defenders. The following sections focus on two of the most pivotal battlegrounds of this new era: the explosion of deepfake-based attacks enabled by AI and the looming threat that quantum computing poses to our foundational security protocols.

Deepfakes: AI-Generated Deception and Its Impact

Figure 5-1 illustrates how deepfake technology can create a synthetic identity by combining face and voice cloning with generated persona attributes.

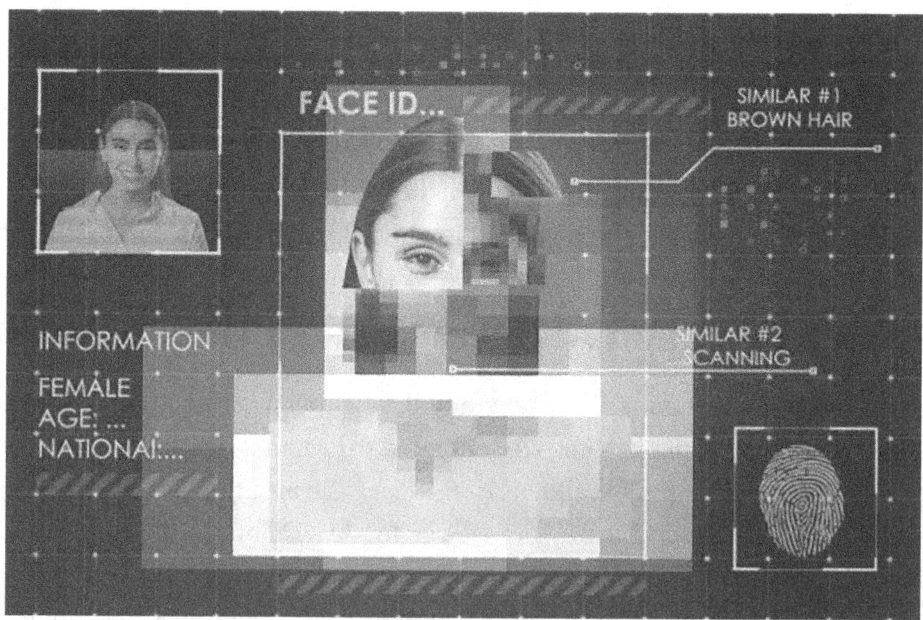

Figure 5-1. *Conceptual illustration of AI-generated identity deception. Deepfake technology can create synthetic personas by cloning a real person's face or voice, making it increasingly difficult to distinguish authentic identity from a fabricated one*

Deepfakes – hyper-realistic fake videos, audio, or images generated by AI – have emerged as a formidable threat in the digital ecosystem. By convincingly mimicking a person's likeness or voice, deepfakes enable a new class of identity deception attacks that were never before possible at scale. Deepfakes have moved from curious internet novelties to practical weapons for fraud, disinformation, impersonation, and sabotage. This section explores how deepfakes are exploited by threat actors, why they are so dangerous to society, and what can be done to combat this rising menace.

The Rise of Deepfake-as-a-Service

One of the most concerning developments is the commercialization and accessibility of deepfake tools. What once required specialized machine learning expertise can now be done by almost anyone, thanks to Deepfake-as-a-Service (DaaS) platforms flourishing on the dark web and even semi-openly online. Deepfake-as-a-Service offerings have become increasingly accessible in criminal and gray-market ecosystems. These services provide user-friendly AI tools to generate fake videos or voices with minimal input – essentially letting a cybercriminal *subscribe* to an AI that can clone voices, swap faces in videos, or create entirely synthetic personas. The barrier to entry for deepfake attacks has thus plummeted. Cybercrime reporting increasingly shows that deepfakes are being incorporated into high-impact corporate impersonation and social engineering schemes. This statistic highlights that a significant portion of fraudsters have already integrated deepfakes into their playbooks to enhance the believability of scams. By using DaaS, even criminals with low technical skill can suddenly conduct highly sophisticated social engineering: imagine a scammer who might barely compose a phishing email before, but now can also attach a *fake audio message from the CEO* or appear in a live video call wearing the *digital face* of an executive, all generated on demand. By lowering technical barriers and costs, the DaaS economy is supercharging the volume and scale of deepfake-enabled attacks.

High-Stakes Impersonations and Fraud

The most direct threat from deepfakes is impersonation fraud, particularly targeting organizations and their financial operations. A dramatic example came to light in early 2024: attackers impersonated a high-ranking executive of a global firm (the CFO of a company, in a case involving the firm Arup) by using an AI-generated *voice and video* deepfake. In a video conference, the fake executive, indistinguishable from the real person in appearance and voice, instructed an employee in the finance department to urgently transfer funds for a confidential transaction. Believing they were following orders from their boss, the employee complied - resulting in a loss of approximately $25 million before the fraud was uncovered. This is not an isolated risk pattern. Similar schemes involving voice cloning, executive impersonation, and synthetic identity cues have appeared in multiple fraud investigations. In Singapore, for instance, criminals leveraged deepfake voice cloning to pose as CEOs and convinced finance staff to redirect millions of dollars to fraudulent accounts. These incidents reveal a stark truth: even well-trained staff can be duped when an attack exploits human trust using the *senses* we rely on - sight and hearing. A voice on the phone that sounds exactly like your CEO, or a video of a colleague giving instructions, will bypass many of the doubt filters an email might raise. Thus, deepfakes allow attackers to *social engineer* at a visceral level, going beyond written words to exploit our inherent trust in what we see and hear.

Beyond direct financial theft, deepfakes have been used in broader fraud and identity crimes. A growing trend is the use of AI to create synthetic identities - fictitious personas stitched together from real and fake data - which are then backed by deepfake images or videos to pass as real people. These synthetic identities can be used to open bank accounts, apply for loans, or trick customer verification processes. By combining stolen personal information (e.g., a real ID number and address) with AI-generated faces and voices, criminals can present what appears to be a legitimate individual on video calls or biometric checks. In one reported case, a bank's "know your customer" video verification process was fooled by a deepfake video of an applicant, allowing a fraudulent account to be opened under a false identity. Such tactics contributed to a significant spike in fraud losses; in the United States alone, recent fraud reporting shows that consumer and financial fraud losses have reached record levels, with AI-assisted schemes adding to the challenge. In sum, deepfakes have turbocharged traditional fraud, making it more convincing and costly than ever.

Deepfakes As a Tool of Misinformation and Chaos

The danger extends far beyond money. Deepfakes pose a national security and public trust threat when used for misinformation, propaganda, or sabotage. In the political realm, we have already seen glimpses of what's possible. During major election cycles, synthetic videos and audio clips have circulated on social media, purporting to show candidates saying or doing scandalous things that never happened. Some clips were debunked, but others seeded confusion and doubt among the electorate. Even when fake content is identified, the damage is done – the target of the disinformation must spend precious time convincing the public the video was fake, and some percentage of viewers will remain convinced by the lie. This phenomenon contributes to what analysts call a "crisis of authenticity" in the digital age: we can no longer take digital media at face value. Authoritarian regimes and rogue actors might use deepfakes to impersonate foreign diplomats or military officials in videos that release false statements, hoping to spark crises or erode trust between allies. Separately, there's the risk of public safety deepfakes – imagine fake emergency broadcasts, or a deepfake of a police officer giving false evacuation orders, causing panic. By enabling *anyone* to fabricate persuasive audio-visual content, deepfakes threaten to undermine societal trust in communications and media.

Even more insidious is the so-called "liar's dividend" effect: the mere existence of deepfakes allows guilty parties to deny reality. If a genuine video emerges showing corruption or wrongdoing, the subject can claim "it's a deepfake" and sow doubt about authentic evidence. Thus, deepfakes erode the foundation of accountability – video or audio evidence can be dismissed as potentially fake, making it harder to hold people responsible for their actions. This erosion of trust can have chilling effects: victims of crimes might struggle to prove something happened if the proof is digital, and the public may grow cynical, believing *nothing* they see, which is equally problematic for democracy and the rule of law.

Challenges in Detection and Response

Confronting deepfake threats is a complex challenge, both technically and organizationally. Researchers are developing detection algorithms that analyze media for signs of manipulation, such as inconsistencies in facial movement, audio timing, lighting, compression artifacts, or biometric features. However, this remains a cat-and-mouse game. As detection improves, deepfake generation techniques also evolve to produce more seamless outputs that evade known detection methods. Human analysts are also increasingly challenged because high-quality fake audio or video may appear credible during a fast-moving business process. Therefore, leaning solely on detection is risky. Organizations need a multi-pronged approach that combines prevention, verified communication channels, out-of-band approvals, employee training, content provenance, and rapid response. A realistic fake voice only needs a few seconds to convince, and a well-crafted fake video can look authentic even on close inspection. Therefore, leaning solely on detection is risky. There is an urgent need for a multi-pronged approach: *prevention, verification, and education.*

Defensive Measures and Verification Techniques

Organizations are adopting various strategies to mitigate deepfake threats. One immediate step is to implement strict verification protocols for any high-stakes requests. For example, if a CFO calls or videos in asking for a funds transfer, companies now require an out-of-band verification - perhaps the employee must call back a known phone number or verify via a secondary channel to confirm it's truly the CFO. This kind of two-factor verification for instructions (especially those involving money or sensitive data) can stop deepfake scams in their tracks by introducing a check that is not easily faked. Some institutions have started using code phrases or pre-arranged challenge questions for executives to use in live communications as an authentication mechanism ("If it's really you, mention the project code we discussed yesterday").

On a larger scale, the tech industry is working on content authenticity frameworks. These involve cryptographically signing legitimate videos or audio at the time of recording to prove their origin and detect any tampering. Initiatives like digital watermarking or the emerging *Content Credentials* (backed by coalitions including major media companies) aim to attach a verifiable ledger of a video's history - if a video has no provenance data or if that data indicates it's been manipulated, consumers and platforms could be alerted. While not foolproof and requiring broad adoption, such measures could help distinguish authentic content from AI-generated media.

Organizations are also investing in threat intelligence focused on deepfakes - monitoring underground forums and early warning signals that their brand or executives might be targeted by synthetic media attacks. Just as companies track data breaches, they now may track if someone is discussing or sharing an AI model of their CEO's voice on the dark web. Rapid takedown efforts are another piece of the puzzle: when a fake video of a company's leader emerges online, having the capability to quickly get it removed or issue clarifications can limit the harm. Some companies maintain "crisis deepfake response" playbooks that outline how to respond if a harmful fake video or audio implicating the company goes viral.

Training and Awareness

Perhaps the most broad-based defense is increasing awareness and skepticism among employees and the public. Businesses are updating their security awareness training to include deepfakes - teaching staff that voices and faces can now be spoofed just like emails. Employees are advised to verify unusual requests through secondary channels and to be on the lookout for subtle inconsistencies in communications. For the general public, there is a push for media literacy in the age of AI. This includes educating people that seeing is not always believing: just because a video shows something, one should consider the source and the possibility of manipulation, especially if the content is shocking or confirms a bias. Paradoxically, the goal is to foster healthy skepticism without sliding into total cynicism.

Governance and Legal Gaps

Finally, it's important to note that while deepfakes proliferate, laws and governance have lagged. Legal frameworks for malicious deepfakes remain uneven and fragmented across jurisdictions. Some countries have started piecemeal efforts - for example, considering whether creating a deepfake of someone without consent could be categorized under identity theft or impersonation laws or, in Denmark's case, attempting to use copyright law to protect one's likeness (a creative but possibly inadequate solution, since copyright doesn't cleanly apply to one's face or voice). There is a growing call for modernizing laws to establish digital identity rights - granting individuals explicit legal ownership of their facial and vocal likeness so that unauthorized replication could be punishable. Regulatory bodies are also examining requiring platforms to detect and label deepfakes, and holding companies accountable if their services knowingly spread harmful synthetic media. We will revisit governance in Section "Governance Principles and Tooling Gaps in the AI and Quantum Era" but suffice it here to say a governance gap exists: deepfakes represent a new kind of threat that our institutions are only beginning to grapple with.

In summary, deepfakes epitomize the dual nature of AI in security - powerful technology that can be used for both amazing creativity and for pernicious deceit. Deepfake-driven attacks have become a clear warning that identity, trust, and media authenticity must be treated as cybersecurity concerns, not only as communications or platform-moderation issues. The silver lining is that awareness is spreading, and collaborative efforts between technologists, policymakers, and organizations are underway to develop countermeasures. The challenge is great: to restore trust in digital content and clamp down on AI-driven fraud without stifling innovation. Navigating that balance is now a key task for cybersecurity leaders and regulators alike.

The Quantum Threat: Risks in the Quantum Computing Era

As we fortify defenses against today's AI-enabled attacks, an entirely different kind of threat is looming on the horizon: the threat posed by quantum computers. Quantum computing is an emerging field of computing that leverages the principles of quantum mechanics to process information in ways impossible for classical computers. While still in its infancy, quantum computing is advancing steadily. Within the next decade or two, it promises breakthroughs in fields from medicine to materials science - but it also harbors a dire risk for cybersecurity. A sufficiently advanced quantum computer could shatter the foundation of modern encryption, rendering many of our current security measures obsolete. This section examines what the quantum threat entails, the current state of quantum technology, and the timeline we face to address this challenge.

Why Quantum Computing Threatens Cryptography

Much of today's digital security relies on certain mathematical problems being extremely hard for classical computers to solve. For example, the security of common encryption and digital signature schemes (like RSA and elliptic-curve cryptography used in HTTPS, VPNs, banking transactions, etc.) is based on problems like factoring large numbers or computing discrete logarithms. These tasks would take classical computers billions of years, making the algorithms effectively unbreakable with brute force. However, in the 1990s, mathematician Peter Shor discovered that a hypothetical quantum computer could run an algorithm (aptly named Shor's algorithm) that solves these problems exponentially faster. In principle, a *sufficiently powerful* quantum computer could factor a 2048-bit RSA key - something impossible for any present-day computer - within hours or days. This means that all encryption that relies on RSA or similar algorithms could be broken, exposing sensitive communications, financial transactions, and state secrets. The day when a quantum computer can do this is often referred to as "Q-Day" - a moment of reckoning for cybersecurity.

It's important to clarify that current quantum computers cannot do this yet. The barrier is not simply the raw number of physical qubits, but the ability to build a fault-tolerant quantum computer with enough high-quality logical qubits, low error rates, and sustained operations to run cryptographically relevant algorithms. Estimates for breaking RSA-2048 or comparable elliptic-curve systems vary and continue to evolve, so security architects should avoid anchoring migration plans to a single qubit count or single predicted Q-Day. However, progress in quantum technology is continuous and non-linear. Laboratories and tech companies are rapidly improving quantum processors each year. The timeline is uncertain - optimists suggest a breakthrough could perhaps arrive in the early 2030s, while pessimists (from a security perspective) say it might take longer, even into the 2040s or beyond. But crucially, surveys of experts show a consensus that a cryptography-breaking quantum computer is *likely to be built within the next 10–15 years*. Even a 10–20% chance that this could happen by around 2035 is enough to raise alarms, given the stakes involved.

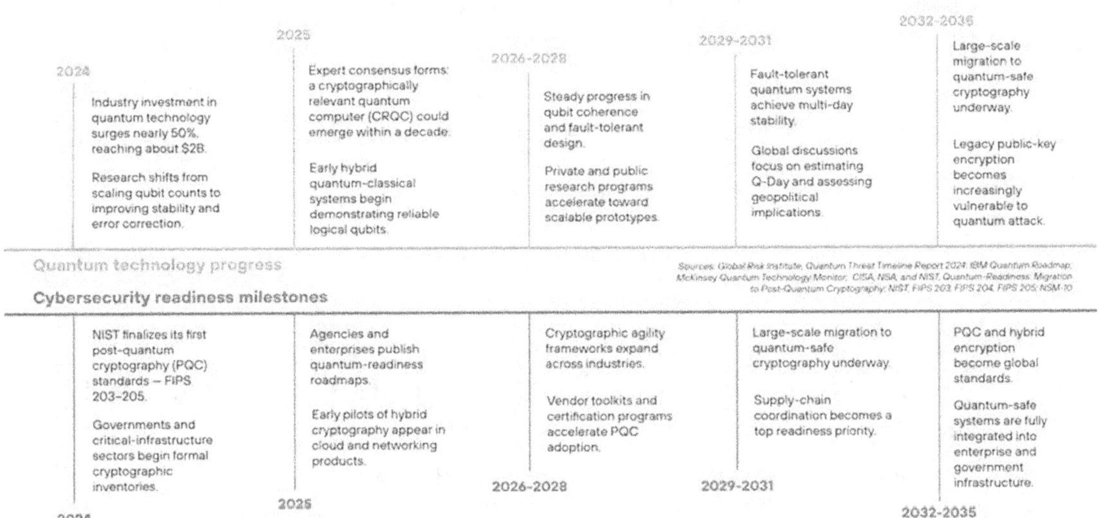

***Figure 5-2.** Projected timeline of quantum computing progress vs. cybersecurity readiness (2024–2035). The upper timeline highlights anticipated quantum technology milestones, while the lower timeline shows planned security responses. In the mid-2020s, investments in quantum research are surging, and early quantum systems are demonstrating small numbers of logical qubits (qubits with error correction). By the late 2020s, quantum prototypes are expected to steadily improve in qubit count and stability, inching toward the thresholds needed for cryptographic attacks. Concurrently, governments and industry are pushing post-quantum cryptography standards and beginning migrations so that by the early 2030s, quantum-resistant encryption is widely deployed before large-scale quantum computers arrive*

The uncertainty of "when" Q-Day will hit should not lull us into inaction. Security experts emphasize that we must act *before* a quantum computer exists that can break our crypto. This is because of a unique threat known as "Harvest Now, Decrypt Later." In this scenario, adversaries (especially well-resourced nation-states) are *already intercepting and storing* vast amounts of encrypted data - everything from internet traffic to stolen archives of sensitive communications - with the expectation that they will decrypt it in the future when quantum capabilities become available. In other words, even if an encrypted document or message is safe against today's computers, if it's intercepted and saved, a quantum computer in ten years could decrypt it and expose its secrets. For certain types of information, like personal data, intellectual property, or military and diplomatic secrets, a decade is not a long time - the information will still be sensitive then. Therefore, each year that passes without quantum-proof encryption in place is a year in which more data accumulates in risk. Intelligence agencies have warned that *starting too late* on the transition - for example, only beginning to swap out algorithms around 2030 - could indeed be "too late" to protect the confidentiality of long-lived information.

Current State of Quantum Computers

To grasp the threat, let's briefly outline where quantum computing stands as of now and what near-term progress looks like. Several tech giants and research institutions (IBM, Google, Intel, universities, and various startups) are building quantum processors. In 2023, IBM unveiled a quantum processor with 1,121 qubits, a milestone in qubit count, though these qubits are *physical qubits*, not corrected for errors. Error rates remain a major hurdle - quantum bits are very fragile and prone to interference, which causes computational errors. To perform the huge numbers of operations needed for something like breaking encryption, the quantum computer must implement error correction, which itself requires many redundant physical qubits to form a single high-quality *logical qubit*. We are still in the stage where demonstrating even a few logical qubits is an achievement. Experts project that reaching the thousands of logical qubits needed for cryptography-breaking will require millions of physical qubits and breakthroughs in stability and error correction. That said, incremental progress is being made: each year brings new records in qubit coherence time (how long they can maintain quantum states), connectivity, and error rates.

Hybrid approaches are also emerging, combining classical and quantum computing for specialized workflows. For instance, early quantum systems are being used in tandem with classical supercomputers to solve specific sub-problems, an approach that might yield useful results sooner than fully quantum solutions. It's conceivable that by the late 2020s, we might have special-purpose quantum accelerators that can do certain tasks faster than classical computers (a phenomenon known as "quantum advantage"), but still not general or stable enough to threaten cryptography. Nonetheless, continuous improvements might suddenly reach a critical threshold where cryptographic computations become feasible.

Quantum Risk Scenarios

The full scope of quantum risks isn't limited to breaking encryption, though that is by far the most consequential. Other potential impacts include breaking digital signatures (allowing forgeries of software updates or documents), undermining blockchain systems (many cryptocurrencies rely on elliptic curve signatures that could be forged, threatening the integrity of blockchain transactions), and even affecting password security (quantum algorithms like Grover's algorithm could speed up brute-force searches, though not as dramatically as Shor's impact on encryption). In secure communications protocols, many use asymmetric cryptography (public key cryptography) for exchanging keys – that initial handshake would be vulnerable, potentially allowing an eavesdropper with a quantum computer to read all subsequently "encrypted" traffic by decrypting the exchanged keys. In short, if we do nothing, a sufficiently powerful quantum computer in the future could crack open a vast swath of the world's stored secrets and ongoing communications, putting everything from financial systems to personal privacy to national defense at risk.

Timeline and Urgency

One might ask: If quantum computers that pose a threat might only arrive 10 or 15 years from now, why act now? The answer lies in the long lead time for cryptographic transitions. Updating encryption across all our digital systems is a massive undertaking. Consider the number of devices, applications, and protocols that use RSA or ECC: every secure website, every ATM, every VPN, IoT devices, industrial control systems, medical devices, etc. Many of these systems (like hardware devices in the field) can take years to upgrade or replace. Standards need to be developed, hardware and software need to implement new algorithms, and data often needs re-encryption. Historically, moving from one encryption standard to another (say, from older 1024-bit RSA to 2048-bit RSA, or from SHA-1 to SHA-256 hashes) took the industry the better part of a decade or more. Given that some experts warn a cryptographically relevant quantum computer could possibly exist by the early-to-mid-2030s, starting migration early is prudent. Governments around the world have recognized this and are issuing directives accordingly (which we will detail in the next section on solutions).

It's also worth noting that recently, *awareness* of quantum risk has grown significantly in executive circles. A few years ago, many business or government leaders might have dismissed quantum threats as purely theoretical or a next-generation problem. Now, surveys show that leadership in finance, government, and critical infrastructure is conversant in the issue and actively planning for mitigation. This shift in awareness is partly due to concerted efforts by security agencies and think tanks to publicize the quantum threat timeline – emphasizing that the timeline has, in fact, accelerated as research investments soar. For example, global investment in quantum R&D grew by nearly 50% in recent years, indicating a strong push toward making large-scale quantum computing a reality sooner than later. We are essentially in a race: *Will we upgrade our cryptography before adversaries achieve quantum codebreaking capabilities?* The next section focuses on the encouraging flipside of this challenge: the development of quantum-resistant cryptography and how we're mobilizing to defend against the quantum threat.

Quantum-Resistant Cryptography: Preparing for a Post-Quantum World

Given the inevitability of quantum computing advancements, the cybersecurity community has been working proactively on a solution: quantum-resistant cryptography, often called *post-quantum cryptography (PQC)*. This refers to new cryptographic algorithms designed to be secure against quantum attacks – meaning even a future quantum computer would not be able to easily break them. Unlike quantum encryption methods (such as quantum key distribution, which uses quantum physics for secure communication but requires special hardware and fiber optics), post-quantum algorithms are implemented in software and hardware much like our current algorithms; they're just built on math problems believed to be hard for both classical *and* quantum computers. In this section, we provide an overview of quantum-resistant cryptography, the current state of post-quantum standards, and practical adoption priorities for organizations preparing for migration.

The Quest for Quantum-Resilient Algorithms

Starting in the mid-2010s, cryptographers worldwide began developing and scrutinizing new algorithms that could withstand quantum attacks. These efforts culminated in a global competition-like process led by the US National Institute of Standards and Technology (NIST). NIST invited researchers to submit candidate algorithms and subjected them to rounds of evaluation, much as was done for selecting the AES encryption standard years ago. After several rounds spanning 2017 to 2022, NIST announced the first group of post-quantum algorithm finalists that would be standardized. By 2024, NIST officially released draft standards for these algorithms. The front-runners include:

- **ML-KEM**, formerly CRYSTALS-Kyber, standardized in FIPS 203 for key establishment. It is intended for use cases such as secure key exchange in protocols that currently rely on RSA, Diffie-Hellman, or elliptic-curve key agreement.
- **ML-DSA**, formerly CRYSTALS-Dilithium, standardized in FIPS 204 for digital signatures. It is intended for use cases such as software signing, document signing, certificates, and authentication workflows that require quantum-resistant signatures.
- **SLH-DSA**, formerly SPHINCS+, standardized in FIPS 205 for stateless hash-based digital signatures. It provides a conservative signature option based on a different mathematical foundation from ML-DSA, though with larger signatures and different performance trade-offs.
- Classic McEliece: an encryption scheme based on error-correcting codes. McEliece has the advantage of having withstood scrutiny for decades (it was invented in the 1970s and still no efficient attack is known, even with quantum). It wasn't as universally chosen due to very large public key sizes, but it remains a standardized option, especially valued in certain niche applications needing long-term security.

NIST has also selected additional algorithms for standardization work. FALCON is expected to be standardized as FN-DSA in FIPS 206, and HQC has been selected as a backup key-encapsulation mechanism to ML-KEM. These should be described as additional or developing standards, not as part of the first three finalized FIPS standards. Governments and large companies have been closely following this process because it essentially provides the toolkit for the future of secure communications.

Standardization and Government Initiatives

In August 2024, NIST released the first official standards for post-quantum cryptography (FIPS 203, 204, 205 for the algorithms mentioned). This was a landmark moment: it signaled to industry that the solutions are ready and it's time to implement them. Governments didn't stop at just publishing standards; they began issuing mandates to ensure adoption. The United States, for example, through directives like the White House's National Security Memorandum-10 (NSM-10) and the NSA's updated cryptographic guidance (the Commercial National Security Algorithm Suite 2.0, or CNSA 2.0), set clear timelines for federal systems. By those policies, starting in 2025, US federal agencies were expected to inventory all their cryptographic usage and identify where they need to migrate to PQC. By 2027, any new systems procured for national security use must be using quantum-resistant algorithms (no new systems launching with old RSA/ECC). And by the early 2030s (2030–2031), all existing sensitive systems must be upgraded or replaced to use the approved PQC algorithms, with legacy non-quantum-safe crypto being phased out entirely.

European bodies have likewise been active. The European Telecommunications Standards Institute (ETSI) has projects and technical reports guiding post-quantum transition (e.g., ETSI TR 103 967 outlines migration considerations). The EU's cybersecurity agency ENISA has been urging member states and companies to start the transition early and working on coordination so that, for example, when banks in different countries or government services communicate, they can agree on common post-quantum protocols. International standards organizations like ISO and ITU are also developing guidelines to ensure global interoperability of quantum-safe cryptography. In Asia, countries like Japan and South Korea have launched their own PQC research initiatives, often aligning with NIST's choices, and are beginning pilot deployments.

***Figure 5-3.** Global quantum readiness landscape – major government and standards-body initiatives for post-quantum migration. The United States has set CNSA 2.0 transition expectations for national security systems, including expectations for new deployments beginning in 2027, unless otherwise specified. Europe is coordinating through ENISA and ETSI for testing and standardizing PQC across member states. Other nations like Japan and Canada are aligning with these standards and running independent trials. A shared global challenge is ensuring all regions progress together, because security is only as strong as the weakest link in a connected world*

The overall message from authorities has been clear: start transitioning now. Government agencies, standards bodies, and industry consortia are publishing quantum-readiness roadmaps and best practices. Organizations are advised to adopt a "crypto agility" approach – meaning designing systems to be flexible in swapping out cryptographic algorithms – to facilitate the transition. Some have already begun deploying *hybrid encryption* in sensitive communications: combining a classical algorithm and a post-quantum algorithm, so that even if one is broken, the other still protects the message. Browser vendors and Internet standards groups have tested adding post-quantum options in TLS (the protocol that secures websites). A notable pilot was a major web browser and CDN provider teaming up to trial a TLS cipher suite that uses both a classical elliptic-curve algorithm and Kyber (post-quantum) together; this kind of experiment foreshadows what a broader Internet-wide rollout might look like.

Challenges in Adoption

Despite clear mandates and the availability of standards, migrating to quantum-resistant crypto is not a flip-the-switch change. There are practical challenges that organizations face, which is why careful planning is needed. One challenge is performance and integration: Some PQC algorithms have much larger key sizes or signature sizes than their classical counterparts. For example, a Kyber public key is a few kilobytes in size, compared to an RSA public key which might be only a few hundred bytes; similarly, Dilithium signatures are larger than RSA signatures. This means protocols and systems that assumed small key sizes might need adjustments (increasing buffer sizes, etc.), and networks might see a slight increase in traffic. Computational performance is also a factor - while most PQC algorithms are efficient on modern CPUs (often as fast as or faster than RSA), they might not yet be optimized on all platforms, especially constrained devices. Embedded systems and IoT devices present another issue: many of them have very limited computing power and memory and may not be able to handle the new algorithms without hardware upgrades.

Another challenge is compatibility: during the transition period, systems that have been upgraded to PQC need to still communicate with systems that have not. This requires careful protocol design to allow a graceful fallback or dual support. It's a bit like the IPv4 to IPv6 Internet transition - it can take a long time for every node to support the new protocols, so interim solutions are needed.

"Crypto-Agility" and Tooling

Crypto-agility has become a practical requirement for post-quantum readiness. This refers to the ability of a system to switch cryptographic algorithms with minimal disruption. Many older systems baked a specific algorithm into their design (for instance, assuming RSA with a fixed key size everywhere). Going forward, organizations aim to design systems that can easily be reconfigured to use different algorithms - not just for the quantum transition, but in case any algorithm gets broken or deprecated in the future. Figure 5-4 explains how crypto-agility is implemented in a typical organization. Achieving crypto-agility might involve adopting standard libraries that support multiple algorithms and keeping an inventory of where and how cryptography is used. Some companies have been surprised to discover just how many places a given algorithm like RSA appears in their infrastructure, from obvious places (VPNs, secure email, databases) to less obvious (internal software license checks, proprietary protocols, etc.). Conducting a thorough cryptography inventory is often the first recommended step: you can't change what you don't know you have.

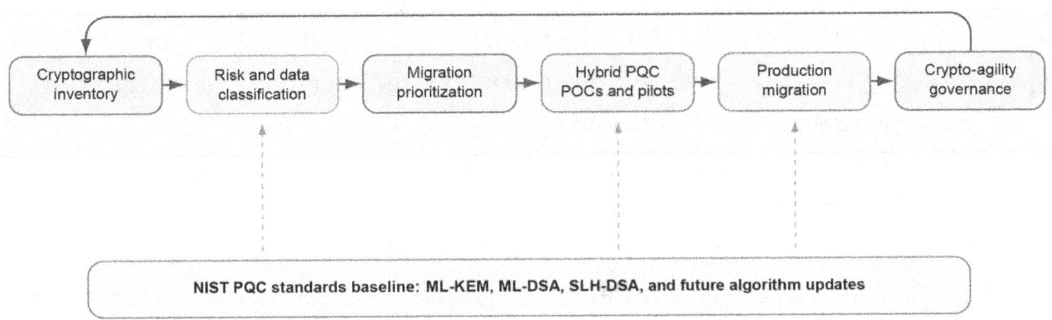

Figure 5-4. *Practical post-quantum readiness lifecycle. The lifecycle begins with cryptographic inventory, moves through risk classification and migration prioritization, then proceeds into hybrid post-quantum pilots, production migration, and ongoing crypto-agility governance. This framing is useful because post-quantum migration is not a single replacement project; it is a continuing governance and engineering process*

Hardware and Infrastructure Upgrades

On the hardware side, vendors of security hardware modules (HSMs, smart cards, trusted platform modules) are rolling out support for PQC. For example, newer HSMs and cryptographic libraries are beginning to add support for standardized post-quantum algorithms such as ML-KEM and ML-DSA, as well as hybrid deployment patterns that combine classical and post-quantum mechanisms during transition. Cloud providers have started offering options for quantum-safe key exchange in their cloud key management services. Telecom companies are thinking about how to update the encryption in 5G/6G systems to PQC in future releases. There's also attention on long-term data archival: if you have data encrypted and stored for long periods (think backups or confidential records that must remain encrypted at rest), you might need to re-encrypt those with quantum-safe algorithms sooner rather than later.

The early phase of post-quantum adoption is moving from standards awareness into product integration, pilot deployments, cryptographic inventory, and migration planning. Organizations should not wait for a cryptographically relevant quantum computer before acting, because long-lived sensitive data and long-lived certificates may already be exposed to harvest-now-decrypt-later risk. We will likely see early adopters – perhaps some banks or government agencies – announcing that their communications are now quantum-safe after upgrades. At the same time, cyber adversaries are aware of this window of time – reports suggest an uptick in espionage activity aimed at stealing encrypted data now ("harvest now") before it becomes inaccessible with new encryption. Thus, paradoxically, the pre-quantum era might see an *increase* in breaches of encrypted data stores, simply to stockpile for later decryption. This adds further incentive for organizations to accelerate migration and also consider encrypting *today's* sensitive data with quantum-resistant algorithms if it absolutely must remain confidential for many years.

Not to be neglected, there's also the human factor and training: cryptographic transitions can introduce misconfigurations or gaps if administrators are not well-versed in the new tech. Companies will need to train their IT security staff on PQC algorithms, how to implement them correctly, and how to manage keys (which might be larger or have different lifecycles). Documentation and best practices are emerging, often guided by bodies like NIST or ENISA, to help with this knowledge transfer.

Alternate Approaches: Quantum and Hybrid Solutions

It's worth noting that post-quantum *algorithms* are not the only line of defense being pursued. Quantum physics itself offers some solutions like Quantum Key Distribution (QKD) – where two parties share encryption keys via quantum particles (photons) so that any eavesdropping is detectable. QKD is already used in some niche applications (like inter-bank communications in Switzerland or between datacenters in China), but it requires special hardware and has distance limitations unless using satellite relays. QKD will likely complement, not replace, post-quantum cryptography, especially for extremely high-security links. Additionally, some researchers are exploring hybrid models combining classical, PQC, and QKD to hedge bets. However, for most of the world, *software-based PQC is the practical solution,* because it can be deployed widely without exotic new infrastructure.

In summary, quantum-resistant cryptography is our primary shield against the quantum threat, and it's a shield that is being forged right now. The progress up to 2025 has been significant: we went from theoretical proposals to standardized algorithms and clear government mandates in roughly a decade. Yet, the hardest part – *deployment at scale* – is just beginning. The next few years (2026–2030) will be critical for ensuring that organizations around the globe actually implement these defenses. The transition is both a technical and a managerial challenge, requiring forward planning and possibly significant investment. But the alternative – being unprepared for Q-Day – is simply not an option. Encouragingly, this is one area of cybersecurity where we aren't necessarily behind the attackers; we know what's coming, and we have the tools; now, it's about execution.

Governance Principles and Tooling Gaps in the AI and Quantum Era

Confronting the dual challenges of AI-driven threats and quantum-era risks isn't just a technical endeavor – it's also a matter of governance. By governance, we mean the frameworks of policies, regulations, ethical guidelines, and organizational practices that ensure technology is developed and used responsibly and safely. As AI and quantum technologies accelerate, governments and industries are scrambling to establish principles to manage their impact. However, there are notable gaps between the risks we face and the tools available (both technical and legal) to mitigate them. In this section, we outline key governance principles emerging for AI and quantum security and highlight areas where current governance or tooling falls short.

AI Governance

Principles for Responsible AI Use – AI's transformative power has led to calls for comprehensive governance to prevent misuse, protect rights, and ensure safety. Several high-level principles are widely advocated: transparency, accountability, fairness, and security in AI systems. In practice, transparency might mean disclosing when content is AI-generated (for instance, watermarking AI images or labeling deepfake media) or making AI decision processes explainable where possible. Accountability means that organizations deploying AI should be responsible for its outcomes – for example, if an

AI used in lending exhibits bias or if an autonomous vehicle AI causes an accident, there needs to be a clear chain of responsibility and potential liability. Fairness requires that AI systems do not unduly discriminate or harm certain groups, aligning with human rights. Security in AI governance implies robust protections against threats *to* AI (like adversarial attacks) and *from* AI (like AI being used maliciously), which ties into the need for things like AI-specific threat modeling as discussed earlier.

Regulators around the world are starting to codify these principles. The European Union's AI Act entered into force in August 2024 and applies in phases. Prohibited AI practices and AI literacy obligations began applying in February 2025, general-purpose AI obligations began applying in August 2025, broader obligations apply from August 2026, and certain high-risk AI system requirements extend into later timelines depending on category.) It is one of the most ambitious attempts: it applies a risk-based framework to AI applications, with stricter requirements (such as transparency, human oversight, and robustness) on "high-risk" AI systems like those in healthcare or law enforcement, and even some prohibitions on uses deemed too dangerous (like real-time facial recognition in public surveillance under most circumstances or social scoring of citizens). The EU AI Act would also likely require makers of generative AI models to implement some safeguards and transparency features (e.g., disclose that output was AI-generated). In the United States, while no single comprehensive AI law exists yet at the federal level, agencies are issuing guidance (the US National Institute of Standards and Technology published an AI Risk Management Framework in 2023 to guide companies in managing AI risks, and there have been executive initiatives on AI safety). Industry groups and international bodies like the OECD have proposed voluntary AI principles that many nations have signed onto. All these efforts reflect a common understanding: governance must accompany innovation in AI, or else we will continually play catch-up to problems after they occur.

The Governance Gap: Case of Deepfakes

Despite these positive steps, there remain glaring gaps in our governance regimes, especially concerning specific AI abuses like deepfakes (as we examined in "Section of Deepfakes above"). Regulations often lag behind the rapid evolution of technology. Taking deepfakes as a case study: most current laws address them indirectly at best. For instance, if a deepfake is used in a fraud, prosecutors might charge fraud; if used to defame or harass, maybe defamation or harassment laws apply. But there are a few laws explicitly forbidding the creation of malicious deepfakes or providing clear remedies to victims whose likeness is stolen. Some jurisdictions have outlawed certain uses (like deepfake pornography without consent is illegal in a few states/countries), yet enforcement is difficult across borders. The EU AI Act, as noted, will have a disclosure requirement for deepfakes, but critics argue this is a minimal measure – essentially requiring that AI-generated content be labeled as such – and doesn't fully address how to handle deepfakes used in crime or foreign influence campaigns.

Governance experts have pointed out that deepfakes slip through the cracks of multiple regulatory domains: they are simultaneously a cybersecurity issue, a media/content issue, a privacy issue, and in some cases a financial crime issue. This fragmentation means no single authority is fully empowered to tackle them, and malicious actors can exploit these silos. One proposal from thought leaders is to designate certain AI applications like deepfakes used for impersonation or large-scale misinformation as "high-risk AI systems" explicitly, thereby subjecting them to mandatory oversight and controls (e.g., requiring AI developers to incorporate authentication measures or traceable watermarks in the output of deepfake generation tools). Another proposal is creating new categories of offenses for synthetic media misuse, so that law enforcement isn't stretching old laws to fit new crimes (e.g., making it clearly illegal to fabricate and use someone's likeness for harmful purposes, with penalties that reflect the severity). There is also discussion about establishing personal property rights over one's digital likeness – so if someone's face or voice is cloned without permission, they have legal grounds to demand removal and sue for damages. Implementing such rights globally is complex, but it shows the kind of fresh legal thinking underway to patch the governance gap.

Quantum Technology Governance

Quantum computing's threat is unusual because, unlike AI (which is here and now causing issues like deepfakes), the quantum threat is *mostly* forward-looking. Governance in this context is largely about risk management and mandating preparedness. Governments have started to weave quantum considerations into cybersecurity policy – for example, by requiring agencies and critical industries to plan for post-quantum migration (as discussed in "Quantum-Resistant Cryptography Section"). Another governance aspect is fostering international cooperation: since a break in cryptography in one country can have global reverberations (think of a stolen encrypted dataset from one country being decrypted by another's quantum computer), countries are sharing research and aligning standards. Forums like the Global Risk Institute or the World Economic Forum have highlighted quantum cyber risks in their annual risk assessments to keep pressure on leaders.

However, not everyone is moving at the same speed. There's a governance gap here, too, in the sense that the private sector's readiness is uneven. Big banks and tech companies are generally aware and investing in crypto agility; smaller businesses or municipalities might not even know about the issue. Thus, one governance challenge is how to incentivize or require broader swathes of the economy to take action. Some ideas include regulatory requirements for sectors like finance and healthcare to prove they have a quantum transition plan (much like how they must have disaster recovery or breach response plans). Financial regulators and industry bodies are increasingly asking whether large institutions understand their quantum exposure and have a migration plan. This expectation may become more formalized through supervisory reviews, cyber resilience programs, third-party risk assessments, and industry cybersecurity certifications.

Ethical considerations in quantum are less about the threat (since the threat is straightforward: broken encryption) and more about the geopolitics and control of quantum technology. Nations are pouring billions into quantum R&D, and there is a quiet race reminiscent of an arms race – whoever gets a cryptography-breaking quantum computer first could, in theory, decrypt a treasure trove of foreign secrets. This raises complex governance issues: Should there be international agreements akin to arms control for not misusing quantum decryption capabilities? If a nation achieves quantum supremacy (the ability to solve certain problems beyond classical reach), will they disclose it or keep it secret? Such questions might seem speculative but are being contemplated in policy circles. Transparency and global norms in the development of quantum tech could become a significant governance topic later in the 2020s. For now, the more immediate governance focus is making sure we "raise the defenses" through PQC and not allow quantum to catch us off-guard.

Tooling Gaps and the Need for Innovation

Effective governance often depends on having the right tools and technologies to enforce or enable it. Here, we identify a few critical tooling gaps in this AI-and-quantum era.

Deepfake Detection and Authentication Tools

As noted earlier, while some tools exist, they are not keeping up with the threat. We need more robust, scalable solutions to verify content authenticity. This could involve AI that can cross-verify multiple signals (e.g., checking if the supposed live video of an executive matches their known physical mannerisms or if the audio spectrum matches known samples). It could also involve broader adoption of digital signing of legitimate content at the source (for instance, cameras that automatically sign footage). One gap is the lack of a widely adopted standard for these content credentials - multiple proposals exist, but no single ecosystem covers all media. Governance could help by endorsing particular standards or requiring platforms to integrate such verification features.

AI System Audit and Monitoring Tools

Organizations deploying AI need better tools to audit their AI models for biases, security vulnerabilities, and compliance with regulations. For example, how does a bank prove that its AI loan approval system is fair and non-discriminatory? It needs tools to explain AI decisions, to log how the AI is used, and to detect if an AI model is drifting into unsafe behavior. This is still an emerging area. We have some AI explainability techniques and bias detection frameworks, but they often require highly skilled teams to use and interpret. A tooling gap exists for more automated, user-friendly AI governance tools that can be plugged into AI development pipelines. Similarly, for security, tools like adversarial ML testing (where you throw many possible attacks at an AI to see if it can be fooled) are still mostly in the research phase or specialized providers - not yet standard in every developer's toolbox.

Cryptographic Agility and Management Tools

Switching to post-quantum crypto is not as simple as installing a patch. Organizations could use better tools for inventorying their cryptographic usage. Today, finding all instances of a certain algorithm in a large enterprise might require manual code reviews and consulting many vendors. Organizations increasingly need cryptographic inventory and crypto-management platforms that can automatically scan and catalog algorithms, keys, certificates, protocols, libraries, and dependencies across enterprise systems, flagging the ones that need upgrading. Some startups and open source projects are beginning to tackle this, but it's not yet common. Also, tools that can handle bulk re-encryption of stored data (e.g., re-encrypt all database records or filesystem contents with a new algorithm seamlessly) would be incredibly useful to facilitate migration. Key management systems will need to handle larger keys and perhaps more diverse algorithms, so upgrades in that area are needed too.

Skilled Workforce and Training

This is more of a human tooling gap – having enough experts who understand both AI and security or quantum and security. Interdisciplinary knowledge is crucial: an AI engineer needs to be aware of security, and a security analyst needs to know a bit about AI to anticipate those threats. Similarly, classical cybersecurity training rarely covered quantum; now it must at least in concept. Organizations and governments are recognizing a skills gap and are pushing for training programs specific to AI security and post-quantum transition. Over time, these topics should become standard parts of security engineering, cloud security, software assurance, and computer science curricula.

Incident Response and Testing Frameworks for New Threats

We have fairly mature protocols for handling a typical data breach or malware infection incident, but how about a deepfake-induced incident (e.g., an employee was tricked by a fake CEO call) or an incident where we suspect a quantum-capable adversary was able to decrypt some traffic? Incident response playbooks need updating to include these scenarios. That includes having policies in place, like "If someone claims a high-ranking person gave an odd instruction, involve a specific chain of verification," or "If quantum decryption is suspected, immediately inform authorities and rotate keys using PQC." Testing (like penetration testing) is also adapting – for instance, some red teams (ethical hackers) are starting to incorporate deepfake phishing calls in their security drills to test if the company procedures can catch it. Expanding these practices will help identify weaknesses before real attackers do.

Collaboration and Cross-Sector Coordination

A recurring theme in governance discussions is that no single entity can solve these issues alone. Public-private partnerships are critical. For AI and deepfakes, tech companies, social media platforms, law enforcement, and civil society need channels to share information and respond rapidly to emerging threats (such as a particularly dangerous deepfake going viral – there may need to be a mechanism to assess it and, if necessary, throttle its spread, without sliding into censorship of legitimate content). For quantum, industry consortia in sectors like banking or energy are working together to ensure consistency in upgrades (e.g., banks exchanging data want to all agree on which PQC algorithm to use to avoid chaos).

Internationally, we see alliances forming: like-minded countries are sharing research on secure AI and quantum risk (for instance, through joint statements or working groups in G7, NATO, etc., focusing on emerging tech security). However, there is also tension as major powers like the United States, the EU, and China each want to lead on standard-setting – a governance challenge will be ensuring that efforts remain interoperable globally. It's a "shared global challenge," to use a phrase often mentioned in this context, because AI and quantum threats don't respect borders.

Ethical and Societal Considerations

Governance is not only about stopping bad outcomes but also about aligning with societal values. In deploying AI for security, for example, one must consider privacy (e.g., monitoring employee communications with AI to detect deepfakes could intrude on privacy if not carefully managed). Or using AI in policing and surveillance brings human rights considerations. Likewise, as we secure systems against quantum threats, we should keep in mind access and equity – we don't want a world where only rich nations or companies have secure communications and others are left vulnerable. This calls for capacity-building: helping developing countries also upgrade their encryption and including diverse voices in AI governance so that solutions work for all communities, not just the most technologically advanced.

In conclusion, governance in the AI and quantum era is as crucial as technical countermeasures. The principles of responsible innovation, risk-based oversight, and global cooperation serve as our compass, but we must fill the gaps between principle and practice. This means investing in better tools and processes, updating our laws and standards continuously, and educating people at all levels about the new norms (e.g., teaching employees that "verify on video calls just like you do on email" or teaching upcoming engineers about crypto agility). The pace of threat evolution is relentless - governance must strive to be anticipatory, not just reactive. Looking ahead, organizations should expect more concrete regulatory, contractual, and audit expectations around AI governance (and perhaps the first enforcement of AI Act type laws) and more concrete requirements in critical sectors to be quantum-ready. Navigating this landscape requires agility not just in code, but in policy and mindset.

Conclusion: Building Resilience for an Uncertain Future

The convergence of AI and quantum technologies with cybersecurity has brought us to a historic inflection point. On one side, AI is turbocharging both attacks and defenses in cyberspace - from deepfakes that can fool our very senses to intelligent security systems that learn and adapt faster than any human. On the other side, the coming quantum revolution threatens to upend the cryptographic shields that have protected our digital world for decades, forcing us into a race to deploy new safeguards in time. Chapter 5 has traversed this complex terrain, highlighting the promise and peril of these developments.

A recurring theme is adaptation. The threats of the 2020s and beyond cannot be met with yesterday's mindset or tools. We must adapt our technology: integrating AI into security operations to handle the scale and speed of modern threats and overhauling our cryptographic infrastructure to be quantum-resilient. We must adapt our governance: crafting laws and policies that address the reality of AI-generated content and that mandate proactive preparation for quantum risks. And perhaps most importantly, we must adapt our culture and awareness: in organizations, this means training employees to be vigilant against AI-enabled scams just as they learned to be wary of phishing links in the past; in society, it means fostering an understanding that not everything we see or hear in the digital realm can be taken at face value and that security is a shared responsibility.

There are reasons for optimism. The same technologies that introduce risk can be harnessed for defense. AI can sift through enormous logs to detect anomalies indicative of a breach or simulate attacks to test our systems before criminals do. Machine learning models are being developed to identify deepfakes with increasing sophistication, and initiatives are underway to authenticate content and restore trust. In the quantum arena, human ingenuity has already produced quantum-proof algorithms and even quantum-based communication methods, proving that we are not helpless in the face of new physics. International collaborations are forming to ensure a coordinated response – a recognition that in a connected world, no nation or company can secure itself in isolation.

Data and foresight have been our allies in this chapter. We cited forecasts and statistics (from the explosive growth of deepfake incidents to the projected timeline of quantum computers) not to alarm, but to anchor our strategies in reality. These data points paint a clear picture that threats are escalating, but they also inform evidence-based action plans. For example, knowing that deepfake fraud losses could approach $40 billion in a few years provides urgency to implement verification controls now; knowing that, while experts differ on exact timelines, many assessments suggest that the probability of a cryptographically relevant quantum computer increases significantly during the 2030s, but near certainty by the 2030s guides us to a reasonable timeline – urgent but not panicked – for completing the cryptographic transition by around 2030. It's a delicate balance between addressing current crises (like ransomware and deepfakes already affecting us) and preparing for future ones (like quantum decryption). The prudent approach, as highlighted throughout, is to tackle both: enhance our current defenses with AI-aware threat modeling and deepfake countermeasures, even as we lay the groundwork for quantum-safe systems.

We also saw that technology alone is not a panacea. Organizational measures (policies, user education, incident response planning) and collaborative frameworks are equally critical. A company might have the best deepfake detector in the world, but if its employees are not trained on new verification protocols or if legal ambiguity slows down response to an attack, the advantage is lost. Similarly, all the brilliant cryptography research means little if businesses do not implement it; hence, governance steps in to provide incentives and deadlines. A key takeaway is the need for holistic resilience: combining technical robustness, human awareness, and adaptive governance. This multi-layered resilience is our best bet to navigate the turbulence of the AI and quantum era.

Looking ahead, AI and quantum security risks will increasingly intersect with identity, software assurance, data protection, and governance. We may see AI and quantum intertwine – for instance, AI might help design better quantum algorithms (for good or ill), or quantum computing might eventually aid AI in breaking encryption in novel ways. The security field will need to continuously reinvent itself. Concepts like *Zero Trust architecture* (never trusting any single input and always verifying) will become even more pertinent in a world of perfect deepfakes and remote workforces. Cryptographic agility might evolve further to *"algorithmic agility"* for AI – meaning systems that can quickly swap in improved AI models or filters when new threats emerge (like a new type of deepfake or an unforeseen model exploit).

In concluding this chapter, we reinforce that while the threats we face are unprecedented, they are not insurmountable. Humanity has a track record of confronting great technological disruptions with equal parts innovation and regulation. Just as we eventually tamed earlier cybersecurity crises with layered defenses and international norms, we can do so again on this new frontier. The keys will be foresight, unity, and a commitment to ethics. By anticipating threats early (as we are doing by addressing quantum risk before Q-Day, or AI risk before it grows uncontrollable), by sharing knowledge and solutions across the globe, and by ensuring that our pursuit of security upholds the values of privacy, freedom, and trust, we stand the best chance of thriving in the AI and quantum era.

In summary, navigating AI and quantum-era threats requires charting a course that embraces cutting-edge security technology, forward-thinking governance, and cultural adaptation. It is a journey already underway – one that will define cybersecurity for a generation. Those organizations and nations that recognize these shifts and act decisively will significantly enhance their resilience. Those that ignore the signs do so at their peril. As we close this chapter, the charge is clear: the future is quantum and AI-driven, so our defenses and governance must be as well. The next chapters will continue to build on these insights, exploring specific domains and case studies where these new principles are put into practice and how we can continuously update our strategies in a world where change is the only constant.

CHAPTER 6

Incident Response and Forensic Readiness

In today's cyber threat landscape, it is no longer sufficient to focus only on preventing attacks – organizations must assume that incidents will happen and prepare to detect and respond swiftly. Incident response (IR) refers to the organized approach to addressing and managing the aftermath of a security breach or cyberattack. Forensic readiness is closely related, describing an organization's preparedness to efficiently collect, preserve, and analyze digital evidence when an incident occurs. Together, these capabilities ensure that when a cyber incident strikes, the damage can be contained and the path to recovery is clear. All industries, from finance and healthcare to manufacturing and government, face cyber threats and therefore require robust incident response and forensic readiness as part of their security architecture.

Building detection and response into the architecture means designing systems, networks, and processes with security monitoring and incident-handling capabilities from the ground up. Rather than treating incident response as an afterthought, leading organizations integrate sensors, logging, alerting mechanisms, and well-defined response plans into their IT infrastructure and business workflows. This proactive approach allows for faster detection of anomalies, limiting of an attacker's dwell time, and more effective containment of threats. It also facilitates forensic investigations by ensuring the necessary data will be available when needed. For example, an ecommerce company with built-in monitoring can quickly spot suspicious transactions or malware activity on servers, and it will have logs and system snapshots ready for forensic analysis if those warnings signal a breach. In contrast, an organization that lacks detection controls may remain unaware of an intrusion for months, and even if it suspects one, it might not have the evidence required to understand or prove what happened.

Another critical driver for strong incident response and forensic readiness is the cost and impact of incidents. Security studies in recent years highlight sobering statistics: the

A. Gupta and S. Mittal, *Foundations of Modern Information Security*,
https://doi.org/10.1007/979-8-8688-2558-3_6

average time to identify and contain a breach can stretch for months, and the financial costs of such incidents continue to rise annually. The cost and operational impact of breaches continue to rise, and organizations face not just direct financial losses but also reputational damage and regulatory penalties. These trends underscore that rapid detection and response aren't just IT problems - they are business imperatives. A well-prepared incident response program can dramatically reduce the mean time to detect (MTTD) and mean time to respond (MTTR) to incidents, thereby limiting damage. Moreover, many industries now have strict regulations requiring prompt reporting of certain security incidents (for instance, data breach notification laws often mandate disclosure within days). Organizations with forensic readiness can more quickly gather the facts needed for such notifications and for informing affected customers or authorities, thereby staying compliant and maintaining trust.

This chapter will explore how to build and mature an incident response capability and achieve forensic readiness in a practical, implementation-focused way. We will examine established frameworks and models - including those from NIST, SANS, and MITRE - that guide incident response planning and operations. We will discuss incident response maturity models that help organizations assess and improve their readiness over time. The chapter also covers how to plan for forensic data collection and evidence handling before an incident ever happens, ensuring that when something does occur, the organization can jump into action with minimal confusion. Communication and containment, two crucial aspects during the heat of incident response, are addressed in detail: we will look at how to coordinate among internal teams and external stakeholders and how to effectively isolate or mitigate threats to prevent further harm. Throughout, the emphasis is on an implementation-focused approach - providing actionable guidance that can be applied across various industries and organizational sizes. By combining best practices from NIST's guidelines, the SANS Institute's process recommendations, and MITRE's threat intelligence frameworks, any organization can embed detection and response into its architecture and cultivate a state of continuous preparedness. The end result is a cyber defense posture that not only guards against attacks but also minimizes the impact of those that inevitably occur.

Incident Response Frameworks and Maturity Models

Before delving into the specifics of building incident response into an architecture, it's important to understand the standard frameworks that define the incident response process. Two widely referenced models come from the National Institute of Standards and Technology (NIST) and the SANS Institute. Both provide structured approaches to incident handling, and they overlap considerably in practice. NIST's incident handling guidance outlines a four-phase incident response life cycle: Preparation; Detection and Analysis; Containment, Eradication, and Recovery; and Post-Incident Activity. In parallel, the SANS Institute teaches a six-step process that expands on similar concepts: Preparation, Identification, Containment, Eradication, Recovery, and Lessons Learned. The difference is mainly in terminology and grouping - SANS separates Identification (detecting and confirming an incident) as its own step and breaks out Containment, Eradication, and Recovery as three distinct steps, whereas NIST's model combines those into a single broader phase. In essence, both frameworks cover the same journey: beforehand you must prepare, during an incident you detect it, contain the damage and eliminate the threat, and afterward you restore operations and learn from the experience. For example, when a malware outbreak happens, both NIST and SANS would have you do the following in some form: recognize there is an issue (Detection/Identification), take immediate actions to stop the malware's spread (Containment), remove the malware from all affected systems (Eradication), bring systems back to normal operation (Recovery), and then analyze how it happened and how to prevent it next time (Lessons Learned/Post-Incident Activity).

While these frameworks tell you what needs to be done at a high level, organizations vary widely in how well they can perform each of these steps. This is where incident response maturity models come into play. An incident response maturity model provides a way to evaluate an organization's proficiency and sophistication in handling incidents. Rather than a binary state of either having or not having an incident response capability, maturity models recognize a spectrum of development. One common approach is based on the Capability Maturity Model (CMM) concept, rating processes on levels from ad hoc and chaotic up to highly optimized. In the context of incident response, a typical five-level maturity scale might be defined as follows:

Initial (Ad Hoc): Incident response processes are unorganized or reactive. There may be no formal plan or team; if a security incident occurs, the response is improvised on the spot. Documentation is minimal or nonexistent. Success depends largely on individual heroics or luck rather than repeatable procedures. At this stage, the organization is often caught off-guard by incidents and might struggle with even basic containment or communication. For example, a small company experiencing its first major cyber incident might scramble to figure out who should do what, since no predetermined roles or playbooks exist.

Repeatable (Basic): Some processes are established and can be repeated for similar incidents, though they may be informal. The organization has perhaps defined a basic incident response plan or designated an incident response lead. There is an awareness of common incident types and a rudimentary ability to respond to them. However, procedures are not comprehensive, and not all staff are trained on them. There is still heavy reliance on a few key people. For instance, the IT department may know to unplug a compromised server and restore from backup if ransomware hits, because they did it once before, but there might not be formal documentation or broader organizational involvement.

Defined (Standardized): The incident response process is fully documented and institutionalized across the organization. There is a formal incident response plan, defined team roles (such as an Incident Manager, a Lead Investigator, a Communications Officer, etc.), and established procedures for various incident types. Playbooks or runbooks exist for handling scenarios like malware infections, denial-of-service attacks, or data breaches. Employees with incident response duties are trained and know their roles. The process is not just in the heads of a few individuals. At this stage, when an incident occurs, the response follows a known workflow, improving consistency and confidence.

Managed (Measured): The organization not only has defined processes but also measures and monitors the effectiveness of those processes. Key performance indicators (KPIs) are tracked, such as how quickly incidents are detected, how long containment takes, or the number of incidents handled per quarter. There is a focus on quality and improvement. The incident response team might use metrics and post-incident analysis to identify bottlenecks or areas for improvement. Also at this level, the organization likely integrates threat intelligence feeds and advanced detection capabilities to better inform incident response. Management is engaged; for example, regular reports on incidents and response performance are provided to senior leadership.

Optimized (Adaptive/Continual Improvement): Incident response at this highest maturity level is a continuously improving, proactive capability. The organization learns from past incidents and from others in its industry, updating its processes, tools, and training regularly. Automation is utilized heavily to speed up response (e.g., using Security Orchestration, Automation, and Response – SOAR – tools to automatically isolate infected endpoints or block malicious IP addresses when certain triggers are met). The incident response function is deeply integrated into the organization's enterprise architecture and risk management. It's not just the security team's concern – system architects, software developers, and business continuity planners all incorporate incident response and recovery considerations into their designs and plans. At this level, the organization might also engage in regular threat hunting (proactively searching for threats that have evaded detection) and red team/blue team exercises or simulations to test and refine its capabilities. Lessons learned from incidents directly drive changes to security controls and even IT architecture (e.g., after a close call with an incident, the network might be further segmented or a new monitoring tool added to cover a visibility gap). The result is an agile, resilient incident response posture that adapts to new threats quickly.

Figure 6-1 presents an incident response maturity ladder ranging from ad hoc to optimized practices.

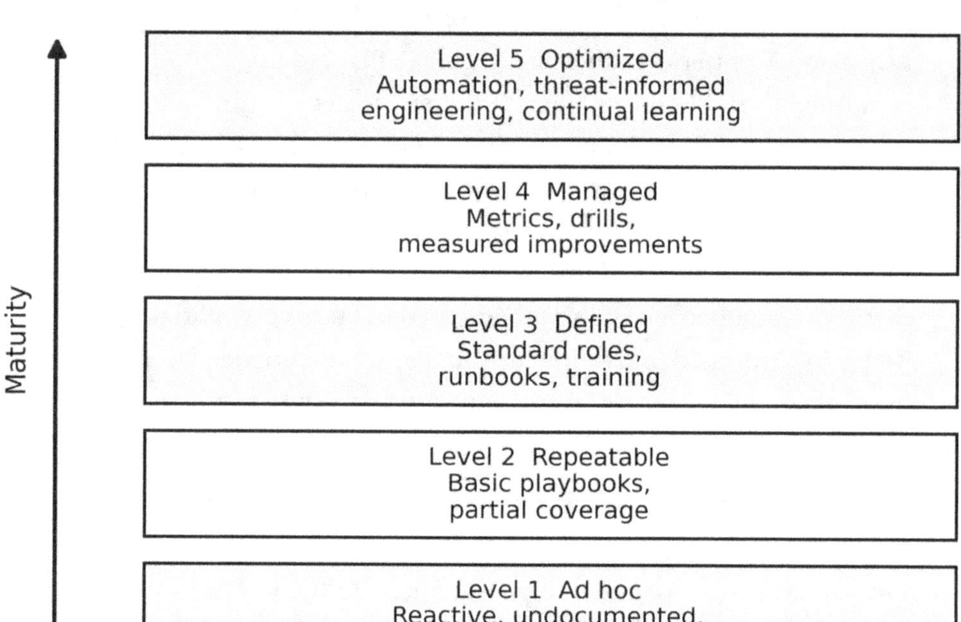

Figure 6-1. *Incident response maturity ladder from ad hoc to optimized*

Organizations can use maturity models to assess their current state and target improvements. For instance, a company might perform an incident response maturity assessment and determine that they are at a "Repeatable" level overall. They have some processes, but they lack comprehensive documentation and metrics. With that understanding, they can formulate a road map to reach the next levels - perhaps focusing on developing formal playbooks and conducting training to achieve the "Defined" level, then later implementing monitoring of response times and regular drills to reach "Managed," and so on. There are tools and frameworks to assist with such assessments. Industry groups like CREST and government bodies like ENISA have published assessment methodologies to quantify incident response maturity on scales (often numeric scales corresponding to levels). These typically evaluate multiple dimensions, including technology, processes, and people. For example, an assessment might look at whether the organization has an incident response policy, whether there is a dedicated team with clearly assigned roles, what technologies (like SIEM, intrusion detection systems, endpoint detection and response agents) are deployed for incident detection, how evidence is collected and preserved, and how lessons learned are fed back into the program. Scoring high in all these areas would indicate a mature capability.

One key insight from maturity models is that advancing in maturity is not just about buying better tools – it's equally about process and governance. Many organizations in the "Initial" or "Basic" stages try to jump straight to using advanced security technologies but may not derive full benefit because their processes and staff readiness are lacking. Conversely, an organization at the "Optimized" stage tends to make effective use of whatever tools they have, because they have solid processes, skilled responders, and a culture of continuous improvement.

As part of achieving higher maturity, organizations often align with well-known frameworks and best practices. NIST's guidelines, like the NIST Cybersecurity Framework, emphasize integrating incident response into overall risk management. NIST Cybersecurity Framework 2.0 aligns incident response activities with the broader lifecycle of cybersecurity risk management: Govern, Identify, Protect, Detect, Respond, and Recover. Preparation and lessons learned processes tie into governance and identification of risks, detection and analysis aligns with the detect function, and response/recovery align with respond and recover functions, respectively. What this means in practice is that a mature incident response is not an isolated technical task – it's embedded in how the organization governs its security and continuity. Meanwhile, the SANS Institute's recommendations (commonly taught in SANS courses and materials) provide very practical checklists and procedures for each phase of incident response, which organizations often adopt in their playbooks. For example, SANS emphasizes having a clear preparation phase including policy, communication plans, and incident response team training; then, during identification, carefully documenting all details; and in lessons learned, writing a post-incident report and holding a follow-up meeting to review what happened.

MITRE's contributions to incident response maturity are somewhat different: MITRE provides frameworks like the ATT&CK knowledge base, which catalogs adversary tactics and techniques observed in real-world attacks. Mature organizations leverage MITRE ATT&CK to improve their detection and analysis capabilities – essentially mapping their security monitoring and alerts to known techniques. For instance, if an organization knows that attackers often use a technique like "PowerShell scripting" for malicious purposes (as documented in MITRE ATT&CK), they will ensure their logging and detection systems are tuned to catch unusual PowerShell usage on their endpoints. MITRE ATT&CK becomes a lens through which they evaluate coverage of potential attack methods, helping to identify gaps. Additionally, frameworks like MITRE D3FEND (a knowledge base of defensive techniques) can guide the selection of countermeasures, and MITRE's Shield framework discusses active defense and deception techniques that advanced (optimized level) organizations might employ. In summary, MITRE's resources help an organization move from a reactive stance to a proactive and threat-informed defense, which is a hallmark of higher maturity.

To illustrate, consider how a very mature Security Operations Center (SOC) team operates during incident detection and analysis: They receive an alert from their SIEM that flags unusual outbound traffic from a server. A less mature team might just see a generic alert and start a slow, manual investigation. But a mature team has context – their SIEM or EDR tool might automatically label the alert with likely ATT&CK tactics (e.g., "Data Exfiltration" technique) and the team, through experience and playbooks, immediately knows to check certain logs (like DNS requests, firewall logs) and to capture a memory dump of the affected server for forensic analysis. They also might cross-reference threat intelligence to see if the detected IP or malware signature is associated with a known threat actor. Because of predefined procedures, they can move quickly to containment while still gathering evidence, rather than scrambling to figure out what to do. This level of orchestration and speed is achieved only after climbing the maturity curve through diligent improvements over time.

In practice, improving incident response maturity is an ongoing effort. Organizations should start by honestly assessing where they stand. If you find that incident responsibilities are ill-defined and responses are chaotic, focus on establishing the basics: create an incident response plan, assign an incident response coordinator, and ensure the team knows the plan. If the basics are there but inconsistent, work on documentation and training to standardize the response. Once standard procedures exist, start collecting data on how well they work – conduct drills or tabletop exercises to simulate incidents and then measure the response (e.g., how long did it take to recognize the incident, were the correct actions taken in the right order, etc.). Use those metrics to drive improvements (maybe you discover that off-hours response is slow because the on-call list is out of date – a fix would be to update contact procedures and rotate on-call duties). At higher levels, consider investing in technologies like centralized log management, intrusion detection systems, and automated response platforms, but integrate them with clear processes. And always incorporate the feedback loop: after each incident (or exercise), do a post-mortem analysis to capture lessons. This might lead to updating policies, adding a new step in a playbook, improving network visibility, or providing additional training to staff. Over time, these incremental improvements, guided by a maturity model, will significantly strengthen the organization's incident response and forensic readiness.

Forensic Planning and Data Handling

A crucial aspect of forensic readiness is thinking ahead about what data will be needed during an incident investigation and how that data will be collected and preserved. Forensic planning involves making deliberate preparations so that if a security incident occurs, the organization can immediately begin gathering evidence without delay or confusion. This reduces investigation time and increases the likelihood of understanding the incident's cause and impact. In parallel, proper data handling ensures that the evidence collected will be admissible (if needed for legal action), trustworthy, and useful for figuring out what happened.

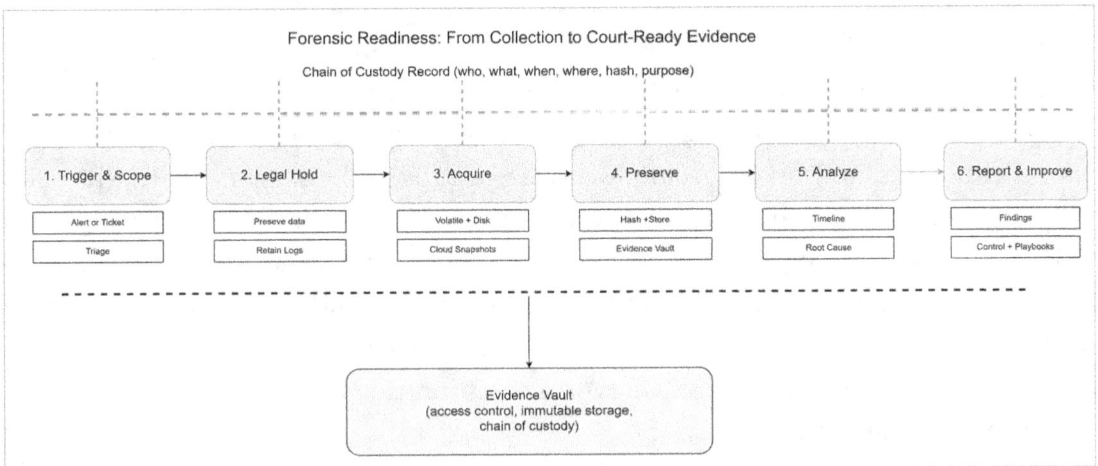

Figure 6-2. *Forensic readiness pipeline from trigger to court-ready evidence*

At its core, forensic readiness can be boiled down to a simple principle: don't wait for a breach to start figuring out where your logs and evidence are. Instead, identify in advance the kinds of incidents that are most likely or most damaging to your business, and ensure that if those incidents occur, you will have the data to respond. One recommended approach is to define a set of likely business scenarios that require digital evidence. For example, scenarios could include the following: an external hacker compromises a server, an insider leaks confidential data, a malware/ransomware outbreak on user workstations, or a fraudulent financial transaction is detected. For each scenario, think about what evidence would be needed to investigate and resolve it. Would you need web server logs? Database transaction logs? Endpoint forensic images? Network traffic captures? By mapping this out, you can highlight which data sources are critical to collect and retain. Often, this exercise reveals gaps – perhaps you realize that while you have firewall logs, you are not logging DNS queries, which might be vital for tracing malware communication. Or you might find that database logs are only kept for one week, which would be insufficient to investigate a stealthy data leak that could span months.

Logging and monitoring are the foundations of forensic readiness. Ensuring comprehensive logging is enabled on systems, applications, and network devices is a primary task of forensic planning. Key systems should have audit logging turned on with sufficient detail. This includes operating system logs (for logins, file access, system events), application logs (especially for any custom or critical applications), database logs (recording queries and changes), and security device logs (firewalls, intrusion detection systems, etc.). It's not enough to just turn on logging; logs must also be collected and centralized, so they aren't lost if a device is compromised. Using a Security Information and Event Management (SIEM) system or a centralized log server is a common practice. A SIEM can ingest logs from various sources across the enterprise - servers, endpoints, network gear, cloud services - and store them in one place while also providing tools to search and correlate events. From a forensic perspective, having logs centralized means investigators have a one-stop shop to query what happened across multiple systems during an incident timeline, rather than having to log in to each device (which might be risky or too slow during an incident). It also means that if an attacker tries to cover their tracks by deleting logs on a compromised machine, copies of those logs still exist in the central repository.

When configuring logging, detail and retention are important considerations. Logs should contain enough detail to be forensically useful. For instance, HTTP access logs on a web server should log client IP, timestamp, requested URL, and response code at minimum. Windows event logs should include authentication events and object access events if possible. Endpoint detection agents might log process creations, loaded modules, or registry changes. It's better to err on the side of logging too much than too little, given modern storage and cloud archive capabilities- but one must also balance noise and signal. Proper tuning (filtering out known benign events, focusing on critical systems) can help manage volume. Retention policies determine how long logs are kept. For forensic readiness, longer retention is generally better, within the constraints of storage and regulations. Some breaches aren't discovered for months; if your logs only go back 30 days, you might miss the early indicators of an attack that began 90 days ago. Many organizations aim to retain critical logs for at least six months to a year. Certain industries and regulations might dictate specific retention periods (e.g., payment card industry guidelines or data protection laws might require retaining security logs for a year or more). The logs should also be protected from tampering - write-once storage or strict access controls should prevent attackers or even admins from modifying historical logs. It's common to implement controls like checksums or digital signatures on log files to detect any tampering.

Beyond logs, planning for data capture during incidents is another key element. Some evidence cannot realistically be collected continuously due to size or sensitivity (e.g., full packet captures of all network traffic would be huge, and recording employees' computer screens or keystrokes at all times would be invasive and impractical). However, you can plan to capture such data selectively when needed. This means having tools and procedures ready. For instance, a good forensic readiness plan will include having "jump kits" or readily available tools for incident responders. A jump kit typically contains portable storage media, forensic software, and hardware tools necessary to collect evidence. In a physical sense, it could be a laptop pre-loaded with analysis software, external hard drives, write blockers (devices that allow you to image a hard drive without accidentally modifying it), bootable USB drives for imaging systems, network tap devices or packet capture tools, and checklists/documentation forms for investigators. In a cloud-centric environment, a jump kit might include scripts or automation playbooks to quickly snapshot virtual machines or copy cloud service logs to a safe repository when an incident is declared.

One example of preparation: ensure that disk imaging and memory capture tools are available and that staff know how to use them. If a critical server is suspected to be compromised, forensic best practice is often to take a full disk image and a memory dump of that server for offline analysis (rather than poking around on the live system, which can alter data). But doing this requires tools such as commercial forensic suites, endpoint response tooling, disk imaging utilities such as dd or dc3dd, and memory acquisition tools such as WinPmem or LiME and knowledge of how to capture the image in a forensically sound manner (using write blockers, verifying hashes of the image). As part of readiness, an organization might pre-install lightweight agents or at least have an approved procedure on each system that can be triggered to collect volatile data. For instance, some companies deploy an agent that can, on command, grab crucial forensic artifacts from an endpoint (running processes, network connections, memory snapshot) and send them to a secure server. This way, when an incident occurs, the team can remotely invoke data capture before an attacker notices and tries to wipe traces.

Data handling procedures are just as vital as data collection. Once evidence is collected, how will it be stored and who can access it? Establishing a clear chain of custody process ensures that evidence is admissible and trustworthy. Chain of custody means you maintain documentation of who collected each piece of evidence, at what time, on what media, and every time it changes hands or is accessed, you log that event. This creates a paper (or digital) trail that could be presented in court to show the evidence was not tampered with and can be trusted as accurate. Even if legal action is not anticipated, maintaining a chain of custody is a good discipline because it reduces the chance of accidental alteration or loss of evidence. A forensic readiness plan might include standard forms or digital tracking systems for evidence handling.

Securing evidence storage is another component. Digital evidence should be stored in a secure, access-controlled repository. This could be an encrypted drive or server that only the incident response and security team can access. Some organizations maintain a dedicated forensic evidence server or vault. It's prudent to isolate this storage from normal network access to avoid it being targeted by adversaries. Also, consider off-site backups of evidence - if the incident is severe (say it involves ransomware that encrypts everything), you wouldn't want your collected evidence to be lost to the same attack. Thus, having offline copies or cloud backups of key evidence might be part of the plan.

Forensic planning also extends to legal and privacy considerations. Data protection laws (like GDPR in Europe, various state privacy laws in the United States, etc.) might restrict what kind of data you can collect and how you can use it. For example, logs that include personal data or employee communications need to be handled in compliance with privacy regulations - you might need to inform employees about monitoring or ensure that certain sensitive personal information is masked or protected. Working with legal counsel when developing forensic readiness policies is advisable to ensure that evidence collection does not inadvertently violate laws or regulations. Additionally, if you suspect that you might involve law enforcement in certain incidents (for instance, if you suffer a major breach of customer data or an incident involving serious criminal activity like extortion), then part of forensic readiness is understanding how to interface with law enforcement. This might include knowing when to call them, what they might ask for, and how to preserve evidence in a way that aligns with their requirements. Law enforcement agencies may even provide guidelines for evidence preservation (in some regions, police or cybercrime units will help organizations by reviewing their incident response plans for forensic soundness).

Let's break down a practical checklist for forensic readiness to illustrate the actions an organization should take:

Identify Critical Assets and Likely Incident Scenarios: Make an inventory of critical systems (servers, databases, cloud services, etc.) and data. Consider how they could be attacked or misused. Prioritize scenarios that would have a high impact on these assets. This prioritization helps focus forensic preparations on what matters most.

Enable and Enhance Logging: For each critical asset and scenario, determine which logs or data sources would provide evidence. Ensure those logs are enabled and configured to capture necessary details. For instance, on critical servers, turn on process tracking and file access auditing; on network devices, turn on connection logging; etc. Configure these systems to send logs to a central SIEM or log server in real time.

Ensure Log Preservation and Protection: Configure log retention to cover a reasonable window (e.g., 6–12 months for important systems). Implement safeguards so that attackers cannot easily erase logs (e.g., logging to a remote server that an attacker on the local machine cannot access). Regularly test that log collection is working (it's unfortunately common to assume logging is happening until an incident reveals that a logging agent was misconfigured months ago and you have gaps).

Deploy Monitoring and Detection Tools: To build detection into the architecture, use tools like Intrusion Detection/Prevention Systems (IDS/IPS) on the network, Endpoint Detection and Response (EDR) agents on hosts, and possibly honeypots or other sensors where appropriate. These tools not only alert you to potential incidents but also record valuable forensic information (e.g., an EDR solution can often show a timeline of processes and events on a host leading up to and during an attack, which is gold for investigators). Make sure these tools cover as much of the environment as possible (including cloud workloads, remote laptops, etc., as relevant).

Establish Evidence Collection Procedures: Document step-by-step procedures for how to collect evidence for different types of incidents. For instance, if malware is detected on a PC, the procedure might state: do not turn off the PC (since valuable memory data would be lost), instead isolate it from the network, then run a memory capture tool and collect pertinent log files, and after that consider shutting down the machine for disk imaging. If an incident involves network intrusion, the procedure might involve capturing a packet trace or flow records from the network at the time of the incident. These procedures should be in simple language and available to the response team (potentially as part of an Incident Response Plan appendix or playbook).

Prepare Forensic Tools and Access: Ensure the team has the necessary software (and licenses if commercial tools are used) readily available. This may include forensic imaging software, analysis tools (for analyzing malware or parsing log data), and hardware (spare storage drives, write blockers, etc.). If certain systems require administrative access to pull data (like a cloud platform or a database), set up a mechanism where responders can get that access quickly (perhaps a break-glass account or an emergency procedure to get admin credentials) without wasting time hunting for passwords in the middle of an incident. The idea is to remove any unnecessary delays between detection and evidence gathering.

Secure Evidence Handling and Storage: Define where digital evidence will be stored and how it will be labeled. For example, decide that any forensic disk images will be stored on an encrypted external drive labeled with the case identifier and that drive will be kept in a locked cabinet (if physical) or in a restricted file share (if digital). Use case or ticket numbers to track evidence items and record details like hash values of files (to detect tampering). Train the team on using hash algorithms (like SHA-256) to fingerprint collected files or images so that if anyone questions integrity later, you can prove the file hasn't changed by comparing hash values.

Integrate Forensic Steps into Incident Response Plans: Make sure your incident response plan or playbooks explicitly include forensic actions. For example, during the detection/analysis phase of the plan, add tasks like "analysts should gather and preserve logs and relevant data from affected systems" and list who is responsible for doing that. During containment, include guidance like "if isolating a system, attempt to collect volatile data (memory, running processes) before cutting power, if possible." Essentially, responders should not have to choose between stopping the attack and saving evidence – the plan should facilitate doing both in sequence and in parallel.

Training and Roles: Identify who on your team will handle the forensic tasks. Not every IT administrator is familiar with forensic techniques, and that's okay – but someone should be. If you have a dedicated security team or SOC, some members should be trained in forensic collection and analysis. If you don't have in-house expertise, consider training programs or having a retainer with a digital forensics firm. Part of forensic readiness might be deciding in advance that "if we face X scenario, we will call in our retained incident response consultants to assist" and having that contract and contact information ready. Many organizations indeed maintain an Incident Response Retainer with a security firm, so that expert help is one phone call away in a crisis.

Practice and Review: Like any aspect of incident response, practicing is key. Conduct drills where the team must collect evidence for a simulated incident. For example, stage a scenario where a file server is acting oddly (perhaps by using a test system and creating some dummy malicious activity), then see if the team can capture the relevant logs, identify the fake malware, and follow chain-of-custody procedures correctly. Afterward, review what went well and what didn't. Maybe the team found that the central log system was missing logs from that server - a gap to fix. Or perhaps the memory capture tool wasn't installed and had to be hurriedly downloaded - a sign to pre-install it. These exercises greatly improve real incident readiness.

It's also useful to consider special data types. For instance, if your business relies heavily on databases, ensure you have database audit logs and maybe even the capability to do point-in-time recovery (which can help in investigating what changed in the database and when). If you maintain web services, consider enabling full HTTP request logging or transaction tracing. For cloud services like Microsoft 365 or AWS/Azure, enable their security auditing features (like AWS CloudTrail logs, Azure Activity Logs, Microsoft 365 audit logs), and make sure you know how to retrieve them quickly. In short, cover each technological environment in use. Mobile devices, IoT devices, and industrial control systems (ICS) each have their own logging and forensic peculiarities - if they are in scope for your organization, include them in the plan. For ICS, for example, forensic readiness might involve regularly backing up configurations of programmable logic controllers (PLCs) and logging operator actions so that if a cyber incident or malfunction occurs, you have baseline data and logs to investigate without halting an entire plant.

Another aspect of data handling is analysis - once data is collected, what do you do with it? Forensic analysis can be complex, involving examining disk images for hidden malware, analyzing memory dumps for signs of injected code, or tracing an attacker's steps through log timelines. As part of planning, ensure analysts have tools to analyze common evidence forms: tools for log analytics (even something simple like grep and text parsing scripts, or more advanced like using the SIEM's query languages), malware analysis sandboxes to detonate suspicious files safely, and forensic suites to comb through disk images. Have reference materials available - like a knowledge base of common artifact locations (e.g., knowing that on Windows, user credentials might be found in certain registry hives, or that browser history is stored in specific files - these details help when analyzing an image). Senior responders should mentor juniors in what to look for during investigations.

Lastly, consider the post-incident data needs. Often, after a major incident, the question arises: How do we ensure this doesn't happen again? The forensic data collected can be turned into lessons and improvements. For instance, forensic analysis might reveal that an attacker used a particular legitimate tool for malicious purposes (living-off-the-land), which bypassed detection. The team can then update monitoring rules to flag that behavior in the future. Or analysis might show the attack timeline, indicating it took 20 minutes from initial compromise to internal pivot – which informs how fast containment needs to be in the future. Capturing these insights and updating both security controls and response plans is part of the continuous improvement we discussed earlier.

In summary, forensic planning and data handling are about being proactive: planning today what data you will need and how you will manage it during tomorrow's breach. By investing time in setting up logging, gathering the right tools, and defining evidence procedures, an organization essentially "front-loads" some of the work, so that during an incident, the team can focus on analysis and decisions rather than scrambling for information. This not only speeds up incident response (since evidence is readily at hand) but also strengthens the organization's position if any legal or compliance issues arise from the incident. It demonstrates due diligence – being able to show, for example, that you have an evidence log and forensic data from a breach can help in regulatory investigations or insurance claims. For all these reasons, forensic readiness is a crucial element of modern cybersecurity architecture. An organization that achieves it will significantly reduce the chaos and uncertainty that otherwise accompany cyber incidents.

Communication and Containment

During a cybersecurity incident, two of the most critical and challenging tasks are communication and containment. Communication refers to how information is shared about the incident – both internally within the organization (among technical teams, management, legal, etc.) and externally (to customers, regulators, law enforcement, and the public). Containment refers to the actions taken to limit the incident's impact and stop the threat from causing further harm. Both must be carried out under pressure, often simultaneously, and, if done poorly, can exacerbate the situation. Therefore, building strong communication protocols and containment strategies into your incident response plan and architecture is essential for a resilient response.

Incident Communication

When an incident strikes, having a clear communication plan is as important as the technical steps of containment. Without organized communication, efforts can become disjointed: teams might duplicate work or overlook critical steps, management might be left in the dark or get misinformed, and external messaging might be inconsistent or legally non-compliant. A well-defined communication plan removes confusion by answering who needs to be informed, about what, how quickly, by whom, and via what channel.

Internal Communication: The moment an incident is identified, the right people inside the organization need to know. Typically, the first person to recognize a potential incident (say, a SOC analyst who sees an alert or an employee who notices ransomware on their PC) should know whom to contact first - often this is the incident response team or a specific Incident Manager on duty. Many organizations set up a dedicated incident response communications channel. This could be a specialized chat channel (e.g., a Microsoft Teams or Slack channel set aside for the incident), a bridged phone line or conference call for real-time discussion (sometimes called a "war room" call), or an incident management system where updates are posted. The method can vary, but the key is that everyone involved in the response is connected and seeing the same information.

One good practice is establishing an incident notification matrix. This is usually a document or table that outlines, for various severity levels of incidents, who must be notified and within what time frame. For example, for a low-severity incident (minor malware on a single workstation), the matrix might say: notify the SOC and the local IT support within one hour, no need to inform upper management immediately. For a high-severity incident (say a widespread ransomware attack crippling multiple systems or a significant data breach), it might require: notify the CISO and CIO immediately (24×7), inform the CEO and board within a few hours, involve legal counsel and corporate communications soon after, and so on. These predefined escalation paths remove ambiguity. During an emergency, people shouldn't be debating "Do we need to tell the executives about this?" - the plan should already specify when it's necessary to escalate.

It's also important to have contact information readily available for all key stakeholders. The incident response plan should include an up-to-date contact list: phone numbers (including after-hours cell numbers) and emails for the incident response team members, IT system owners, department heads, corporate communications team, legal team, external partners (like a cyber insurance breach coach or forensics firm if you have a retainer), and law enforcement contacts if appropriate. Some organizations even maintain encrypted contact lists on physical paper or offline in case systems are down during an incident (e.g., a ransomware event might take out email systems, so having hard copies of phone trees can save time).

Using standard communication tools is helpful. Many companies adopt an incident management platform or even use ticketing systems to track incident status and communications. The advantage is that all updates, decisions, and actions taken can be logged in one place, creating a timeline that is useful both for managing the incident in real-time and for later analysis. It also helps shift work between team members as shifts change, because the history is recorded. Even if a formal tool isn't used, at minimum maintain a written log of events and actions as the incident unfolds.

Maintaining a clear chain of command is another factor in internal communication. It should be clear who the Incident Commander or Manager is for a given incident. This person is responsible for overall coordination – they don't necessarily do all the technical work, but they ensure that communication is flowing and that tasks are assigned. They will call in additional resources if needed, escalate issues that require management decisions (like shutting down a critical system), and make sure the team isn't missing anything obvious. When people know who is in charge, they are more likely to route information to that person and follow the decisions made, preventing chaos. Larger organizations often have trained incident commanders or a rotating duty officer for this role. In smaller setups, it might be the IT manager or security lead by default.

Incident response also depends on the well-being and effectiveness of the people doing the work. During a long-running incident, security analysts, IT operators, application owners, business teams, legal, communications, and recovery teams may all be working under high pressure for many hours or days. If these teams are exhausted, missing information, or unclear on decision rights, the quality of response decisions will decline. A strong incident communication plan should therefore include not only technical updates but also basic support for the responders themselves.

The incident commander should establish a sustainable operating rhythm early. This includes assigning shifts, rotating responders before fatigue becomes a problem, making sure food and rest breaks are available during extended response windows, and keeping a clear handoff record when teams change shifts. The response team should also know where to find current facts, open decisions, recovery priorities, and business constraints. Without that shared context, teams may repeat work, make conflicting changes, or delay recovery because they are unsure who can approve a decision.

Organizations should also be ready to augment teams when the incident exceeds internal capacity. This may include bringing in additional infrastructure staff, application owners, legal support, communications staff, cloud platform specialists, or external incident response partners. The goal is not only to recover faster, but to recover safely. A tired team working without clear information can accidentally destroy evidence, restore infected systems, or make public statements before facts are confirmed. Taking care of responders is therefore part of operational resilience, not a soft or secondary concern.

External Communication: Depending on the nature of the incident, you may have obligations or strategic needs to communicate outside the company. This includes customers, regulators, law enforcement, partners, and possibly the media/general public. This aspect requires careful handling and often the involvement of legal and public relations experts. As part of your incident response plan, have a communications or public relations plan template ready for incidents. Many organizations prepare "breach notification" templates in advance - boilerplate language that can be quickly adapted to a specific incident to notify customers or the public. These templates are reviewed by legal and PR beforehand, because during an incident, you won't have much time to draft messages from scratch and get all the necessary approvals.

Regulatory communications are a big factor, especially as cybersecurity disclosure expectations continue to mature. Many jurisdictions have laws requiring notification of certain breaches within a tight timeframe. For example, GDPR in the EU generally requires notification to authorities within 72 hours of confirming a personal data breach, and various US state breach notification laws require notice to affected individuals without unreasonable delay. Sector-specific regulations, such as HIPAA for healthcare, may impose additional requirements. Public companies in the United States must also consider the SEC's cybersecurity disclosure rules. Under Item 1.05 of Form 8-K, a domestic registrant must disclose a material cybersecurity incident within four business days after determining that the incident is material, not simply four business days after discovery. The disclosure focuses on the material aspects of the nature, scope, and timing of the incident, as well as the material impact or reasonably likely material impact on the company. The materiality determination must be made without unreasonable delay and should consider both quantitative and qualitative factors, including operational, reputational, customer, vendor, litigation, and regulatory impacts. SEC guidance also distinguishes between incidents determined to be material, which belong under Item 1.05, and voluntary disclosure of incidents that are not yet determined to be material or are determined not to be material, which may be disclosed under another Form 8-K item such as Item 8.01. It is generally advisable to notify law enforcement in cases of serious incidents, such as deliberate cyberattacks by external actors (especially nation-state or organized crime), extortion attempts (like ransomware with a demand), or incidents involving large-scale theft of sensitive information. Law enforcement agencies can offer assistance, and involving them might also be part of legal/insurance requirements. Your plan should note when to consider contacting law enforcement (and which agency – local police, national cybercrime units, FBI in the US, etc., depending on jurisdiction and severity). However, this decision may depend on leadership approval and the specifics of the incident. Some companies may initially involve external incident response consultants who then coordinate with law enforcement on the company's behalf.

When communicating externally, consistency and accuracy are paramount. Mixed messages or incorrect information can cause panic or loss of trust. Typically, one person or team is designated as the spokesperson. For public/media, that's usually a communications executive or someone trained in crisis communication. Staff should be instructed not to discuss the incident publicly or on social media unless authorized – all external queries should be directed to the official spokesperson or PR team. Internally, employees might be curious or concerned; it might even be wise to send an internal memo once you have basic facts, to prevent rumors (e.g., "We are experiencing a network issue that appears to be a cybersecurity incident. The IT security team is responding. If you notice any suspicious activity, please report it to X. In the meantime, please do not turn off your computers unless instructed," etc.). This keeps your workforce informed and cooperative.

One must also consider communication security during an incident. If you suspect that your internal systems (like corporate email or chat) are compromised or being monitored by the attackers (which has happened in some breaches), you may need alternative channels for the response team. Some companies keep out-of-band communication methods for incident responders – for example, personal cell phones or a separate chat server that's isolated from the possibly breached network. The idea is to avoid tipping off an intruder that you're aware of them, especially if it's an insider threat or a sophisticated actor who might have visibility into your communications. Planning this in advance is wise: e.g., having a private WhatsApp group or phone call tree as a backup if corporate email is down or untrusted.

To illustrate good communication practice: Consider a scenario of a data breach where customer information is stolen. Internally, the incident team immediately sets up a conference bridge to coordinate the technical response. The incident manager notifies the CISO and legal counsel within the first hour. After initial containment steps, they draft an internal report of what is known so far. The CEO and other execs get a briefing by hour 3. Legal confirms that under relevant law, customer notification is required, so the communications team begins working with legal to draft a customer notice and press statement by hour 24. By hour 36, law enforcement is contacted with a summary of the breach and indicators of the attackers (IP addresses, etc.). Throughout this, the company releases a controlled public statement acknowledging a security incident and that an investigation is underway and promises to update with more details. They avoid speculation or admitting fault until facts are verified, in line with legal advice. Such a measured and pre-planned approach can greatly reduce reputational damage compared to a disorganized response where news leaks out before the company has formulated a response.

Containment Strategies

Containment is the act of limiting the scope and impact of an incident. Once you have detected a malicious activity or breach, you want to stop the "bleeding" as quickly as possible so that the problem does not worsen. However, containment is not as simple as pulling the plug on everything; it must be done thoughtfully to be effective without causing unnecessary collateral damage.

Different types of incidents require different containment tactics, but broadly speaking, containment can be viewed in two time horizons: short-term (immediate) containment and long-term (sustained) containment.

Short-Term Containment: These are quick actions taken to halt the attacker's activity or the spread of malware right now. They often involve isolating affected systems. For example, if a workstation is infected with ransomware and actively encrypting files, a short-term containment might be to disconnect that machine from the network (to stop it from accessing any more files or spreading to shared drives). If an intruder is actively exfiltrating data from a server, short-term containment could involve blocking the server's network connections or shutting down certain services. In a web application attack, it might mean temporarily taking the web application offline or enabling a web application firewall rule to block malicious traffic. These actions sometimes degrade service availability (like disconnecting a server will disrupt whatever business process it serves), but they are critical to prevent further compromise or data loss. A rule of thumb is to contain in the least destructive way possible, but prioritize stopping harm. For instance, instead of powering a server off immediately (which stops the attack but also wipes memory), one might simply disconnect its network cable or virtually isolate it so the attacker can't communicate with it, but the system stays running (allowing memory to be captured for evidence and possibly maintaining some services for users).

Long-Term Containment: After immediate threats are halted, there's often a need for interim solutions that allow some operations to continue while the environment is being cleaned and rebuilt. Long-term containment might involve applying temporary patches or workarounds, increasing monitoring on certain systems, or migrating operations to safe environments. For example, if a database is compromised, a long-term containment might be to fail over to a standby instance (that you have verified as clean) and sever connections from the compromised one, then keep the compromised system offline for a thorough forensic investigation. In a network breach scenario, long-term containment could include adding network segmentation – say you segment an affected part of the network off from the rest of the corporate network until you're sure the threat is eradicated. Users might be given alternate ways to do their work if their usual systems are isolated. The idea is to keep the business running in some capacity (albeit possibly reduced or with workaround processes) while you eradicate the threat and ensure systems are safe to fully restore.

Containment strategies should be planned during the preparation phase of incident response. Your incident response plan can include specific actions for containment for different scenarios. For instance, in a ransomware playbook, a containment step might read: "Disable file sharing on infected devices; remove affected devices from the network by disabling switch ports or network access control; temporarily take critical servers offline if there's evidence of infection spreading." In a suspected data breach playbook, you might have: "Geoblock network traffic to known attacker regions; change passwords or disable accounts that were used by the attacker; increase logging level on critical systems to catch any further malicious activity." Having these pre-planned saves time and ensures consistency.

Tools and architecture can significantly aid in containment. If your network is designed with segmentation (like isolating sensitive servers in their own VLANs, using internal firewalls), it's easier to cut off a segment that's affected from the rest of the environment. If you have endpoint management solutions, you might remotely quarantine a device (some EDR tools allow one-click isolation of a host, where it's cut off from all network except a connection back to the EDR server). If an organization has a software-defined network, it might push new rules rapidly across the network to block malicious traffic or quarantine subnets. Cloud environments offer security groups and access control lists that can be quickly tweaked – for instance, if an AWS server is compromised, you could apply a restrictive security group to it immediately to block all but investigator IP addresses.

It's crucial to identify all affected elements to be effectively contained. If you isolate one infected machine but the attacker has already moved to another, containment will fail. That's why the detection and analysis phase feeds into containment – you must rapidly scope out the incident. Using clues like logs of connections, the presence of malware on systems, or unusual account activity, responders should try to map out all machines, user accounts, or network segments that are part of the incident. Containment actions should then cover the entire scope. This might mean deploying an enterprise-wide script to cut off certain processes or block certain accounts if you suspect a widespread issue.

Another consideration is the balance between acting fast and preserving evidence. There is often a trade-off: the fastest way to stop something might be to power off a machine, but doing so will lose volatile memory that contains valuable forensic evidence (like the malware running in RAM or an attacker's in-memory tools). A best practice is to capture evidence before or concurrently with containment, if feasible and if it will not greatly delay stopping the damage. For example, if you can afford five extra minutes before disconnecting a server, use that time to dump its memory or copy key log files. In some cases, however, the risk is too high – e.g., a malware could be actively exfiltrating data or deleting files, and thc priority is to stop it immediately. Each situation calls for judgment, and that judgment improves with training and experience (hence why drills help, to practice making those calls). Document in your plan what the priorities are; generally, safety and preventing further harm come first, then evidence collection if possible second. If human safety or critical operations are at risk (consider incidents in industrial environments – sometimes the decision might involve shutting down a system that controls physical processes to prevent damage or injury), containment actions might even override concerns about data loss.

Who executes containment is another planning point. The incident response team will coordinate it, but you might need help from various IT ops teams. If you need to shut down a server, who has access to do that? If you need to block an IP at the firewall, is the network team on standby to assist? Identifying the people or teams responsible for specific containment actions and including them in the plan (or at least having their contact info) is important. Involving those teams in incident response exercises will ensure they know how to respond quickly when asked ("Network team: please block all traffic to our database subnet except from the application servers" – they should be able to do that without a long approval process in an emergency). Some organizations give the incident commander the authority to enact emergency changes, skipping normal change management, with the understanding that it's only done in critical situations and documented after the fact.

Let's consider some concrete containment techniques by scenario for clarity:

> **Malware Outbreak (e.g., Ransomware):** Immediately isolate infected machines from the network (unplug cable, turn off Wi-Fi, or use endpoint agent isolation). Temporarily disable shared network drives or put them in read-only mode to prevent encryption spread. If you know the malware's indicators (filenames, processes), use enterprise security tools to block or kill those processes on other machines. Possibly take down certain services (like an email server, if the malware is spreading via email) until they can be checked and cleaned. Notify users not to use certain systems if needed (e.g., "do not open email attachments until further notice" broadcast if that's the vector).
>
> **Unauthorized Access/Data Breach in Progress:** If an intruder is active in your environment, containment might involve cutting off their access. That could mean disabling the compromised user accounts (reset passwords or lock accounts thought to be hacked). If they came in through a VPN or remote access, cut that session and block the user or IP. If a web application is being exploited, you might change firewall rules or routing to redirect traffic from that app or even take the app offline for a short time. A fine point: sometimes incident handlers choose to monitor an intruder briefly before kicking them out, to understand what they're after or to identify all compromised systems. This is risky but can be useful. It requires coordination and is not typical unless working with intelligence teams or law enforcement who might want to trace the attacker. Most often, containment = kick them out as soon as you can do so thoroughly.

Denial of Service Attack: Containment might involve activating DDoS protection services, blocking offending IP addresses, or temporarily dropping certain types of traffic. This is a different kind of incident (availability impact rather than data loss), but the principle is to minimize service disruption.

Insider Threat: If an employee is identified as performing malicious actions (like an IT admin stealing data), containment might be more about access control: revoke their credentials, escort them off premises if serious, and secure any systems they had access to (change admin passwords, review accounts). It's a sensitive situation, often involving HR and legal.

Physical Device Loss (like a stolen laptop containing sensitive info): Containment includes remotely wiping the device if possible and changing credentials that were stored on it. It's partly IR, partly IT ops.

Containment in cloud environments has its nuances as well. In the cloud, you might not have a cable to pull - but you can isolate an instance by adjusting its security group (essentially a firewall policy). You can quarantine a workload by moving it to a separate virtual network. Many cloud providers have incident response guidance for containment, such as using versioning and immutability on storage (so an attacker can't easily delete logs or backups) or using cloud automation to quickly replicate a system to analyze it while stopping the original.

During containment, it's important to keep evaluating potential side effects. You should ask: If we shut this system down, what business process breaks? If we block this network segment, who will be impacted (perhaps the finance team cannot reach their servers, etc.)? That's where having the asset inventory and knowing the business importance of systems, which should be part of preparation, comes into play. Sometimes you deliberately choose a less disruptive containment method to avoid unnecessary business impact. For example, instead of shutting down a critical database that's under attack, you might temporarily disable just the account the attacker is using or block their IP, allowing legitimate users to continue working. Or you might put the database in read-only mode if the attack is trying to alter data, as a containment step that still allows queries. These nuanced decisions often need input from system owners or business stakeholders. In incident drills, including those stakeholders helps them understand that in a real incident, they might have to help decide trade-offs (like "we can contain now but it will cause an hour of outage, or we can wait 30 minutes to do it in a cleaner way but risk 30 more minutes of exposure - what do we do?").

After immediate containment, verifying that containment was successful is crucial. If malware was spreading, confirm that no new infections are happening. If an attacker was in the network, monitor to ensure they aren't still in via another backdoor. This often involves increased monitoring for a while after containment. In some cases, you might set traps - for instance, leave a honeypot system out to see if the attacker touches it now that their known access is cut (which could reveal another method they have). But generally, once contained, you move to eradication (cleaning everything up) and recovery (restoring services).

Communication and containment intersect heavily. When you are about to contain, communication is needed: technical teams need to know ("We are taking server X offline now"), management might need a heads-up if the containment will cause a visible outage ("We are temporarily disconnecting the customer portal, expect service disruption for 30 minutes"), and employees could need instructions ("All staff: as a precaution, please disconnect from the corporate VPN until further notice while we handle an issue"). Miscommunication here can lead to chaos - imagine the security team isolates a segment, but the IT helpdesk isn't told, and they get flooded with user complaints, or an executive sees a major system go down and panics because they weren't aware it was intentional containment. Thus, coordination is key: ideally, the Incident Manager coordinates the timing of containment actions with communications. Often, very fast-moving incidents mean containment comes first and explanations right after, which is fine as long as those explanations do come and are honest about what's being done.

One should also plan for containment failure scenarios. If an initial containment attempt doesn't work (say you block one network route but the attacker finds another or the malware re-infects systems from a hidden source), have plan B. This might mean escalating to more drastic measures - e.g., completely shutting off internet connectivity for the company temporarily (that's extreme but has happened in cases like aggressive ransomware outbreaks). Knowing the "big red button" options and their consequences in advance is useful. For example, deciding "In an absolute emergency, we can disconnect our data center from the network - but that will cut off all our services. This is only if everything is spiraling out of control" should be thought about ahead of time, not in the heat of the moment.

In conclusion, effective containment limits damage and buys you time to eradicate and recover, while effective communication ensures everyone involved in or affected by the incident remains informed and can act appropriately. By pre-planning both aspects, an organization can respond to incidents in a calm, coordinated manner rather than a panicked scramble. The integration of incident response into the organization's architecture and culture - having the communication pathways and technical capabilities ready - truly shows its value when containment is achieved quickly and stakeholders from IT staff to executives to customers feel that the situation was handled transparently and competently.

Building Detection and Response into the Architecture

For many organizations, incident response still lives as a set of documents and a handful of experts. Building response into the architecture changes that: monitoring, evidence capture, and containment controls become first-class design requirements, the same way availability and performance are. When this is done well, responders do not rely on luck to find the right logs or to isolate the right asset. The environment itself makes the next step obvious.

Telemetry As a Product: Designing for Visibility

The fastest way to lose an incident is to discover, mid-breach, that critical signals were never collected, were overwritten too quickly, or were stored on the same system that got compromised. Treat telemetry like a product with customers (responders, threat hunters, auditors) and with requirements (coverage, quality, retention, integrity, and cost). A useful mental model is to design telemetry so that it answers four questions quickly: what happened, when it happened, where it happened, and what changed as a result.

A practical blueprint is shown in Figure 6-3. It separates sources, aggregation, normalization, integrity controls, detection, and response. The separation matters: sources are owned by platform teams; aggregation and integrity are often owned by security engineering; detections are owned by detection engineers; response actions span security and operations. The blueprint clarifies ownership and helps avoid gaps.

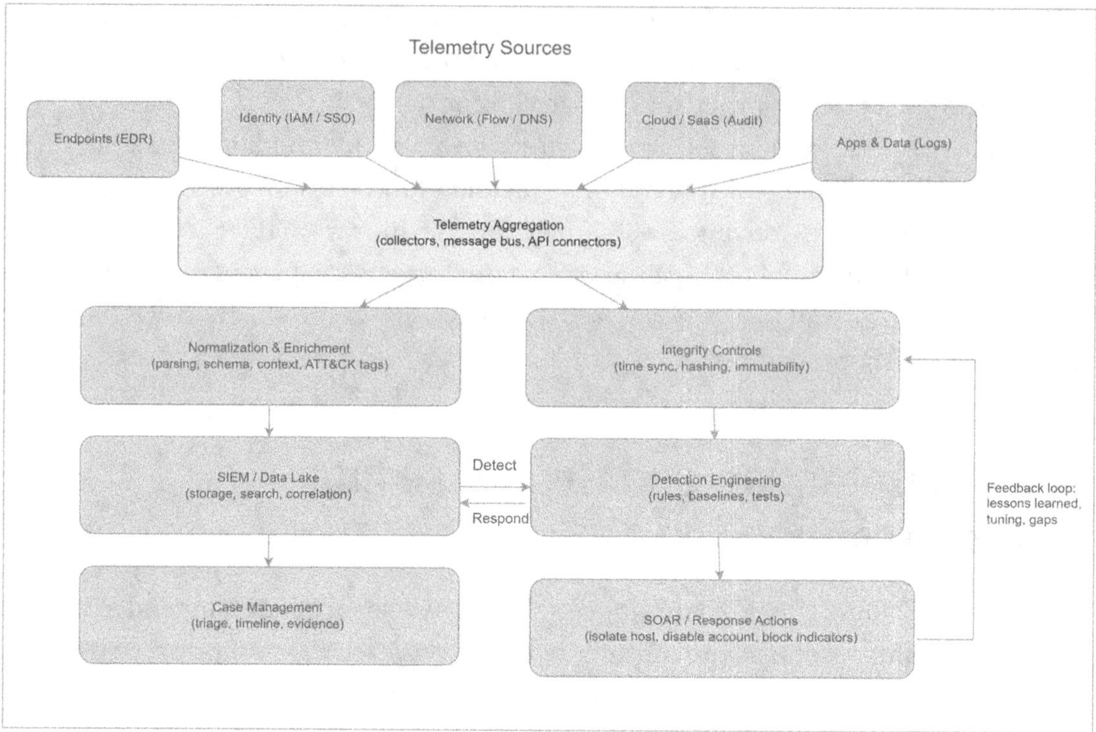

Figure 6-3. *Telemetry-to-response architecture for building detection and response into the platform*

Implementation requirements that tend to matter across industries are listed below. They are written as design constraints that architecture reviews can enforce.

- **Coverage**: Ensure identity, endpoint, network, cloud, and application telemetry exist for every tier that can affect material risk.
- **Consistency**: Adopt a common schema and naming conventions so queries, dashboards, and playbooks behave predictably across teams.
- **Time Accuracy**: Standardize time synchronization and record time zones; small drift turns timelines into arguments.
- **Integrity**: Forward logs off-host, restrict delete permissions, and use immutable storage for high-value streams.
- **Retention**: Keep high-value telemetry long enough to reconstruct realistic dwell times and support regulatory needs.

- **Access Control**: Enforce least privilege for log access; responders need broad read access, but write/delete access should be rare.
- **Cost Controls**: Tier data so you can retain the right signals longer without bankrupting the program.

Telemetry Coverage and Retention Matrix

A simple way to operationalize visibility is to publish a coverage matrix that platform teams must satisfy. Table 6-1 provides a starting point. Adapt it to your environment and data sensitivity, then treat it as a contract: new systems cannot go live without meeting the minimum telemetry requirements.

Table 6-1. *Baseline telemetry and retention requirements (starting point)*

Domain	Examples of Sources	Minimum Evidence to Capture	Practical Retention Target
Identity	SSO, MFA, IAM, PAM, directory services	Auth success/failure, MFA events, token issuance, privileged sessions, group changes	12+ months for core events; longer for privileged access
Endpoint	EDR agent, OS audit logs	Process start, parent/child lineage, command line, network connections, file and registry changes (where feasible)	90 days high-detail; 12+ months summary/alerts
Network	Firewall, VPN, DNS, proxy, flow logs	Egress destinations, DNS queries, VPN sessions, inbound rule hits, east-west flows for critical segments	6–12 months; longer for high-risk segments
Cloud and SaaS	Cloud audit logs, SaaS admin logs	Admin actions, API calls, IAM policy changes, storage access, mailbox or file share access	12+ months where available; export regularly
Applications	Web access logs, API gateways, app audit logs	User identity, request IDs, key transactions, permission checks, error and security events	6–12 months; longer for regulated data flows
Data Platforms	Database audit logs, object storage logs	Privileged queries, schema changes, bulk export actions, object reads/writes, encryption key events	12+ months for audit trails; keep key events longer

Threat-Informed Detection Engineering with MITRE ATT&CK

MITRE ATT&CK is most useful when you treat it as a planning and testing tool rather than a vocabulary list. The practical workflow is as follows: choose a set of likely attack paths for your industry and technology stack, map those techniques to available telemetry, write detections that are as behavior-based as you can make them, and continuously validate those detections with safe simulations.

Many modern breaches begin with valid credentials, token theft, abuse of remote management tools, and cloud misconfigurations. That pattern pushes detection programs to focus heavily on identity, administrative actions, and unusual access paths. Network malware signatures still matter, but identity-driven detections often decide whether you detect early or late.

A practical way to apply ATT&CK is to build a detection map for a small number of high-impact tactics first, then expand. Table 6-2 shows examples of techniques and the evidence you should expect to use when building detections. The goal is not to cover everything at once; the goal is to cover the techniques that would materially change your incident response outcomes.

Table 6-2. *Example ATT&CK-driven detection map (illustrative)*

Attack Goal	Example Behaviors to Detect	Primary Telemetry	Response Hook
Initial access and execution	Suspicious script execution; unusual installer behavior; unexpected scheduled tasks	Endpoint process and task logs; application execution logs	Quarantine host; collect volatile artifacts
Credential access	Password dump tools; token replay; MFA fatigue patterns; abnormal privilege elevation	Identity and PAM logs; endpoint security events	Disable or reset credentials; revoke sessions
Persistence	New startup items; service creation; new OAuth app or API key	Endpoint change logs; cloud audit logs	Remove persistence; rotate keys; increase monitoring

(continued)

Table 6-2. (*continued*)

Attack Goal	Example Behaviors to Detect	Primary Telemetry	Response Hook
Privilege escalation	Abuse of admin tools; anomalous group changes; policy updates	Directory and IAM logs; change management logs	Rollback policies; require approvals; investigate actor
Lateral movement	Remote exec from non-admin endpoints; unusual SMB or RDP patterns; cloud role chaining	Network flows; endpoint remote exec; cloud identity trails	Segment network; block protocols; isolate accounts
Exfiltration	Bulk downloads; unusual egress destinations; repeated API exports	Proxy and DNS logs; SaaS audit; data platform logs	Block egress; apply legal hold; start evidence capture

Automation and SOAR: Speed Without Self-Inflicted Outages

Automation becomes valuable when the response action is low-risk and time-critical. In practice, most teams start with enrichment and ticket hygiene (pulling context, assigning owners, linking related alerts) and then move to containment actions for specific scenarios with strong guardrails.

A useful policy is to classify actions into three categories: automatic, assisted, and manual. Automatic actions can trigger without human approval because the blast radius is small and reversible. Assisted actions prepare the change but require a human to approve. Manual actions are complex, high-risk, or legally sensitive, and they require explicit command decisions.

1. **Automatic**: Block a known-bad domain at the proxy, revoke a single suspicious session token, or isolate a single endpoint that is clearly executing ransomware behavior.

2. **Assisted**: Disable a user account, quarantine an entire subnet, rotate service credentials, or lock down a cloud storage bucket.

3. **Manual**: Shut down a revenue-critical application, cut Internet connectivity, notify regulators, or engage law enforcement.

Architecturally, automation works best when response hooks are designed into platforms. Examples include an endpoint isolation API, an identity provider session revocation API, a network segmentation control plane, and a cloud policy rollback mechanism. If responders must improvise these controls during an incident, automation will be brittle or unsafe.

Incident Response Execution: From Alert to Recovery

Frameworks become useful when they translate into repeatable decisions under stress. The combined NIST and SANS lifecycle can be implemented as a set of gates: confirm an incident, decide the containment boundary, preserve evidence, remove the threat, restore service safely, and close the loop with improvements. This section provides implementation details and checklists you can adapt to your organization.

Preparation: Roles, Access, and Muscle Memory

Preparation is not a policy document; it is the ability to execute. Two things tend to break responders during real incidents: missing access and unclear authority. If the response team cannot isolate an endpoint, revoke a session, pull cloud audit logs, or snapshot a workload without waiting for a separate team, response time will be measured in hours instead of minutes.

A practical preparation package includes an on-call roster, a clear incident commander role, break-glass access that is tested monthly, a shared evidence repository, and a small library of playbooks for high-frequency scenarios. Treat these as operational assets with owners, testing schedules, and change control.

Detection and Analysis: Triage, Scoping, and Timeline Building

Detection begins when an alert becomes a hypothesis. The first goal is not root cause; it is to reduce uncertainty fast enough to make safe containment decisions. High-performing teams use a structured triage loop: validate the signal, collect context, decide severity, scope affected assets, and preserve perishable evidence.

A practical triage method is to answer five questions in the first 30 minutes: What is the indicator, what asset is involved, what user or identity is involved, what is the likely tactic (credential misuse, malware, misconfiguration, insider), and what could be the worst plausible impact if you wait. If you cannot answer these questions, you do not yet have enough context to decide containment.

Timeline building should start early. Use a single time standard, gather the key events from identity, endpoint, network, and cloud sources, and record every action taken by the response team. That record becomes the backbone of the final report and prevents the incident from becoming a debate about who did what.

Containment: Choosing the Boundary

Containment is a design problem disguised as a crisis. You must decide what to isolate: a single device, a user account, an application tier, a network segment, or an entire region. The right boundary depends on attacker speed, business criticality, and confidence in scoping.

A useful decision rule is to contain at the narrowest boundary that stops the attacker while preserving evidence and keeping the business running. If you are uncertain about the scope, choose a boundary that prevents spread. For example, if you suspect a privileged account is compromised, it is usually safer to revoke sessions and disable the account immediately than to watch longer for confirmation.

Eradication: Removing Persistence and Closing the Door

Eradication is where many teams accidentally reintroduce the attacker. The goal is not only to remove malware or stop the observed behavior; it is to remove persistence mechanisms and to fix the initial weakness that enabled the incident.

Practical eradication actions usually include reimaging compromised endpoints, rotating credentials and API keys that were reachable from affected systems, patching exploited vulnerabilities, removing malicious scheduled tasks or cloud access policies, and hunting for secondary footholds. In cloud and SaaS environments, eradication often means revoking tokens, rotating secrets, and reviewing all administrative actions during the attack window.

Recovery: Restoring Service Safely

Recovery is not the moment you turn systems back on; it is the moment you can explain why turning them back on is safe. Use gated recovery: verify integrity, validate business functions, monitor closely, and gradually restore connectivity.

In modern environments, recovery is faster when infrastructure and configuration are reproducible. Golden images, infrastructure-as-code, and automated configuration management reduce the temptation to "fix it live" on a compromised host. If you must do live repair, record every change and assume you will need to rebuild later.

Post-Incident Activity: Converting Pain into Improvement

Post-incident work is where maturity is built. The output should include a concise executive summary, a detailed technical timeline, evidence handling notes, quantified impact, and a prioritized improvement backlog with owners and due dates.

Avoid vague lessons like "improve monitoring." Instead, record specific gaps and changes: add DNS logging for the egress resolver, increase SaaS audit log retention, require approvals for privileged role assignments, or add an automated response that isolates hosts when a ransomware signature is observed.

Incident Severity and Escalation Model

Severity should be determined by business impact, attacker capability, and confidence in scope, not by how scary an alert looks. A simple severity model improves decision speed because it ties response actions and communication requirements to predefined thresholds, as summarized in Table 6-3.

Table 6-3. Example incident severity levels and required actions

Severity	Typical Indicators	Required Response	Communication Trigger
S1 (Low)	Single endpoint malware blocked; low-confidence alert	Triage within business hours; collect minimal evidence; close or monitor	Notify SOC lead; no external communication
S2 (Moderate)	Confirmed compromise of one asset; suspicious credential use with limited scope	Contain affected asset; preserve evidence; validate no spread	Notify security manager and system owner
S3 (High)	Multiple assets affected; privileged account involvement; possible data access	Activate incident commander; start war room; containment within hours; begin legal and PR readiness	Notify executives on a schedule; legal engaged
S4 (Critical)	Active ransomware; confirmed sensitive data theft; disruption of critical operations	Full incident response activation; aggressive containment; consider disaster recovery; 24×7 operations	Immediate executive notification; regulator/ customer planning; external partners engaged

Roles, Responsibilities, and Decision Rights

Incidents fail when everyone assumes someone else is handling the hard decisions. Establish clear roles and decision rights, then test them in exercises. The incident commander owns coordination and prioritization. Technical leads own containment and eradication. Legal and communications own external messaging. Business owners decide on acceptable downtime and operational trade-offs.

***Table 6-4.** Example RACI for incident response activities*

Activity	Incident Commander	Security Engineering/SOC	IT Operations/ Platform	Legal/ Comms
Declare incident and set severity	R	A	C	C
Collect and preserve evidence	C	R	C	C
Isolate endpoint/ segment network	A	R	R	C
Disable accounts/ revoke tokens	A	R	C	C
Restore service and validate	C	C	R	C
External notifications	C	C	C	R
Post-incident report and backlog	R	R	C	C

Forensic Readiness Deep Dive: Cloud, SaaS, and Ephemeral Workloads

Traditional forensics assumes you can seize a machine, image a disk, and analyze it at leisure. Modern environments complicate this: workloads are ephemeral, logs are provider-managed, and identity is often the real control plane. Forensic readiness therefore shifts toward rapid acquisition of cloud audit trails, snapshots, and identity timelines, combined with strong evidence handling practices.

Cloud Control Plane Evidence

In cloud incidents, the most valuable evidence often comes from the control plane: who created or modified resources, who changed policies, and which API calls were made. Ensure that cloud audit logging is enabled in every account and region, that logs are exported to a security-controlled location, and that retention is long enough to cover slow intrusions.

When an incident is declared, prioritize acquisition of the following artifacts: audit log slices for the incident window plus buffer time, a list of recent privileged actions, changes to identity policies and role assignments, and inventory snapshots of affected resources. Capture them into an evidence vault as read-only copies. Do not rely on the cloud console as your only record; export and preserve data in formats your investigators can analyze offline.

SaaS Evidence: Email, Collaboration, and Business Systems

SaaS platforms often hold the most sensitive information, but their logs can be fragmented across multiple admin pages and licensing tiers. Build a SaaS forensic checklist per provider that answers: where are the audit logs, how long are they retained, how do you export them, and what permission is required to access them.

For email and collaboration platforms, prioritize sign-in logs, token issuance and consent events, mailbox access logs, bulk download indicators, forwarding rule changes, and administrative actions. For customer or finance platforms, prioritize admin activity, permission changes, data export actions, and API token creation. Always preserve the raw exports in your evidence vault before you start manipulating data for analysis.

Containers, Serverless, and Short-Lived Hosts

Ephemeral compute breaks disk-based assumptions. If a container is replaced every few minutes, the most valuable evidence is not a disk image; it is telemetry captured while the workload ran: container runtime logs, orchestrator audit events, image provenance, and network flows.

Implementation tactics include enabling orchestrator audit logging, shipping container runtime logs off-host, storing build and deployment metadata (image digests, build pipelines, signer identities), and capturing egress telemetry at the network layer. For high-risk clusters, consider on-demand packet capture or flow logging for east-west traffic so lateral movement is visible.

Handling Volatile Data Under Time Pressure

Volatile data (memory, running process state, active network connections, temporary tokens) can disappear quickly. Decide in advance which systems merit volatile capture and how you will do it safely. In some environments, remote capture via an endpoint agent is feasible. In others, capturing memory may be too disruptive, and you will rely on endpoint telemetry and log trails instead.

If you do perform volatile capture, standardize the workflow: record the reason for capture, identify the operator, capture to trusted media, compute cryptographic hashes, and move the evidence into the vault immediately. This discipline prevents accidental contamination and makes later reporting defensible.

Communication and Containment in Practice

Good technical containment can still become a business failure if communication is late, inconsistent, or overly speculative. The objective is to keep decision-makers informed, keep responders aligned, and protect legal and regulatory posture without slowing down urgent technical work.

Internal Communications: War Room Operating Rhythm

Use a predictable cadence. Establish a single incident channel for detailed technical updates and a separate executive update thread for concise summaries. Assign a scribe. Every update should include current severity, affected services, confirmed facts, hypotheses, actions completed, actions in progress, and next decision points.

The following template can be copied into your incident ticket or incident channel as a standing update format.

```
Incident update (time):
Severity:
Summary (one sentence):
What we know (facts):
What we suspect (hypotheses):
Impacted services/users:
Containment actions completed:
Evidence captured:
```

```
Risks/unknowns:
Next actions (owner, ETA):
Decisions needed from leadership:
```

Keep the format stable. Consistency reduces confusion when teams rotate during long incidents.

Containment Decision Checklist

Before executing a containment action with significant business impact, walk through a short checklist. It does not prevent action; it prevents accidental self-harm.

- **Objective**: What behavior are we trying to stop (spread, exfiltration, command and control, privilege escalation)?
- **Boundary**: Which assets and identities are in scope, and what is our confidence in that scope?
- **Evidence**: What volatile or perishable evidence must be captured before containment, and can we capture it safely?
- **Blast Radius**: What business process will break, and who must approve the trade-off?
- **Reversibility**: Can we undo the containment quickly if it is a false positive?
- **Monitoring**: How will we confirm containment is effective and detect secondary footholds?

External Communications: Regulatory and Customer Readiness

External notifications usually require verified facts and legal review. The best way to move fast is to prepare in advance: define notification triggers by severity, maintain contact lists, and pre-approve message templates that can be filled in during an incident.

Avoid technical speculation in early statements. Share what is confirmed, what you are doing to contain and remediate, and what recipients should do next (e.g., password resets or monitoring accounts). Maintain a single public voice to avoid contradictions.

Incident Response Playbooks (Implementation)

This section provides practical playbooks that can be adapted to most industries. They assume the combined lifecycle described earlier and emphasize evidence preservation alongside containment. Customize the actions to your tools and governance model.

Playbook 6-A: Credential Theft, Session Hijack, or Account Takeover

Identity-driven incidents are common across industries. The attacker may not drop malware at first; they may use valid credentials, stolen session tokens, or repeated MFA prompts to obtain access. The priorities are to stop active access, preserve identity timelines, and determine whether the compromise is limited to one identity or indicates broader token or device compromise.

Triggers and Declaration Criteria

Use the following triggers as starting points. Escalate severity when privileged identities, regulated data, or business-critical services are involved.

- Repeated MFA prompts reported by users, especially outside normal hours or geographies
- New device registrations, recovery email/phone changes, or suspicious password resets
- Impossible travel patterns or unusual sign-in locations for privileged users
- Unexpected consent grants or new OAuth applications connected to enterprise data
- Admin actions executed from endpoints or networks not normally used by administrators

First 15 Minutes

Focus on stopping active harm and preserving perishable evidence. Keep actions reversible when you are still validating the incident.

- Confirm the identity and the scope of access (which tenant, which account, which privileges).
- Revoke active sessions and refresh tokens for the affected account; force reauthentication.
- Disable the account temporarily if privileged access is suspected or if activity is ongoing.
- Preserve identity logs and admin audit logs for the incident window plus buffer time.
- If the user endpoint may be compromised, isolate it and collect endpoint telemetry before reissuing credentials.

Evidence to Collect

Collect evidence early and store raw exports in the evidence vault before processing. Prefer centralized logs over pulling data directly from compromised hosts where possible.

- Sign-in logs, MFA events, token issuance/revocation events, and conditional access decisions
- Privileged access and role assignment changes and group membership changes
- SaaS audit logs for data access (mailbox access, file downloads, exports)
- Endpoint telemetry for the user's primary devices (processes, browser activity indicators, VPN usage)
- Network telemetry for unusual egress or proxy activity associated with the account

Containment

Contain at the smallest boundary that stops the spread. If the scope is uncertain, choose a boundary that prevents expansion and protects sensitive data.

- Reset the password and enforce strong authentication; rotate recovery options if they were changed.
- Revoke all sessions across devices; remove any newly registered or untrusted devices.
- Disable newly created OAuth apps, API tokens, or forwarders until validated.
- Increase monitoring for related identities (same department, same admin groups, same IP ranges).
- If the compromise is tied to a phishing campaign, block sender domains and quarantine similar messages.

Eradication

Eradication removes the adversary's foothold and prevents immediate re-entry. It should include credential and secret hygiene, not only malware removal.

- Identify the initial compromise path: phishing, password reuse, token theft, device compromise, or misconfiguration.
- Remove malicious mailbox rules, forwarding rules, and suspicious delegated access.
- Hunt for persistence through API keys, service principals, and admin roles.
- Rebuild or reimage compromised endpoints; verify browser extensions and credential stores.
- Update conditional access and privileged access workflows (e.g., require step-up authentication for admin actions).

Recovery

Use gated recovery and heightened monitoring. Assume the attacker will try to return or pivot during restoration.

- Restore account access with verified strong authentication and monitored sign-in conditions.

- Validate that data access has returned to normal baselines; watch for renewed token abuse.
- Communicate clear user actions (password changes, device health checks) without creating panic.
- For privileged identities, require re-enrollment into MFA and revalidation of devices.
- Run a short after-action review focused on identity telemetry gaps and approval workflows.

Communications

Maintain disciplined messaging. Keep technical details in internal channels and focus external messages on impact, actions taken, and next steps for stakeholders.

- Notify the system owner and identity governance owner; confirm decision rights for disabling accounts.
- If regulated data may be affected, engage legal early and preserve audit exports.
- Provide helpdesk guidance for user reports of MFA prompts and suspicious sign-ins.
- If customer accounts are affected, prepare customer messaging with steps and reassurance.
- Record the final scope: accounts impacted, data accessed, and remediation actions.

Playbook 6-B: Ransomware and Destructive Malware

Ransomware response is a race between attacker spread and defender containment. The technical steps must be paired with business decisions on operational continuity. Many ransomware events now also include data theft and extortion, so evidence preservation and communications readiness are critical.

Triggers and Declaration Criteria

Use the following triggers as starting points. Escalate severity when privileged identities, regulated data, or business-critical services are involved.

- Multiple endpoints reporting encrypted files, ransom notes, or mass file rename activity
- High volume of file access errors or unusual write operations on shared storage
- Backup systems showing unexpected deletions, encryption, or privilege changes
- Security tools reporting known ransomware behaviors (process injection, credential dumping, lateral movement tools)
- Sudden loss of availability across business applications without an obvious infrastructure cause

First 15 Minutes

Focus on stopping active harm and preserving perishable evidence. Keep actions reversible when you are still validating the incident.

- Isolate affected endpoints and servers from the network using endpoint isolation or network controls.
- Disable shared drives or set them to read-only where feasible to stop encryption spread.
- Preserve volatile evidence on key systems if safe (running processes, network connections).
- Identify and disable the accounts used for lateral movement, especially privileged accounts.
- Protect backups: isolate backup networks, and pause replication if it risks copying encrypted data.

Evidence to Collect

Collect evidence early and store raw exports in the evidence vault before processing. Prefer centralized logs over pulling data directly from compromised hosts where possible.

- EDR timelines from affected endpoints and one or two likely patient-zero systems
- Authentication and privileged access logs for the suspected intrusion period
- Network flow and DNS logs for command-and-control and lateral movement paths
- Storage access logs for mass delete or mass modify operations
- Copies of ransom notes, file extensions, and any attacker communications

Containment

Contain at the smallest boundary that stops the spread. If the scope is uncertain, choose a boundary that prevents expansion and protects sensitive data.

- Segment the network aggressively: separate user networks from server networks and backup networks.
- Block known indicators at the proxy, firewall, and email gateway; update deny lists.
- Disable remote management protocols temporarily where they are not essential.
- Quarantine compromised hosts; do not reconnect them to production networks until rebuilt.
- If encryption is spreading rapidly, consider a controlled shutdown of vulnerable services to preserve data.

Eradication

Eradication removes the adversary's foothold and prevents immediate re-entry. It should include credential and secret hygiene, not only malware removal.

- Reimage affected endpoints and servers from trusted golden images; do not rely on partial cleanup.
- Rotate credentials broadly, prioritizing privileged credentials, service accounts, and secrets in automation tools.
- Patch exploited vulnerabilities and remove exposed services used for initial access.
- Hunt for persistence mechanisms and secondary backdoors before restoring network trust.
- Validate that backups are clean and that restore points predate the intrusion.

Recovery

Use gated recovery and heightened monitoring. Assume the attacker will try to return or pivot during restoration.

- Restore critical services first based on business priorities and dependency mapping.
- Use clean restore validation: scan restored systems, validate configurations, and monitor closely.
- Reintroduce network connectivity gradually; keep high-risk protocols restricted initially.
- Monitor for renewed attacker activity and for extortion follow-up attempts.
- Document recovery times, data loss, and operational workarounds to improve resilience planning.

Communications

Maintain disciplined messaging. Keep technical details in internal channels and focus external messages on impact, actions taken, and next steps for stakeholders.

- Engage executive leadership early due to operational impact and potential extortion dynamics.
- Coordinate with legal and communications on any external messaging and negotiation posture.
- Provide clear internal guidance: do not power off systems unless instructed; report symptoms immediately.
- If data theft is suspected, begin legal hold and prepare notification workflows.
- Maintain a single record of decisions: containment boundary, restore priorities, and risk acceptance.

Playbook 6-C: Cloud Access Key Leak or Over-privileged Identity

Cloud incidents often move fast because infrastructure changes are automated. A leaked API key or an over-privileged role can enable rapid resource creation, data access, and persistence through new identities. The priorities are to stop the credential, preserve the cloud audit trail, and review all policy and resource changes during the compromise window.

Triggers and Declaration Criteria

Use the following triggers as starting points. Escalate severity when privileged identities, regulated data, or business-critical services are involved.

- Detection of API calls from unusual geographies, networks, or automation fingerprints
- Unexpected creation of compute resources, storage buckets, or network rules

- IAM policy changes, new roles, new keys, or permission escalations without a change ticket
- Unusual data access patterns: bulk reads, exports, or snapshots of sensitive data stores
- Billing anomalies that suggest unauthorized resource creation

First 15 Minutes

Focus on stopping active harm and preserving perishable evidence. Keep actions reversible when you are still validating the incident.

- Disable or rotate the suspected key or credential immediately; revoke tokens and sessions where possible.
- Snapshot the relevant audit logs and export them to the evidence vault before further actions.
- Identify the principal associated with the key and its permissions; determine reachable assets.
- Lock down high-risk resources (object storage, key management, identity management) with temporary restrictive policies.
- If you suspect automation compromise, pause pipelines that can create or modify cloud resources.

Evidence to Collect

Collect evidence early and store raw exports in the evidence vault before processing. Prefer centralized logs over pulling data directly from compromised hosts where possible.

- Cloud audit logs for the incident window plus buffer time, including identity and policy changes
- Inventory snapshots of affected resources: instances, storage, access policies, network rules
- Key management logs: key usage, creation, rotation, and decryption events

- SaaS or CI/CD logs if credentials could have leaked from build systems or secrets managers
- Network egress logs and flow records for suspicious outbound traffic from cloud workloads

Containment

Contain at the smallest boundary that stops the spread. If the scope is uncertain, choose a boundary that prevents expansion and protects sensitive data.

- Rotate secrets in a controlled order: stop the leak first, then rotate dependent services to avoid cascading outages.
- Remove or disable newly created identities, keys, and roles that are not validated.
- Apply temporary deny rules for risky actions (e.g., public bucket changes, new admin role grants).
- Quarantine suspicious workloads by moving them to an isolated security group or subnet.
- Increase monitoring for administrative actions, especially around identity and network configuration.

Eradication

Eradication removes the adversary's foothold and prevents immediate re-entry. It should include credential and secret hygiene, not only malware removal.

- Identify the leak source: exposed repository, misconfigured secrets store, compromised developer endpoint, or third-party integration.
- Remove unauthorized policies, role bindings, and network rules; restore from known-good configurations.
- Rebuild compromised workloads and rotate credentials that were accessible from those workloads.

- Review all persistence vectors: new service principals, scheduled jobs, and cross-account trust relationships.
- Implement preventive controls: short-lived credentials, tighter identity boundaries, and approval workflows for high-risk actions.

Recovery

Use gated recovery and heightened monitoring. Assume the attacker will try to return or pivot during restoration.

- Validate that production workloads are running with known-good identities and policies.
- Re-enable pipelines after secrets and access controls are verified.
- Run post-recovery monitoring focused on admin actions and data access anomalies.
- Update infrastructure-as-code baselines so future drift detection catches similar changes quickly.
- Add a tabletop scenario focused on cloud identity compromise to test the improved controls.

Communications

Maintain disciplined messaging. Keep technical details in internal channels, and focus external messages on impact, actions taken, and next steps for stakeholders.

- Notify cloud platform owners and business owners for impacted services early.
- If sensitive data stores were accessible, engage legal and begin a data access assessment.
- Coordinate internal messaging to avoid unapproved manual changes to cloud policies during the response.
- Document the sequence of secret rotations and policy rollbacks for auditability.
- Prepare external notifications if data exposure is confirmed.

Playbook 6-D: Web Application or API Compromise

Web and API compromises can involve exploitation of vulnerabilities, credential stuffing, or abuse of exposed administrative endpoints. The priorities are to protect users and data, preserve transaction evidence, and prevent the attacker from using the application as a pivot into internal systems.

Triggers and Declaration Criteria

Use the following triggers as starting points. Escalate severity when privileged identities, regulated data, or business-critical services are involved.

- WAF or gateway alerts indicating exploitation attempts or abnormal request patterns
- Unusual spikes in errors, authentication failures, or admin endpoint access
- Unexpected changes to application code, configuration, or deployment pipelines
- Database anomalies such as unusual query patterns, schema changes, or bulk export activity
- Fraud signals: abnormal transactions, account changes, or data access patterns

First 15 Minutes

Focus on stopping active harm and preserving perishable evidence. Keep actions reversible when you are still validating the incident.

- Stabilize: consider rate limiting or temporarily disabling risky endpoints while you confirm scope.
- Capture evidence: preserve web access logs, gateway logs, and application audit logs for the time window.
- Identify the affected endpoints, user accounts, and data stores; classify sensitivity.

- Check deployment and configuration changes; freeze risky deployments if compromise is suspected.
- If active exploitation is confirmed, block exploit patterns and isolate the application tier if needed.

Evidence to Collect

Collect evidence early and store raw exports in the evidence vault before processing. Prefer centralized logs over pulling data directly from compromised hosts where possible.

- Web server and API gateway logs with request IDs, user IDs, IPs, and response codes
- Authentication logs, session creation logs, and MFA events
- Application audit logs for privilege changes and sensitive transactions
- Database audit logs for privileged queries, exports, and schema modifications
- CI/CD pipeline logs and artifact digests for recent releases

Containment

Contain at the smallest boundary that stops the spread. If the scope is uncertain, choose a boundary that prevents expansion and protects sensitive data.

- Block known exploit payloads and suspicious IPs; enable temporary stricter WAF rules.
- Disable or restrict administrative endpoints; require step-up authentication.
- Rotate application secrets and keys if they may have been exposed.
- Disable suspicious user accounts and invalidate sessions involved in malicious activity.
- Segment the application from internal systems; restrict outbound connections to approved destinations.

Eradication

Eradication removes the adversary's foothold and prevents immediate re-entry. It should include credential and secret hygiene, not only malware removal.

- Patch the exploited vulnerability and validate with tests; do not rely on blocking alone.
- Review code and dependencies for malicious changes; redeploy from a trusted build pipeline.
- Remove backdoors: web shells, unauthorized admin accounts, and malicious config changes.
- Hunt for lateral movement from the application tier into databases or internal services.
- Strengthen preventive controls: input validation, secure defaults, and least-privilege service identities.

Recovery

Use gated recovery and heightened monitoring. Assume the attacker will try to return or pivot during restoration.

- Restore service with heightened monitoring, especially for repeated exploit attempts.
- Verify data integrity for critical transactions; reconcile if needed.
- Re-enable temporarily disabled endpoints in phases after confirming safety.
- Update monitoring to detect the technique used (e.g., unusual admin endpoint access, unusual query patterns).
- Perform a structured post-incident review with development and platform teams.

Communications

Maintain disciplined messaging. Keep technical details in internal channels, and focus external messages on impact, actions taken, and next steps for stakeholders.

- Inform product and customer support teams early if users may see disruptions or account actions.
- If data exposure is possible, coordinate legal review and draft notification triggers.
- Provide clear customer guidance if password resets or session invalidation are required.
- Record the precise attack window and affected endpoints for regulatory reporting if needed.
- Share internal lessons with development teams to prevent recurrence.

Playbook 6-E: Insider Data Exfiltration or Misuse

Insider incidents require careful coordination because actions can affect employment, legal posture, and privacy. Technically, the focus is to preserve evidence and prevent further access without tipping off the actor prematurely, when that could lead to the destruction of evidence.

Triggers and Declaration Criteria

Use the following triggers as starting points. Escalate severity when privileged identities, regulated data, or business-critical services are involved.

- Unusual bulk downloads from sensitive repositories or collaboration platforms
- Repeated access to data outside the user's normal role or project scope
- Use of personal cloud storage, external email forwarding, or unusual removable media activity

- Access to sensitive systems from atypical devices or networks
- Reports from managers or HR about suspicious behavior correlated with technical indicators

First 15 Minutes

Focus on stopping active harm and preserving perishable evidence. Keep actions reversible when you are still validating the incident.

- Engage the incident commander and legal/HR liaison; confirm decision rights for account actions.
- Preserve evidence quietly: export audit logs and access histories for the suspected assets.
- Assess whether immediate access revocation is required to prevent ongoing harm.
- If you must restrict access, prefer actions that preserve evidence (session revocation rather than wiping devices).
- Begin a controlled scope assessment: which datasets were accessed, exported, or shared.

Evidence to Collect

Collect evidence early and store raw exports in the evidence vault before processing. Prefer centralized logs over pulling data directly from compromised hosts where possible.

- SaaS audit logs for file access, downloads, shares, and exports.
- Identity logs for sign-ins, device registrations, and privilege changes.
- Endpoint telemetry for data staging behavior (archive tools, large file moves, external device use).
- Network egress logs and proxy logs for uploads to external destinations.
- Ticketing or approval records that show what access the user was legitimately granted.

Containment

Contain at the smallest boundary that stops the spread. If the scope is uncertain, choose a boundary that prevents expansion and protects sensitive data.

- Restrict the user's access to sensitive datasets; disable high-risk privileges first.
- Revoke active sessions and remove access tokens; force reauthentication where needed.
- Disable or restrict external sharing features for the impacted repositories temporarily.
- Preserve and secure the user's corporate devices following legal guidance.
- Increase monitoring for related identities or collaborators if collusion is possible.

Eradication

Eradication removes the adversary's foothold and prevents immediate re-entry. It should include credential and secret hygiene, not only malware removal.

- Remove unauthorized shares, links, or access grants; rotate secrets that were exposed.
- Fix control weaknesses: overbroad access groups, lack of approval workflows, and weak monitoring on exports.
- If endpoint compromise is suspected, perform a forensic acquisition and rebuild the device.
- Document a clear chain of custody for all collected evidence.
- Review offboarding processes and access reviews for similar roles.

Recovery

Use gated recovery and heightened monitoring. Assume the attacker will try to return or pivot during restoration.

- Restore normal sharing and access gradually after validating controls and monitoring.
- Perform a data impact assessment: what was accessed, what left the environment, and what remains uncertain.
- Update data loss prevention rules or alerting for bulk access behaviors.
- Run a targeted access review to reduce standing privileges for sensitive systems.
- Hold a post-incident review that includes security, HR, legal, and the data owners.

Communications

Maintain disciplined messaging. Keep technical details in internal channels, and focus external messages on impact, actions taken, and next steps for stakeholders.

- Keep communications tightly controlled to protect privacy and legal process.
- Coordinate with HR and legal before interviewing employees or taking disciplinary action.
- Provide executives with a fact-based summary without unnecessary personal details.
- If customer data is involved, prepare notification workflows once facts are confirmed.
- Ensure the final report distinguishes facts from interpretations to prevent disputes later.

Playbook 6-F: Third-Party or Supply Chain Compromise

Third-party incidents include compromised vendors, poisoned software updates, malicious open source components, or breaches in shared services. The challenge is to identify exposure quickly, contain dependencies, and coordinate communications with external parties while maintaining evidence and service continuity.

Triggers and Declaration Criteria

Use the following triggers as starting points. Escalate severity when privileged identities, regulated data, or business-critical services are involved.

- Trusted vendor alerts of compromise or emergency patch notifications
- Detection of unexpected outbound connections from software components
- New binaries or container images with unknown provenance in the environment
- Compromised integration accounts or API tokens tied to partners
- Multiple customers or business units reporting similar suspicious behavior linked to the same product

First 15 Minutes

Focus on stopping active harm and preserving perishable evidence. Keep actions reversible when you are still validating the incident.

- Identify the dependency: which systems, versions, and environments use the vendor component.
- Apply a temporary containment boundary: isolate affected services or block suspicious update channels.
- Preserve evidence: capture version information, hashes, and audit logs before changing systems.
- Disable or rotate partner integration credentials if compromise is suspected.
- Engage vendor incident contacts and internal procurement or third-party risk owners.

Evidence to Collect

Collect evidence early and store raw exports in the evidence vault before processing. Prefer centralized logs over pulling data directly from compromised hosts where possible.

- Software inventory: versions, package manifests, container image digests, and build pipeline records
- Network telemetry for suspicious connections tied to the component
- Endpoint or host telemetry for new processes started by vendor software
- Vendor communications and advisories; internal change management records
- Logs from integration points (API gateways, service accounts, webhook configurations)

Containment

Contain at the smallest boundary that stops the spread. If the scope is uncertain, choose a boundary that prevents expansion and protects sensitive data.

- Block known malicious domains and IPs associated with the compromised component.
- Disable auto-update mechanisms until verified safe; pin to known-good versions.
- Isolate systems that received the suspicious update; prevent lateral movement.
- Limit the permissions of vendor integrations temporarily (least privilege emergency mode).
- If compromise is widespread, consider a controlled shutdown of dependent services to stop harm.

Eradication

Eradication removes the adversary's foothold and prevents immediate re-entry. It should include credential and secret hygiene, not only malware removal.

- Remove the compromised component and replace with a known-good version or alternative.
- Rotate credentials used by the component, including API tokens and secrets in CI/CD systems.
- Validate build and deployment pipelines for tampering; reissue signing keys if needed.
- Hunt for persistence created by the compromised component (new users, scheduled jobs, cloud roles).
- Strengthen supply chain controls: signed artifacts, provenance checks, and dependency scanning.

Recovery

Use gated recovery and heightened monitoring. Assume the attacker will try to return or pivot during restoration.

- Restore services using verified components; validate functionality and security baselines.
- Increase monitoring specifically for the techniques used in the supply chain compromise.
- Audit the environment for additional instances of the compromised version.
- Review third-party dependency mapping and improve inventory accuracy.
- Use the incident to justify improvements in vendor monitoring and contract requirements.

Communications

Maintain disciplined messaging. Keep technical details in internal channels and focus external messages on impact, actions taken, and next steps for stakeholders.

- Coordinate messaging with the vendor while maintaining independence in your own assessment.
- Inform internal stakeholders about service risk and containment actions early.
- If customer impact exists, provide clear timelines and guidance without blaming external parties prematurely.
- Maintain documentation of vendor communications for later reporting and contracts.
- Update third-party risk teams on the root cause and the control improvements required.

Exercises, Validation, and Continuous Improvement

Incident response capability degrades if it is not exercised. Staff change, tools change, and architectures evolve. The goal of exercises is not theater; it is to validate that the team can execute the high-risk actions: isolate assets, revoke access, preserve evidence, make business trade-offs, and communicate clearly.

Tabletop Exercises

Tabletops are low cost and high value. Start with scenarios that stress decision-making: ransomware disrupting operations, suspected data theft, or a cloud credential leak. Use a facilitator, keep a timeline, and record decisions. After the exercise, convert observations into backlog items with owners.

Purple Teaming and Detection Testing

Detection programs improve fastest when defenders test their detections against realistic techniques. Purple teaming combines red-team techniques with blue-team measurement. Use safe simulations to generate telemetry, then confirm that alerts fired, that they were routed correctly, and that playbooks produced the expected actions.

If you cannot safely run simulations in production, build a test environment that mirrors production telemetry and run simulations there. The objective is to test end-to-end: telemetry ingestion, normalization, detection logic, case creation, and response actions.

Metrics That Matter

Maturity improves when you measure it. The most useful metrics are those that reveal bottlenecks and drive architectural improvements. Avoid vanity counts of alerts and focus on timing and outcomes.

- **Time to Triage**: From first alert to incident declaration or closure
- **Time to Contain**: From declaration to stopping active harm
- **Time to Eradicate**: From containment to removal of persistence and credential rotation completion
- **Time to Recover**: From eradication to safe restoration of business services
- **Evidence Completeness**: Percentage of incidents with a complete timeline and preserved raw artifacts
- **Repeat Incident Rate**: How often the same root cause reappears

After-Action Review Agenda

Use a repeatable agenda, so reviews produce improvements instead of blame. Keep the discussion fact-based and focus on decisions and system behavior.

1. **Timeline Review**: What happened and when.
2. **Decision Review**: What decisions were made, by whom, and based on what evidence.
3. **Control Gaps**: What telemetry was missing or unreliable.
4. **Process Gaps**: Where handoffs, approvals, or communications slowed response.

5. **Recovery Validation**: What worked and what created risk during restoration.

6. **Backlog**: Prioritize improvements with owners and due dates.

Implementation Road Map

Many programs stall because the scope feels infinite. A phased road map helps: establish a minimum viable capability quickly, then expand coverage and automation over time. The road map below assumes a starting point where incident response exists but is inconsistent or under-documented.

First 30 Days: Establish the Minimum Viable Program

- Appoint an incident commander role and define escalation paths and severity levels.
- Create an on-call roster and a single incident communications channel.
- Identify the top five incident scenarios and draft short playbooks (start with ransomware and identity takeover).
- Validate break-glass access for identity, endpoint isolation, and critical cloud accounts.
- Confirm that central logging works for identity, endpoint, and key cloud audit streams.

Days 31–90: Expand Coverage and Evidence Discipline

- Publish a telemetry coverage and retention matrix and enforce it in architecture reviews.
- Stand up an evidence vault with access control and basic chain-of-custody tracking.
- Run two tabletop exercises and one detection validation exercise; convert outputs into backlog items.

- Create a standard incident report template and require timeline documentation for all high-severity incidents.
- Begin ATT&CK-driven detection mapping for a small set of high-impact techniques.

Months 4–12: Optimize and Automate

- Implement SOAR-assisted response for selected low-risk, high-frequency actions (enrichment, single-host isolation, session revocation).
- Harden identity with privileged access controls and step-up authentication for high-risk actions.
- Improve segmentation and egress controls so containment boundaries are easier to apply.
- Expand forensic readiness for cloud, SaaS, and container workloads, including export automation and retention improvements.
- Introduce regular purple teaming and a quarterly incident response exercise calendar.

Appendix: Templates and Checklists

The templates in this appendix are designed to be copied into your incident management system. Keep them short and consistent. The goal is to remove decision friction during an incident and to improve documentation quality.

Evidence Log Template

Use one line per evidence item. Store the raw evidence separately and record hashes after acquisition. If your organization has strict legal requirements, align this template with counsel.

```
Evidence item ID:
Incident ID:
Collected by:
```

```
Date/time (UTC):
Source system:
Artifact type (log export, disk image, memory capture, screenshot, email
export):
Collection method:
Hash (SHA-256):
Storage location:
Access restrictions:
Notes:
```

Executive Summary Template

Executives need clarity and decisions, not raw logs. Keep the summary to one page when possible.

```
Incident title:
Severity:
Status (active/contained/recovering/closed):
Business impact:
What happened (plain language):
What we know (facts):
What we are still investigating:
Actions taken:
Customer or regulatory considerations:
Decisions required:
Next update time:
```

First-Hour Checklist

This checklist is designed for the incident commander and technical leads. It emphasizes containment, evidence, and communications setup.

- Confirm the incident commander and assign a scribe.
- Establish the incident channel and a bridge call if needed.
- Set initial severity and document the reason for the rating.

- Preserve perishable evidence (identity logs export, key endpoint telemetry, cloud audit slice).
- Execute the first containment boundary, favoring reversible controls when the scope is uncertain.
- Identify affected business services and notify the service owner.
- Set an update cadence and a next-decision checkpoint.

Post-incident Backlog Template

Convert lessons into trackable work. Without owners and due dates, post-incident reviews become storytelling sessions instead of improvements.

```
Finding:
Impact:
Root cause (technical and process):
Recommended control change:
Owner:
Due date:
Validation method:
Status:
```

Conclusion

Incident response and forensic readiness are architecture concerns, not just security team tasks. When visibility, evidence capture, containment boundaries, and recovery mechanisms are designed into platforms, response becomes faster, safer, and more consistent. When they are not, incident response becomes improvisation under pressure.

The practical approach in this chapter combines the structure of the NIST and SANS lifecycles with threat-informed engineering using MITRE ATT&CK. The result is a program that can scale across industries and technologies: a clear operating model, disciplined evidence handling, and playbooks that translate uncertainty into action.

As environments continue to shift toward cloud services, identity-driven access, and highly automated deployments, readiness must shift as well. Programs that succeed are those that treat telemetry as a product, automate with guardrails, and build recovery as a verified capability rather than a hope. The goal is not to avoid every incident. The goal is to detect early, contain confidently, preserve evidence, recover cleanly, and learn fast.

CHAPTER 7

Frameworks and Certifications

In today's complex cybersecurity landscape, organizations rely on well-established frameworks and skilled professionals with recognized certifications to secure their systems. Frameworks provide structured, high-level guidance to manage security risks and ensure governance and compliance, while certifications validate an individual's expertise across these best practices. This chapter bridges foundational cybersecurity knowledge with practical governance frameworks and certification readiness. We will explore major vendor-neutral security frameworks – from the NIST Cybersecurity Framework to ISO/IEC 27001, CIS Critical Security Controls, and MITRE ATT&CK – explaining how each guides an organization's security program. In parallel, we examine how professional certifications like CISSP and CCSP encompass these governance principles, preparing practitioners to align security domains with risk management and compliance. Throughout the chapter, we highlight how to map and align controls across frameworks for audits, provide examples of crosswalks between standards, and offer tips for audit preparation and evidence collection. Both newcomers and seasoned readers will gain a high-level view of frameworks and certifications, coupled with detailed insights to apply these tools in the real world. By the end, you will understand how to integrate frameworks into a cohesive security program and leverage certification knowledge to strengthen governance in the AI-driven era of cloud and data security.

Major Cybersecurity Frameworks

Cybersecurity frameworks are comprehensive guides that help organizations manage and reduce security risk in a structured way. They usually consist of categorized best practices or controls that organizations can implement and often map to each other. In this section, we provide an overview of four influential frameworks: the

A. Gupta and S. Mittal, *Foundations of Modern Information Security*,
https://doi.org/10.1007/979-8-8688-2558-3_7

NIST Cybersecurity Framework, the ISO/IEC 27001 standard (and related ISO 27xxx standards), the CIS Critical Security Controls, and the MITRE ATT&CK framework. Each of these plays a distinct role in governance and risk management, from broad risk-based management systems (NIST CSF, ISO 27001) to prescriptive security controls (CIS Controls) and adversary techniques for threat-informed defense (MITRE ATT&CK). Understanding their scope and focus will help in aligning your organization's security program with recognized best practices and preparing for audits or assessments.

NIST Cybersecurity Framework (CSF)

The NIST Cybersecurity Framework (CSF) is a widely adopted voluntary framework developed by the US National Institute of Standards and Technology. First released in 2014 and updated through version 1.1 (2018) and version 2.0 (2024), the NIST CSF provides strategic guidance for managing cybersecurity risk in any organization. It is composed of three main elements: the Core, Implementation Tiers, and Profiles.

- **CSF Core**: The Core is a set of cybersecurity activities, outcomes, and references that are common across critical infrastructure sectors. It is organized into Functions, Categories, and Subcategories, along with Informative References to other standards. The Core establishes a common lexicon for cybersecurity. Functions are the highest level and represent the primary pillars of a security program. In CSF version 1.1, there were five core Functions – Identify, Protect, Detect, Respond, and Recover. In CSF 2.0, a sixth Function, "Govern," was added to emphasize cybersecurity governance and executive oversight. These Functions are carried out concurrently and continuously; for example, activities in Govern, Identify, Protect, and Detect are ongoing, while Respond and Recover actions occur during and after incidents. Beneath each Function are Categories (groups of related security outcomes) and Subcategories (specific outcomes or technical/control activities). Each Subcategory includes Informative References mapping to practices in other standards (like ISO 27001 controls, COBIT, NIST 800-53, etc.), illustrating how CSF connects to detailed controls and regulations.

- **Implementation Tiers**: The CSF Implementation Tiers describe the maturity of an organization's cybersecurity risk management practices, ranging from Tier 1 (Partial) to Tier 4 (Adaptive). They help organizations assess how closely their security activities align with their risk objectives and regulatory requirements. A higher Tier indicates more formalized and adaptive risk processes. Tiers are not meant to be a simple maturity score, but rather a way to view the degree of rigor and integration of cybersecurity into business practices. For instance, Tier 1 organizations may have ad hoc security measures, whereas Tier 4 organizations adapt their defenses based on lessons learned and predictive indicators.
- **Profiles**: A CSF Profile represents an organization's unique alignment of the Framework Core with its business requirements, risk tolerance, and resources. Essentially, profiles are used to identify the current "Current Profile" (where an organization's cybersecurity program stands) and a "Target Profile" (desired state of security). By comparing these, organizations can pinpoint gaps and prioritize improvements. Profiles are highly useful for communicating cybersecurity posture to stakeholders and for planning future state improvements in a tailored way.

Under NIST CSF Core Functions, each function covers an essential aspect of cybersecurity management:

- **Govern**: (Introduced in CSF 2.0) Develop and oversee the organization's cybersecurity strategy, risk management, and governance processes. This function ensures senior leadership engagement and integration of cybersecurity into enterprise risk decisions. It involves establishing policies, roles, and oversight mechanisms for cybersecurity.
- **Identify**: Develop an organizational understanding of cybersecurity risks to systems, assets, data, and capabilities. This includes asset management, business environment understanding, governance (policies and legal requirements), risk assessment, and supply chain risk management. In practical terms, the Identify function ensures you know what you have (assets and data), the business

context and dependencies, and the risks facing those assets. For example, identifying all hardware and software assets (inventory) is a key Category in this function. Identifying risks and vulnerabilities (through risk assessments) and understanding compliance requirements also fall here.

- **Protect**: Design and implement appropriate safeguards to ensure delivery of critical services. The Protect function encompasses controls like access control, data security, maintenance, and protective technology management. The goal is to prevent or contain cybersecurity events. Example Categories include Identity Management and Access Control, Awareness and Training, Data Security, Information Protection Processes and Procedures, Maintenance, and Protective Technology. An outcome might be "access to assets is limited to authorized users, processes, and devices" - achieved via controls like account management and network segmentation.
- **Detect**: Implement activities to promptly identify the occurrence of cybersecurity events. This function covers continuous security monitoring, threat detection processes, and anomaly detection. Categories include Anomalies and Events, Security Continuous Monitoring, and Detection Processes. Effective detection means an organization can quickly spot unusual activity or known attack patterns in their environment. For example, having a centralized logging and SIEM (Security Information and Event Management) system supports the Detect function by correlating events to find indicators of compromise.
- **Respond**: Take action regarding a detected cybersecurity incident to contain the impact and eradicate the threat. The Respond function involves incident response planning, communications, analysis, mitigation, and improvements. Key Categories are Response Planning, Communications (coordinating with stakeholders, law enforcement), Analysis (investigating the incident), Mitigation (containing/remediating), and Improvements (lessons learned) to ensure incidents are handled efficiently and do not recur. A simple example is having an up-to-date incident response plan and team ready, which allows a coordinated reaction when an intrusion is detected.

- **Recover**: Implement recovery plans to restore any capabilities or services impaired by cybersecurity incidents. This includes activities like recovery planning, improvements, and communication of recovery progress to stakeholders. Categories such as Recovery Planning, Improvements (post-incident), and Communications ensure that after an incident, operations are brought back to normal and improvements are made. For example, regularly tested data backups and a business continuity plan are crucial subcomponents of the Recover function, enabling restoration of systems and data after events like ransomware attacks.

It's important to note that these CSF functions are high-level and iterative; organizations continuously perform identify-protect-detect and govern activities as part of normal operations and stand ready to respond and recover when incidents occur. NIST designed the framework to be "sector-, country-, and technology-neutral," meaning it can be applied by any organization globally to improve cybersecurity risk management. Over time, the CSF has indeed been adopted internationally in various industries as a best-practice framework for cybersecurity governance. In fact, CSF 2.0 explicitly broadened its scope from critical infrastructure to all organizations, reflecting its global usefulness.

Governance Emphasis in CSF 2.0: One of the major updates in NIST CSF 2.0 (released in February 2024) was the introduction of the "Govern" function and emphasis on cybersecurity governance. This addition underscores that cybersecurity must be treated as an enterprise risk, on par with financial, reputational, and other risks considered by senior leadership. The Govern function deals with how organizations make informed decisions, establish oversight, and direct and monitor their cybersecurity risk management. It includes activities like defining a risk management strategy, ensuring adequate resources and roles for security, and integrating cyber risk into enterprise risk governance. By including Govern, CSF 2.0 encourages organizations to have top-down support and accountability for security. It aligns with trends in which boards and executives are expected to actively oversee cybersecurity strategy. Notably, the Center for Internet Security updated its own controls (v8.1) to add a similar Governance element for alignment, illustrating how frameworks are coalescing around governance as a core pillar.

Using NIST CSF: Practically, organizations use the NIST CSF as a road map to compare their current practices against the framework's recommended outcomes. A common approach is to perform a gap analysis by listing the CSF Subcategories (e.g., "PR.AC-1: Identities and credentials are managed for authorized devices and users") and determining whether the organization has controls in place for each. The Informative References in the CSF Core link to detailed controls in standards like ISO/IEC 27001 Annex A, NIST SP 800-53, COBIT, etc., which help practitioners identify specific measures to implement. The CSF does not replace those standards but rather provides a high-level structure to organize and communicate the security program. Many organizations start with the CSF to get a broad view of their security posture, then dive into specific standards for implementation guidance. As an example of its flexible use, a small business might use CSF as a checklist of fundamental practices and track improvement over time, whereas a large enterprise might align all its departmental security activities to CSF functions to ensure comprehensive coverage. Because the CSF is not a prescriptive control checklist but a framework of outcomes, it allows mapping to practically any other framework or compliance requirement, making it a powerful tool for aligning diverse security efforts.

Relationship to Other Frameworks: NIST CSF is explicitly designed to be compatible with and mapped to other standards. It adopts a risk-based approach similar to ISO/IEC 27001, focusing on identifying and treating risks in alignment with business objectives. Both emphasize continuous improvement (CSF via iterative assessments, ISO via the Plan-Do-Check-Act cycle). The CSF Core's Categories and Subcategories include mappings to ISO controls and other best practices, serving as a Rosetta stone between frameworks. For example, the CSF Protect function's category for Data Security (PR.DS) can be directly mapped to ISO/IEC 27001 controls on cryptography and data protection or to specific CIS Controls. NIST has also published crosswalks such as mappings between NIST CSF and the CIS Critical Controls and CSF to NIST's own 800-53 control catalog (via SP 800-53's Appendix mappings). This means an organization can use CSF as an umbrella to ensure nothing is missed, even if they ultimately undergo an ISO 27001 certification or follow CIS benchmarks internally. We will explore such mappings in a later section, but it's worth noting here that CSF acts as a unifying framework. It is often recommended as a starting point for organizations building a cybersecurity program because of its flexibility and scalability. Smaller or less mature organizations appreciate CSF's simplicity and adaptability, whereas highly regulated or larger entities often use CSF in tandem with a certifiable standard like ISO 27001 to get the best of both worlds.

In summary, the NIST Cybersecurity Framework provides a high-level, function-oriented approach to cybersecurity governance and risk management. It has six core Functions (as of CSF 2.0) that cover the lifecycle of managing cyber risk, from governance and identification of assets and risks to protection, detection, response, and recovery. Its risk-based, flexible nature makes it applicable to any organization, and it complements other detailed standards by offering a common language and structure. Organizations adopting NIST CSF create Profiles to track their current and target security postures and use the framework to prioritize improvements. By doing so, they ensure all fundamental areas of cybersecurity are addressed and can more easily communicate their program status to executives, auditors, and partners. As one source aptly notes, "NIST CSF is more focused on general best practices and guidelines... a foundational body of knowledge for integrating security practices into a complex organization." Used effectively, it aligns technical security initiatives with business-level risk management and prepares organizations to meet various compliance obligations through a unified, strategic approach.

ISO/IEC 27001 and Related ISO Standards

ISO/IEC 27001 is an internationally recognized standard for establishing and operating an Information Security Management System (ISMS). Published by the International Organization for Standardization (ISO) and International Electrotechnical Commission (IEC), ISO/IEC 27001 provides a comprehensive framework for managing an organization's information security in a systematic, risk-based way. While NIST CSF is a voluntary guidance framework, ISO 27001 is a certifiable standard - organizations can be audited and certified compliant with ISO 27001 by accredited certification bodies. This distinction makes ISO 27001 especially popular among organizations that need to demonstrate security assurance to customers, partners, or regulators.

ISMS and Structure: At its core, ISO/IEC 27001 defines requirements for an Information Security Management System - essentially, the policies, processes, and controls by which an organization secures its information assets. It follows the classic management system model of Plan-Do-Check-Act (PDCA) for continuous improvement. The standard is divided into ten main clauses (four through ten) which outline mandatory requirements for establishing the ISMS (such as defining context, leadership commitment, planning, support, operation, performance evaluation, and improvement). These clauses include things like conducting risk assessments, setting up security objectives, training staff, and internal auditing of the ISMS. In the 2022 version of ISO 27001, these clauses remained largely consistent with the 2013 version, emphasizing that organizations must demonstrate leadership involvement, resource allocation, communication, and routine evaluation of the ISMS's effectiveness.

A critical part of ISO 27001 is Annex A, which is a reference list of security controls. Annex A is not exhaustive or mandatory in itself; rather, after performing a risk assessment, an organization selects which Annex A controls are relevant to treat identified risks (documenting any exclusions). In ISO/IEC 27001:2013, Annex A contained 114 controls organized into 14 domains (such as Asset Management, Access Control, Cryptography, Physical Security, etc.). In the updated ISO/IEC 27001:2022, Annex A was revised to align with the new ISO 27002:2022 guidance. The current Annex A has 93 controls grouped into four high-level categories or "themes":

- **Organizational Controls (37 Controls)**: Covering policies, governance, risk management, supplier security, incident management, etc.
- **People Controls (8 Controls)**: Covering HR security, training and awareness, etc.
- **Physical Controls (14 Controls)**: Covering facility security, equipment protection, etc.
- **Technological Controls (34 Controls)**: Covering IT-specific controls like access control, encryption, network security, system acquisition and development, etc.

This reorganization was intended to remove some redundancy and modernize the control set (e.g., adding controls for cloud services, threat intelligence, and data leakage prevention in the 2022 update). Each control in Annex A is fairly high-level (e.g., "Access control policy" or "Physical entry controls"), and organizations are expected to implement them in a way that fits their context and risk. For more detailed implementation guidance, ISO 27002 provides best practices for each control, but ISO 27001 itself just requires that the controls (or alternative controls) be implemented according to the identified risks.

Risk-Based Approach: A key similarity between ISO 27001 and NIST CSF is their risk-based approach to security management. ISO 27001 requires organizations to systematically assess information security risks (considering threats, vulnerabilities, and impacts), determine risk treatment options, and then apply controls (from Annex

A or others) to mitigate those risks in line with an overall risk appetite. This ensures that security resources are directed where they are most needed. Both frameworks aim to align security efforts with the organization's specific context and threat landscape. In ISO 27001, this is formalized: you must have a risk assessment methodology and maintain a Statement of Applicability (SoA) that lists which Annex A controls are applied or not, with justifications. The SoA acts as a bridge between identified risks and selected controls, demonstrating that all relevant risks have been addressed with some control measure.

Certification and Global Adoption: One of the attractions of ISO/IEC 27001 is that an organization can earn a certificate to show it meets the standard. An external auditor (from an accredited Certification Body) will perform an audit of the ISMS - examining documentation, interviewing personnel, and checking that controls are operating - to determine if the requirements of the standard are met. If successful, the organization is issued an ISO/IEC 27001 certificate, typically valid for three years with surveillance audits annually. This certification is globally recognized and often used as a trust signal. For example, a cloud service provider may achieve ISO 27001 certification to assure customers that it follows internationally vetted security processes. ISO/IEC 27001:2022 should now be treated as the current baseline for new and maintained ISMS programs. Organizations that previously held ISO/IEC 27001:2013 certification were required to complete their transition to the 2022 version by the October 2025 transition deadline. For current planning, audit preparation, and control mapping, organizations should align to ISO/IEC 27001:2022 and its updated Annex A control structure. This reflects the continuous evolution of the standard to address new security challenges (the update from 2013 to 2022 integrated lessons from the past decade, including the rise of cloud computing and more emphasis on cybersecurity in supply chains).

Globally, ISO 27001 is one of the most popular security frameworks for formal compliance. It is often required or strongly preferred in industries dealing with sensitive data or by multinational clients who seek consistent security assurance. ISO 27001's strength lies in its comprehensive governance model - it not only lists controls but ensures there is an overall management system wrapping around those controls to verify they are appropriate and effective (through internal audits, management reviews, corrective actions for issues, etc.). The result is a cycle of continuous improvement in security. An ISMS per ISO 27001 helps organizations fulfill legal, contractual, and regulatory requirements by providing structure and documentation (for instance, ISO 27001 can support compliance with laws like GDPR because it requires data protection controls and an inventory of data assets, among other things).

Related ISO 27xxx Standards: ISO/IEC 27001 is part of the ISO 27000 family of standards which cover various aspects of information security and privacy. Some notable related standards include

- **ISO/IEC 27002**: A code of practice providing detailed security control guidelines. While ISO 27001 says "what" to do (as requirements), ISO 27002 offers advice on "how" to implement controls and is a very useful companion. The 2022 edition of ISO 27002 aligns with the new 93 controls.
- **ISO/IEC 27017**: Security controls for cloud services (augmenting ISO 27002 with cloud-specific guidance).
- **ISO/IEC 27018**: Focuses on the protection of personally identifiable information (PII) in public clouds.
- **ISO/IEC 27005**: Guidelines for information security risk management (supporting the risk assessment process required by ISO 27001).
- **ISO/IEC 27701**: An extension to 27001/27002 for privacy information management (mapping to GDPR and other privacy laws, effectively a "privacy extension" to an ISMS).
- **ISO/IEC 27031**: Guidelines for ICT readiness for business continuity (related to the incident and business continuity controls).
- **ISO/IEC 22301**: Business continuity management systems, often used in conjunction since ISO 27001 has a section on business continuity (Annex A domain A.17 in the 2013 version).

Organizations often use ISO 27001 as a baseline and integrate other frameworks or standards as needed. For example, one can run a combined ISO 27001 and ISO 27701 (privacy) management system to cover both security and privacy in one audit/certification. Similarly, if an organization must comply with sector-specific regulations (like healthcare HIPAA or financial PCI DSS), an ISO 27001 ISMS can be the umbrella under which those specific requirements are managed. ISO 27001 shares significant overlap with other frameworks; one source notes it facilitates compliance with PCI DSS, HIPAA, and others due to this overlap. Essentially, achieving ISO 27001 means you have solid processes that likely cover many common controls required elsewhere. However,

ISO certification doesn't automatically mean compliance with all other standards – mappings and perhaps additional controls might be needed – but it sets a strong foundation.

ISO 27001 vs. NIST CSF and Others: While ISO 27001 and NIST CSF are often discussed together, they have different use cases. ISO 27001 is auditable and formally recognized, making it suitable when you need a credential or when consistent, repeatable processes are crucial (e.g., in a large enterprise or for regulatory reasons). NIST CSF is flexible and not certifiable, making it easier to adopt initially or in environments where formal certification is not required. A useful analogy from one source compares them: NIST CSF provides a high-level road map and emphasizes voluntary improvement, whereas ISO 27001 provides a structured ISMS and stresses documented procedures, audits, and continual compliance. The two can work in tandem – for instance, an organization might use NIST CSF to guide and prioritize operational security improvements while simultaneously building an ISO 27001-compliant ISMS to get certified. The frameworks are certainly not mutually exclusive; in fact, many of the controls and outcomes map closely. For example, NIST CSF's Identify (ID) function with category Asset Management (ID.AM) corresponds to ISO 27001's requirements for asset inventory (Annex A.8). The CSF's Protect (PR) function includes categories like Data Security (PR.DS) and Access Control (PR.AC) which align with ISO's controls for cryptography, backup, access control policies, etc. There are published crosswalks mapping NIST CSF Core Subcategories to ISO 27001 Annex A controls, highlighting these correspondences. Such crosswalks help organizations "speak both languages" – for instance, a company could tell a US partner that they meet all NIST CSF subcategories and simultaneously tell a European partner that they're ISO 27001 certified, with both statements referring to the same underlying practices.

Benefits and Considerations: Adopting ISO/IEC 27001 brings a disciplined approach to security governance. It forces organizations to think of security not as a one-time project but as an ongoing process embedded in business operations. Top management must be involved (signing the security policy, reviewing ISMS performance), which elevates the priority of cybersecurity in the organization. It also clarifies roles and responsibilities, requires security awareness training, and ensures incidents are formally managed and learned from. For companies seeking external validation, ISO 27001 certification can be a competitive advantage – it demonstrates to clients and regulators that the company has met an international benchmark for security. On the other hand, preparing for ISO 27001 certification can be resource-intensive: it requires thorough documentation (policies, procedures, risk assessments, treatment plans, etc.) and evidence that controls are working overtime. Many organizations start with a gap assessment against ISO 27001, remediate any shortcomings, run the ISMS for a few months to gather records, and then call in auditors for a certification audit.

In summary, ISO/IEC 27001 provides a holistic, auditable framework for information security management, aligning people, processes, and technology under a continuous improvement model. Its related standards (ISO 27002, 27017, 27005, etc.) support specific areas like implementation guidance and risk management. The standard emphasis on risk assessment and control selection means it's tailorable: you implement only what's relevant to your organization's risks, but you must justify and manage that systematically. In the context of governance frameworks, ISO 27001 represents the gold standard for formal security management - a high-level framework that ensures all aspects of security are considered (from physical security of facilities to technical controls and legal compliance) and that the organization can demonstrate accountability through documentation and audits. We will later discuss how ISO controls can be mapped alongside other frameworks (like NIST, CIS) to ensure comprehensive coverage and efficient compliance.

CIS Critical Security Controls (CIS Controls)

The CIS Critical Security Controls (formerly known as SANS Top 20 and often just called the CIS Controls) are a prescriptive, prioritized set of best practice security measures maintained by the Center for Internet Security (CIS), a nonprofit organization. Unlike high-level frameworks (NIST CSF, ISO 27001), the CIS Controls focus on specific actionable safeguards that organizations can implement to protect against common threats. They are frequently described as a minimum baseline of cybersecurity hygiene - especially for small and medium-sized enterprises that need practical guidance on "where to start" in securing their environment.

Structure and Evolution: As of version 8.1 (released in October 2023), there are 18 CIS Controls, each representing a broad area of cybersecurity (e.g., Inventory of Assets, Vulnerability Management, Email and Web Browser Protection, Malware Defenses, Incident Response, etc.). Each Control is further broken down into Safeguards (formerly called Sub-Controls), which are specific actions or technical controls. In CIS v8, the term "Safeguards" was introduced to denote these individual best practices. There are a total of 153 Safeguards across the 18 Controls in v8. Each Safeguard is phrased as a specific defensive action like “Establish and Maintain an Inventory of Enterprise Assets” or “Enable Logging for Network Sessions.”

One key feature of CIS Controls is prioritization through Implementation Groups (IGs). The Safeguards are divided into three Implementation Groups: IG1 (basic cyber hygiene), IG2, and IG3, reflecting the progressively more complex needs of larger or more at-risk organizations. Implementation Group 1 includes a foundational subset of Safeguards (approximately 56 of them) that every organization should implement as a minimum baseline. These typically address the most common attacks and fundamental practices (asset inventory, secure configurations, patching, etc.). IG2 builds upon IG1, adding more safeguards for organizations with moderate resources and risk (often mid-sized organizations), and IG3 includes the most advanced practices for organizations with significant risk (like large enterprises or targets such as finance, defense). This IG approach allows companies to phase their implementation: start with IG1 to cover the basics, then expand to IG2 and IG3 as appropriate. For example, Control 1 (Inventory of Enterprise Assets) might have a basic Safeguard in IG1 to maintain an asset inventory and additional Safeguards in IG2/IG3 about using automated discovery tools or tracking unauthorized devices.

The CIS Controls have gone through several revisions. Version 8 (released in 2021) was a major update from version 7, reorganizing and consolidating controls (from 20 controls down to 18) and making them more activity-focused rather than device-focused. For instance, previous separate controls for desktops, mobile, and IoT were merged into a single control for asset management. The update also considered cloud services and remote work. The minor update to v8.1 in 2023 introduced adjustments like updated mappings to other frameworks and notably the addition of a “Governance” function or tag to align with frameworks like NIST CSF 2.0. This reflects that even a technical control set like CIS recognizes the role of governance.

Focus on Top Threats: The philosophy behind the CIS Controls is to prioritize security efforts on areas that stop the most common and damaging attacks. The controls were originally derived from analyzing attack patterns and consulting a community of experts to identify what basic things, if done, would mitigate a large percentage of incidents. As such, the Controls cover things like knowing what hardware and software is in your environment (so you can secure it), reducing the attack surface via secure configurations and vulnerability management, controlling use of administrative privileges, deploying malware defenses, and so on. Empirical data (from threat reports, real incident statistics) has influenced their content. The CIS Community Defense Model is a companion analysis that maps how the CIS Controls defend against specific attack techniques; for example, it quantifies that implementing certain controls will help thwart ransomware, web application hacking, insider threats, etc.

Prescriptive and Measurable: Each CIS Safeguard is written in a way that is testable – e.g., "Use Multi-Factor Authentication for All Administrative Access" or "Ensure Portable Devices are Encrypted." This makes the CIS Controls very practical for IT and security staff to implement and audit. Organizations can self-assess or use CIS's CSAT (CIS Security Assessment Tool) to measure how many safeguards they have in place. It's very common to use CIS Controls as a checklist for hardening an environment. In fact, some regulatory bodies and state laws reference CIS Controls as an example of reasonable security practices. For instance, several US states require government agencies or contractors to implement cybersecurity best practices and explicitly cite the CIS Controls as a framework to use. This effectively elevates the CIS Controls to a de facto standard for baseline security.

Relation to Governance Frameworks: While the CIS Controls are tactical, they are often mapped to broader frameworks and compliance requirements. The CIS organization provides mapping documents showing how each CIS Control/Safeguard maps to other standards like NIST CSF, NIST 800-53, ISO/IEC 27001, PCI DSS, HIPAA, etc. For example, CIS Control 5 (Account Management) will align with NIST CSF category PR.AC (access control) and various ISO 27001 Annex A controls on user access management. Such mappings help organizations that choose the CIS Controls as their operational checklist to also demonstrate compliance or alignment with higher-level frameworks. It essentially creates an "on-ramp" to compliance – implement CIS Controls, and you will have covered many requirements of common regulations. A healthcare organization, for instance, can map CIS Safeguards to HIPAA Security Rule criteria to ensure nothing is missed.

Using CIS Controls: Many organizations adopt the CIS Controls as a starting baseline, especially if they do not have a full governance program in place yet. It's not uncommon for a small company to say: "Let's implement CIS IG1 this year," which would give them a solid foundation of about 56 essential safeguards (inventory, patching, antivirus, backups, etc.). Because the controls are prioritized, this helps simplify the approach to threat protection – focusing on the most critical things first. Once IG1 is done, they might progress to IG2, adding more sophisticated controls like security monitoring (SOC) and penetration testing. The prescriptive nature of CIS Controls also makes them attractive for internal audits or assessments. An internal auditor can literally check if each Safeguard is in place and find evidence (e.g., check that an asset inventory exists and is updated, check that administrative accounts are reviewed, etc.). Organizations sometimes create their own spreadsheets or use GRC tools to track the implementation of each Safeguard and assign owners.

Example Controls: To give a sense of coverage, here are a few of the CIS Controls (v8) with brief descriptions:

- **Control 1: Inventory and Control of Enterprise Assets**: Keep a detailed inventory of all devices and systems (incl. cloud and IoT) connected to the network and manage them actively. Rationale: You can't secure what you don't know about; unmanaged devices are a common entry point.
- **Control 2: Inventory and Control of Software Assets**: Track all software and ensure only authorized software is installed and running. Rationale: Prevent malware or unauthorized apps; patch known software promptly.
- **Control 3: Data Protection**: Develop processes and technical measures to classify and secure data (encryption, data retention and disposal policies, etc.). Rationale: Protecting sensitive data is crucial for privacy and compliance.
- **Control 5: Account Management**: Use tools/processes to manage user accounts and their authorization, including for admins and service accounts. Rationale: Accounts are the keys to systems; ensuring proper creation, monitoring, and removal of accounts helps prevent unauthorized access.
- **Control 7: Continuous Vulnerability Management**: Continuously scan for vulnerabilities and remediate them (patching, updates). Rationale: Unpatched vulnerabilities are frequently exploited; regular scanning reduces exposure.
- **Control 8: Audit Log Management**: Collect, alert, and review logs of events, especially for security-relevant activities. Rationale: Logging and monitoring are needed to detect and investigate incidents.

- **Control 13: Network Monitoring and Defense**: Perform network monitoring, intrusion detection/prevention, to identify anomalous traffic. Rationale: Early detection of intrusions via network patterns can significantly reduce incident impact.
- **Control 17: Incident Response Management**: Establish an incident response plan and management process. Rationale: So that when incidents occur, the damage is contained and recovery is faster.

Each control has several Safeguards; for instance, under Control 17 (Incident Response), Safeguards include having a written incident response plan, assigning roles, conducting incident response exercises, etc. These details make the CIS Controls a practical playbook for security operations.

Community and Updates: The CIS Controls are maintained via a global community consensus process. Experts from various industries volunteer to update the controls based on emerging threats and feedback. This community aspect ensures the controls remain relevant. For example, in v8, new Safeguards were added to address cloud services and working from home - reflecting changes in technology use. The CIS also releases companion guides like "CIS Controls Cloud Companion Guide" or mappings for specific sectors. Additionally, the CIS Benchmarks (secure configuration guides for systems like Windows, Linux, and cloud provider settings) complement Control 4 (Secure Configuration of Enterprise Assets and Software). By using CIS Benchmarks to harden systems, an organization in effect fulfills many of the requirements of CIS Control 4.

Alignment with Governance: Although the CIS Controls themselves are largely technical, implementing them can be an integral part of an organization's governance and risk management strategy. They can be seen as the implementation layer that feeds into frameworks like NIST CSF or ISO 27001. For instance, an organization might use NIST CSF to set high-level objectives ("we need to protect our assets and detect threats") and use CIS Controls as the concrete steps to achieve those objectives ("inventory assets, apply patches within 14 days, deploy EDR for malware defense, etc."). The CIS Controls provide a common language between security practitioners and auditors/regulators for what specific measures are in place.

Notably, because of their compliance mappings, the CIS Controls can help organizations kill multiple birds with one stone. By following CIS Controls, a company simultaneously moves toward compliance with multiple regulations. CIS even states that by implementing the Controls, you create an "on-ramp" to meet the requirements of laws like PCI DSS, HIPAA, GDPR, and others. It simplifies compliance efforts by unifying them under one actionable checklist. This is especially helpful for internal and external audits, as we'll discuss later – evidence can be collected against CIS Safeguards, which then satisfies auditors for different frameworks.

In summary, CIS Critical Security Controls are a highly practical and prioritized set of cybersecurity actions that organizations of any size can use to improve their security posture. They distill the vast array of possible security measures into a focused list of the most essential defenses against real-world threats. By starting with IG1 and progressing through IG3, organizations can systematically bolster their defenses. The CIS Controls complement higher-level governance frameworks by providing the "how-to" details for technical and operational controls. They are also a valuable tool for compliance and audit preparation, due to the extensive mappings available. Thousands of organizations and many government entities leverage the CIS Controls as a baseline; as one source notes, they are considered a "minimum standard of information security" for establishing reasonable security practices. Ultimately, incorporating the CIS Controls into your security program helps ensure that your defense strategy is aligned with known threats and consensus best practices, making it a solid foundation for any broader security or compliance initiatives.

MITRE ATT&CK Framework

The MITRE ATT&CK framework is quite different from the governance and control frameworks discussed above. Rather than prescribing what security measures to implement, ATT&CK is a knowledge base of adversary tactics and techniques – essentially a structured way to describe how attackers operate and how defenders can detect or mitigate their methods. Developed by MITRE, a US federally funded research organization, ATT&CK (which stands for Adversarial Tactics, Techniques, and Common Knowledge) has gained global prominence as a foundation for threat intelligence, threat-informed defense, and cybersecurity operations.

What ATT&CK Is: MITRE ATT&CK is a globally accessible knowledge base of cyber adversary behaviors, based on real-world observations of attacks. It is organized as a set of matrices. The most well-known is the Enterprise ATT&CK Matrix, which covers tactics and techniques used against enterprise IT environments (Windows, Linux, macOS, cloud, networks, etc.). There are also specialized matrices for Mobile (tactics/techniques used against mobile devices) and ICS (industrial control systems). The Enterprise matrix is further sub-divided; for example, MITRE maintains sub-matrices for different domains like Cloud, Containers, Microsoft 365, etc., but they all integrate under the enterprise scheme.

In an ATT&CK matrix, the columns represent Tactics - the adversary's tactical goals or the phases of an attack (the "why" of an action) - and under each tactic column are specific Techniques (the "how" - the methods used to achieve that tactic). The Enterprise ATT&CK matrix defines 14 tactic categories, arranged roughly in the order of an attack lifecycle. These tactics range from Reconnaissance (gathering information before the attack) and Initial Access (penetrating the target) through Execution, Persistence, Privilege Escalation, Defense Evasion, Credential Access, Discovery, Lateral Movement, Collection, Exfiltration, and finally Impact (disrupting or destroying systems). Each tactic is a goal like "Establish Foothold" or "Move Laterally," and within each are numerous techniques adversaries use. For example, under the "Privilege Escalation" tactic, there might be techniques like Bypass User Account Control, Exploitation for Privilege Escalation, or Valid Accounts usage.

There are hundreds of defined techniques and sub-techniques in ATT&CK, and the framework is updated regularly as adversary behavior evolves. Because technique counts change over time, it is better to reference ATT&CK as a continuously maintained knowledge base rather than freezing the chapter to a specific count. Each technique is identified by a unique ID (e.g., T1548 for "Abuse Elevation Control Mechanism") and includes a description of what the adversary does, what it achieves, known threat actors or malware that utilize it, platforms it applies to, and references to real-world incidents. Importantly, ATT&CK entries also include mitigation suggestions and detection suggestions for each technique - meaning it's not only a catalog of threats, but also a guide for defenders on how to address those threats.

Use Cases of ATT&CK: The MITRE ATT&CK framework has become a lingua franca for cyber threat intelligence and a tool for SOC (Security Operations Center) teams, penetration testers, and red/blue teams. Some of its key uses include

- **Adversary Emulation**: Security teams can simulate attacks using known ATT&CK techniques to test defenses (e.g., using red team exercises that emulate a ransomware actor's known behavior, drawn from ATT&CK). This helps identify gaps in detection and response.

- **Threat Intelligence**: Analysts classify and share information about cyber threat groups in terms of the ATT&CK techniques they employ. For instance, an intel report might say "Group X commonly uses T1566 (Phishing) for initial access and T1059 (Command-Line Interface) for execution." This structured description makes it easier to understand and compare threats.
- **Detection and Monitoring**: SOCs map their detection capabilities or SIEM use-cases to ATT&CK techniques. For example, ensure there are alerts for suspicious use of PowerShell (Technique T1059.001) or unusual persistence mechanisms. By mapping which techniques are covered by logging and analytics, teams can find blind spots (e.g., "we have no visibility into technique T1027 Obfuscated Files/Scripts"). Many SIEM and EDR vendors even present detections in an ATT&CK context.
- **Assessment of Security Coverage**: Organizations use ATT&CK to measure how well their controls cover known adversary behaviors. For example, MITRE's CTID (Center for Threat-Informed Defense) produced a mapping of NIST 800-53 controls to ATT&CK techniques. This can tell a defender which controls help mitigate or detect which techniques. If certain techniques have no corresponding controls, that might indicate a gap. The idea is to ensure that for every step an attacker might take (according to ATT&CK), the organization has some defense or detection in place. Indeed, the NIST 800-53 to ATT&CK project yielded over 6,300 mappings of controls to techniques, providing a resource for assessing coverage against real-world threats. The goal is to integrate threat knowledge into the risk management process, so that when you design or evaluate controls, you consider the specific threats they address.
- **Incident Response and Investigation**: When analyzing an attack, responders can use the ATT&CK framework to categorize what was observed and ensure they look for related techniques. For instance, if you found evidence of lateral movement via remote desktop (T1021.001), you might also check for credential dumping (T1003) or other persistence mechanisms (tactics that often go hand-in-hand). It provides a checklist of sorts for investigation and helps communicate what the adversary did in standardized terms.

Differences from Traditional Frameworks: Unlike NIST, ISO, or CIS, the ATT&CK framework is not about what you should implement organizationally; it's about understanding the threat side of the equation. It doesn't directly tell you to "implement multi-factor authentication" or "install an IDS" – instead, it might highlight that attackers commonly steal credentials from memory (Technique T1003, Credential Dumping), which in turn implies that you should have controls to prevent or detect that (like system lockdown, credential guard, or log alerts for certain process accesses). In other words, ATT&CK helps you think like an attacker and then choose defensive measures accordingly. It is thus a perfect complement to control frameworks: the control frameworks ensure you have broad best practices in place, and ATT&CK ensures you are aware of and watching for how those controls might be circumvented. As one source explains, MITRE ATT&CK is focused on specific tactics and techniques from real incidents, giving insight into how attackers circumvent defenses, whereas NIST CSF focuses on general best practices and integration of security into the organization. Both can be effective if implemented well, and in fact, organizations are encouraged to map between the two: for any practice in NIST CSF, consider which ATT&CK techniques it mitigates; conversely, for any ATT&CK technique of concern, ensure you have a CSF-aligned practice or control to address it.

ATT&CK in Governance and Risk Management: While ATT&CK itself is not a governance framework, it has started to influence higher-level strategies. The concept of threat-informed defense means integrating threat intelligence (like ATT&CK data) into governance and risk management decisions. For example, when doing a risk assessment (as required by ISO 27001 or NIST RMF), an organization could use ATT&CK to systematically identify what techniques might be used against their crown jewels and then evaluate if controls are in place for those. This makes risk assessments more empirical and aligned to actual adversary behavior. Additionally, some organizations build custom threat models or attack simulations to test their security program's effectiveness, effectively using ATT&CK as a yardstick: e.g., "Can we detect and respond to the top ten techniques that ransomware groups use? If not, improve controls in those areas."

From an audit and compliance perspective, auditors traditionally check control existence ("Do you have AV? Do you have logging?"). But forward-looking security audits (especially internal ones or in frameworks like SOC 2's "description criteria") might also ask, "How do you know your controls cover relevant threats?" Mapping controls to ATT&CK can provide evidence of due diligence: it shows the organization has thought about specific threats. Regulators are increasingly interested in outcomes (are you secure against likely attacks?) rather than just checklists, and ATT&CK is a way to demonstrate that outcome-based perspective. As an example, a defense contractor complying with NIST 800-171 could use ATT&CK mappings to show that each required control helps mitigate certain techniques used by APTs targeting their industry, thereby reinforcing why those controls are critical.

Keeping ATT&CK Updated: MITRE maintains the ATT&CK knowledge base with input from the community. New techniques are added as threat actors evolve. For instance, in recent years, new tactics for cloud environments (like compromising cloud authentication tokens) have been incorporated. The framework version is incremented periodically (v10, v11, etc.) with new content. Users of ATT&CK need to stay updated; fortunately, MITRE provides ATT&CK in various formats (online website, STIX/TAXII feeds, spreadsheets) to integrate into tools and processes.

In conclusion, the MITRE ATT&CK framework is a powerful tool for linking the world of offense to defense. It does not replace control frameworks but augments them by ensuring that a security program is threat-aware. Where frameworks like CIS or ISO tell you what to do in general, ATT&CK tells you what you're up against. Organizations that leverage ATT&CK alongside their governance frameworks gain a more granular understanding of their security posture: they can identify exactly which adversary behaviors they can stop or detect and where the gaps are. As one CISO guide suggests, mapping your security controls to ATT&CK tactics and techniques can highlight defensive gaps and guide investments. For example, you might realize you have strong protection against initial access (phishing defenses, web filters) but poor visibility into lateral movement (no internal network monitoring). That insight comes from an ATT&CK-oriented view. The outcome is a more robust security program that not only meets best practices on paper but is demonstrably effective against the tactics real attackers use in the wild. In the era of advanced persistent threats and AI-augmented attacks, such a threat-informed approach is increasingly seen as essential to modern information security governance.

Professional Security Certifications and Governance Alignment

Achieving professional cybersecurity certifications is a way for individuals to validate their knowledge and skills across a broad range of security topics. In the context of governance and frameworks, certifications often include content on risk management, security management practices, and regulatory compliance, ensuring that certified professionals are well-versed in aligning security programs with business and regulatory requirements. This section focuses on two prominent certifications - CISSP and CCSP - and discusses how the domains of knowledge in these certifications map to governance frameworks and risk management practices. Understanding this alignment can help practitioners see the connection between what they study for exams and what is expected in implementing frameworks like NIST CSF, ISO 27001, or in managing controls for audits.

CISSP: Certified Information Systems Security Professional

The CISSP is a globally respected certification for information security professionals, governed by $(ISC)^2$. Often dubbed "the gold standard" of security certs, CISSP certifies that an individual has deep knowledge across a range of security domains and the ability to design and manage an overall security program. CISSP is inherently vendor-neutral and covers managerial and technical aspects of security, which makes it very relevant for governance and high-level coordination of security efforts.

Domains of CISSP: The CISSP Common Body of Knowledge (CBK) is divided into eight domains: (1) Security and Risk Management, (2) Asset Security, (3) Security Architecture and Engineering, (4) Communication and Network Security, (5) Identity and Access Management (IAM), (6) Security Assessment and Testing, (7) Security Operations, and (8) Software Development Security. Each domain represents a cluster of concepts, best practices, and techniques that a security professional should know. Several of these domains tie directly into governance, risk, and compliance:

- **Domain 1: Security and Risk Management**: This domain is foundational and heavily focused on governance, risk, and compliance (GRC). It covers security governance principles, compliance requirements (laws, regulations, standards), professional ethics, security policies, and risk management concepts (like quantitative vs. qualitative risk analysis, risk appetite, etc.). For example, a CISSP candidate must learn about frameworks (such as ISO 27001, NIST SP 800-53), security control categories, confidentiality/integrity/availability concepts, and business continuity planning. This directly aligns with establishing an overall security program - e.g., understanding how to align security strategy with business goals, how to manage security risk through frameworks, and ensuring compliance with external requirements. In essence, CISSP Domain 1 teaches the importance of having governance structures (policies, roles, processes) in place and making sure security efforts are in line with organizational objectives and obligations. It also introduces the idea of security being a continuous, managed process (just like the PDCA cycle in ISO 27001 or the iterative improvement in NIST CSF).

- **Domain 2: Asset Security**: This domain involves managing information assets - classification, handling, and data lifecycle - which ties into governance through policies on data classification, data retention, and privacy requirements. It ensures professionals know how to protect information according to its value and sensitivity, a key part of compliance regimes (for instance, GDPR requires knowing where personal data is and protecting it accordingly).
- **Domain 5: Identity and Access Management**: IAM is often covered by technical controls (access control systems, authentication, etc.), but it also has governance aspects like defining access policies, least privilege, and managing identities across their lifecycle - which are reflected in frameworks (NIST CSF has an entire category on Access Control, ISO 27001 has controls on user access management). A CISSP must understand both how to implement IAM and how it fits into an overall policy (e.g., joiner-mover-leaver processes, role-based access control aligned to business roles).

- **Domain 7: Security Operations**: This includes incident management, logging and monitoring, disaster recovery – all of which require governance planning (incident response plans, DR plans, continuous monitoring strategies). It touches on frameworks like NIST's incident response guidance or ISO's requirements for incident management and continuity. A certified professional is expected to know how to organize an incident response capability, which aligns with implementing the Respond/Recover functions of NIST CSF or ISO's incident management controls.
- **Other Domains**: The remaining domains (Security Architecture and Engineering, Network Security, Software Security, Security Assessment) are more technical, but each has governance elements. For instance, Security Assessment and Testing covers audit techniques and control assessment, which is directly relevant to preparing for compliance audits or internal audits of controls (e.g., how to design test plans for controls, use of penetration testing). Software Development Security covers secure development processes, which align with governance policies requiring security in the SDLC (as mandated by many frameworks for organizations that develop software).

The breadth of CISSP means a certified individual should be able to understand and contribute to an organization's entire security program. How does this align with frameworks and risk management? Significantly. For example, when studying CISSP, candidates learn about security governance frameworks and standards as part of Domain 1. This includes high-level familiarity with NIST standards, ISO 27000 series, COBIT (for governance of IT), and risk frameworks like ISO 31000 or NIST's Risk Management Framework (RMF). Thus, a CISSP holder is not expected to have every control memorized, but they are expected to recognize the names and purposes of major frameworks and to know how to apply them for aligning security with business. A CISSP should know, for instance, that "ISO/IEC 27001 is an international standard for an ISMS, which can be used to manage and certify an organization's security program" or that "NIST SP 800-53 is a comprehensive catalog of security controls often used in government and mapping to NIST CSF." They should understand concepts like control selection based on risk, which directly plays into how one would use a framework like ISO 27001 (perform risk assessment, choose controls).

Furthermore, CISSP emphasizes the alignment of security with business and compliance – things like legal and regulatory issues (intellectual property law, privacy laws, export controls, etc.) are part of the curriculum. This means a CISSP is aware of compliance drivers and can help an organization integrate those into the security program (e.g., if an organization is subject to HIPAA, a CISSP would know that means strong controls for protecting health data are needed, aligning with specific frameworks or additional standards).

From a governance perspective, a CISSP is being trained to eventually take roles like Security Manager, Director, or CISO (indeed, ISC^2 markets CISSP as ideal for people who might become CISOs, security consultants, auditors, etc.). Those roles require a broad understanding to build policies, perform risk analysis, choose appropriate frameworks, and ensure the security program meets both internal goals and external requirements. CISSP's content on risk management (covering risk assessment methods, risk treatment options, and the importance of a risk register) directly translates to implementing enterprise risk management in alignment with corporate governance. A CISSP should be able to map risks to controls – for example, identify that a risk of data breach can be mitigated by controls in areas of encryption, DLP, access control, and monitoring, which relate to various domains and to certain NIST CSF categories or ISO controls.

Example of Alignment: Consider the CISSP Domain 1 knowledge: it highlights that governance and compliance are "pivotal" and stresses aligning security with regulations and standards. This is essentially the same goal as frameworks: to ensure an organization's security measures are not random, but rather aligned with best practices and obligations. A CISSP preparing, say, to secure a cloud deployment might recall from Domain 1 that they should consider relevant frameworks (like maybe CSA's Cloud Controls Matrix or ISO 27017 for cloud security) and regulatory demands, then ensure the chosen controls meet those – a process analogous to creating a compliance mapping or a controls matrix in an organization.

In practice, many organizations rely on CISSP-certified professionals to lead or audit their framework implementations. For instance, an internal audit function may require auditors to be CISSPs to validate that ISO 27001 controls are in place. Or a company aiming for SOC 2 or NIST 800-171 compliance might hire a CISSP as a consultant, confident that the person understands what controls need to be in place and how to structure policies (since CISSP covers policy development and security program management).

CISSP and Audits: CISSP knowledge also prepares professionals for audits. Domain 6 (Security Assessment and Testing) covers the basics of audits, security control testing, and reporting. A CISSP knows about audit concepts like sampling, evidence collection, and assessment methodologies (e.g., how to verify a control is working). This is directly useful when aligning and mapping controls for an external audit - the CISSP can interpret an audit requirement and map it to the organization's controls, then gather appropriate evidence. We will delve more into evidence in a later section, but the point here is that certifications incorporate these practices in their curriculum.

In summary, the CISSP certification domains align closely with governance and risk management functions. It instills a broad understanding of frameworks, controls, and processes that collectively form an information security program. A CISSP professional is expected to be able to take something like the NIST CSF or ISO 27001 and see how the various technical and procedural controls they've learned fit into those structures. The certification's emphasis on risk management and compliance means that CISSPs are often the ones ensuring that security efforts are not only technically sound but also legally and organizationally sound. This prepares them to map security controls across frameworks or to develop internal policies that satisfy external standards. As evidence of this alignment, one training resource notes that CISSP Domain 1 explicitly integrates governance, risk, and compliance, stressing aligning organizations with regulations and standards. This ethos permeates the CISSP CBK and is a big reason why CISSPs are valued in roles that involve designing or auditing comprehensive security programs.

CCSP: Certified Cloud Security Professional

The CCSP is a certification offered by $(ISC)^2$ in cooperation with the Cloud Security Alliance (CSA) that focuses on cloud security expertise. As organizations rapidly adopt cloud services, CCSP was created to ensure professionals have the knowledge to secure cloud environments in a manner consistent with global standards and best practices. CCSP covers both technical cloud security issues and the governance and risk management aspects of using cloud services. Given that cloud computing introduces unique security challenges (like loss of control over infrastructure, shared responsibility with providers, multi-jurisdictional legal issues, etc.), CCSP includes significant content on risk, compliance, and governance in the cloud context.

Domains of CCSP: The CCSP is organized into six domains: (1) Cloud Concepts, Architecture and Design; (2) Cloud Data Security; (3) Cloud Platform and Infrastructure Security; (4) Cloud Application Security; (5) Cloud Security Operations; and (6) Legal, Risk, and Compliance. We'll highlight Domain 6 in particular, as it directly pertains to governance, but it's worth noting that each domain has some GRC elements.

- **Domain 6: Legal, Risk, and Compliance**: This is the domain explicitly about governance in the cloud. It teaches candidates about the legal requirements in cloud environments (such as data privacy laws, e.g., GDPR, and how they apply to cloud providers and customers), the unique risks associated with cloud computing, compliance frameworks for cloud (like the CSA Cloud Controls Matrix (CCM), or how ISO 27001/17 apply to cloud, etc.), and audit processes for cloud services. Essentially, Domain 6 is where CCSP holders learn to "speak the language of lawyers and risk managers" in a cloud context, bridging technology and governance. Topics in this domain include cloud regulatory issues (data location, cross-border data flow, privacy, etc.), contract management and procurement (like understanding cloud service agreements and SLAs), risk assessment methods for cloud deployments, and compliance considerations like aligning cloud security controls with standards such as PCI DSS (for cloud cardholder data), HIPAA (for cloud-stored health data), or FedRAMP (for US government cloud). It also covers cloud-specific audit and assurance methods (e.g., understanding SOC 2 reports from cloud providers or ISO 27017 certification of providers). The inclusion of audit processes in the cloud is significant – CCSPs learn how to prepare for and undergo audits of cloud security, including what evidence might be needed from both the cloud customer and provider.
- Domains 1–5 (summary):
    - **Cloud Concepts, Architecture, and Design**: This sets the stage by explaining cloud computing concepts, service models (IaaS/PaaS/SaaS), deployment models (public, private, hybrid, etc.), and the fundamental shared security responsibilities between cloud provider and customer. Governance tie: understanding

these concepts is crucial for risk management – e.g., knowing in IaaS the customer is responsible for OS security, whereas in SaaS the provider handles it, which influences risk decisions and contractual governance.

- **Cloud Data Security**: Covers data lifecycle in the cloud, cloud data storage types, and controls like encryption, tokenization, and data loss prevention (DLP) for cloud. Governance tie: data classification policies must extend to the cloud, and compliance like GDPR needs techniques like encryption for data in the cloud.
- **Cloud Platform and Infrastructure Security**: Focuses on securing the underlying cloud infrastructure and virtualization, as well as understanding how to design secure cloud architectures. Governance tie: includes continuity and disaster recovery in the cloud, which relates to contractual and risk planning (e.g., ensuring providers meet certain uptime or that you have multi-region deployments to meet continuity requirements).
- **Cloud Application Security**: Discusses securing software in the cloud, DevOps/DevSecOps, using cloud-native security services, etc. Governance tie: ensuring software development in the cloud follows secure SDLC and that any compliance requirements for software (like OWASP ASVS or certain coding standards) are enforced.
- **Cloud Security Operations**: Addresses operations like logging, monitoring in the cloud, incident response in the cloud, managing cloud identities and access, and more. Governance tie: incident response roles and processes when using cloud (e.g., contractually defining how the cloud provider supports incidents) and ensuring continuous monitoring of cloud as part of the security program (aligning with frameworks that require log monitoring, etc.).

Across these domains, CCSP's content heavily references existing frameworks and standards. For example, candidates learn about the CSA's Cloud Controls Matrix (CCM), which is a framework specifically mapping cloud security controls to other standards (ISO, COBIT, etc.). They also learn about attestations and certifications relevant to cloud – such as ISO/IEC 27017 (cloud security controls), ISO/IEC 27018 (cloud privacy), SOC 1/SOC 2 reports, FedRAMP (a US government cloud compliance program), and regional standards like the EU's Cloud Code of Conduct. Thus, CCSP holders are prepared to align cloud security practices with these frameworks. They would understand, for instance, how to use the Cloud Controls Matrix to ensure a cloud deployment meets ISO 27001 or NIST CSF controls or how to interpret a cloud provider's SOC 2 Type II report and use it as evidence of certain controls when undergoing an audit.

Alignment with Governance: CCSP's emphasis on risk and compliance means that a certified professional knows how to incorporate cloud into an organization's overall GRC framework. Many organizations struggle with extending their security program to the cloud (a classic question: "How do we demonstrate compliance when we've outsourced infrastructure to AWS/Azure?"). A CCSP would have learned methodologies to do this – for instance, by using the shared responsibility model to delineate which controls the cloud provider must fulfill vs. which the customer must and then ensuring both sides' controls meet the required frameworks. They would also know the importance of cloud governance policies (like cloud usage policies, approving cloud services, etc.) and how they tie into risk management.

For example, part of governance is ensuring that new cloud services are assessed for risk and compliance before use (to avoid shadow IT issues). CCSP covers such governance controls by addressing cloud procurement and vendor management. It advises on due diligence: checking certifications of cloud providers, including contractual terms for security SLAs, right-to-audit clauses, data ownership, and breach notification – all of which are governance measures aligning with frameworks that require supply chain and vendor risk management (like ISO's supplier security controls or NIST's ID.SC category for supply chain risk).

Risk Management in Cloud: CCSP Domain 6 also delves into risk management for cloud. It teaches how to evaluate cloud risks (which may include multi-tenancy risks, hypervisor vulnerabilities, data loss, compliance violations, etc.) and how to adjust risk assessment processes to cover cloud technologies. This aligns with organizational risk management frameworks – e.g., if you use ISO 27005 or NIST RMF, a CCSP can contribute by identifying cloud-specific threats and vulnerabilities to include. Moreover, CCSP stresses that risk management in the cloud is not a one-time thing; it must be continuous and adapt to the dynamic nature of cloud (e.g., auto-scaling, serverless, etc., which can spin up and down rapidly). This again reinforces the concept that governance in the cloud era needs agility and continuous oversight, something the NIST CSF "Govern" function also highlights (supply chain and dynamic risk management).

Legal and Compliance Focus: Cloud often complicates legal compliance due to data residency and privacy laws. CCSP ensures professionals are aware of these issues. A CCSP knows that storing EU personal data in a US-based cloud might invoke GDPR concerns or using a cloud provider in another country might raise data transfer issues. They also learn about eDiscovery in the cloud, forensic readiness (which often requires coordination with providers), and contractual compliance commitments. Therefore, they are equipped to align cloud operations with frameworks and standards that an organization uses. If an organization is ISO 27001 certified and moves to the cloud, a CCSP would be able to map the ISO controls to the cloud environment and ensure the ISMS still covers things like physical security (now at the provider's data center – the CCSP would likely check the provider's ISO 27001 certification for that), or access control (ensuring integration with cloud IAM), etc.

CCSP vs. CISSP for Governance: While CISSP is broader, CCSP zeros in on cloud. Many CISSPs pursue CCSP to deepen their cloud-specific governance knowledge. The domains in CCSP align in part with CISSP's but with a cloud lens. For instance, CISSP has a domain on Security Operations and on Legal/Compliance, CCSP has one combined, focusing specifically on cloud operations and cloud legal/compliance. The synergy is such that a lot of foundational GRC knowledge from CISSP is built upon in CCSP but with the nuance of cloud shared responsibility, provider-consumer relationships, and cloud service models.

For governance frameworks: A CCSP-certified professional will be familiar with the CSA's Cloud Controls Matrix (CCM) and the related STAR registry (where cloud providers publish their compliance). They will know how CCM maps to NIST CSF, ISO 27001, etc., meaning they can help an organization cross-reference its cloud security controls with those broader frameworks. For example, if using NIST CSF, a CCSP can help ensure that for each CSF category, the relevant cloud controls (either the customer's or provider's) are identified. Many organizations create a cloud security governance addendum to their main frameworks, and CCSP content empowers professionals to do that systematically.

In Practice: Suppose an enterprise is migrating some systems to AWS. A CCSP on the team might lead the creation of a cloud risk assessment and controls mapping. They would identify risks like "unauthorized access to S3 buckets" or "cloud misconfiguration leading to data leak" and then map which controls mitigate those (e.g., enabling encryption, access logging, configuration audits). They'd align those controls with the company's overall security framework – e.g., say the company follows CIS Controls, the

CCSP might map specific CIS Safeguards to AWS configurations (like CIS Control 3 Data Protection Safeguards to enabling S3 encryption and lifecycle policies). They could also prepare evidence for an ISO 27001 audit showing that cloud systems are within scope and are controlled via both the provider's attestations and the customer's configurations. Essentially, CCSPs ensure cloud is not a black box in governance – they make it transparent how cloud workloads meet the same security and compliance requirements.

To quote an example from CCSP training: Domain 6 frames the CCSP as someone ready to "become the bridge between cloud technology and corporate governance," ensuring cloud solutions are not just technically sound but also legally compliant and risk-aware. This nicely encapsulates the role: CCSPs bring the cloud piece of the puzzle into alignment with overall security governance.

In summary, the CCSP certification equips professionals with knowledge to manage and secure cloud environments in line with governance frameworks and compliance needs. It covers cloud-specific interpretations of risk management, legal requirements, and security controls, enabling alignment of cloud security with an organization's existing GRC program. Cloud services often involve external providers, so CCSP emphasizes third-party risk management, contracts, and assurance – all governance concerns. With cloud now an integral part of most organizations' IT, having CCSPs means the organization can confidently extend their security program (be it NIST CSF, ISO 27001, CIS Controls, etc.) to the cloud rather than treating cloud separately or informally. Thus, CCSP and similar cloud certifications (like AWS's specialty certs, or CompTIA Cloud+, etc.) complement general certifications in preparing professionals to maintain a consistent, compliant security posture across all platforms.

Aligning Certification Knowledge with Frameworks and Risk Management

Both CISSP and CCSP (as well as other certifications like CISM, CRISC, etc.) share a common theme: they aim to produce security leaders who can align security initiatives with business goals and compliance requirements. The domains in these certifications map conceptually to various components of governance frameworks:

Risk Management: A heavy component in CISSP Domain 1 and CCSP Domain 6, risk management knowledge aligns with the risk-based approach of frameworks like NIST CSF and ISO 27001. A certified professional will know how to conduct risk assessments and can apply that to ensure the organization's use of frameworks is informed by actual risk priorities (e.g., focusing on high-risk areas in a CSF implementation or selecting ISO controls based on risk).

Governance Structures: Understanding roles, policies, and processes (CISSP Domain 1) means a certified pro can help set up governance committees, write charters, and define KPIs for security – all of which ensure the framework adoption (like NIST CSF's "Govern" function or ISO clause 5 Leadership) is effective. They know, for instance, the importance of senior management support and can communicate risk in business terms thanks to their training (CISSP even covers creating business cases for security).

Control Mapping: Professionals who have studied a broad array of standards can serve as translators between them. A CISSP/CCSP might be comfortable reading a law or standard and devising a controls checklist to comply. For example, if a new privacy law comes out, their broad knowledge helps them map its requirements to existing controls (perhaps referencing ISO 27701 or other frameworks) and integrate it into the ISMS or control framework the company uses.

Audit and Compliance: As noted, CISSP Domain 6 and CCSP Domain 6 cover preparing for audits, collecting evidence, and the importance of consistent processes. When it comes to internal or external audits, a certified professional is more likely to be prepared with proper documentation and evidence mapped to each control requirement, thereby streamlining the audit. Certifications like CISA (Certified Information Systems Auditor) also explicitly train on mapping and auditing, but even CISSP touches this area.

By aligning certification domains with frameworks, one can create a personal road map to ensure nothing is overlooked. For example, a CISSP knows that asset security is crucial (Domain 2) – so in any framework (be it NIST CSF Identify/Asset Management or ISO 27001's asset management controls), they will prioritize making sure asset inventories and classification are in place. Similarly, a CCSP knows legal and compliance issues in cloud – so if the organization adopts, say, CIS Controls, the CCSP might ensure an additional control for cloud contract review is added (since CIS Controls are somewhat generic, a CCSP might supplement them with cloud-specific checks).

To conclude this part: professional certifications reinforce and complement the knowledge needed to implement governance frameworks. The domains of CISSP and CCSP ensure that certified individuals can not only recall facts but also apply holistic thinking to secure an organization. They act as a bridge between theory and practice: the frameworks provide the structure, and the certified professional provides the expertise to fill that structure with effective policies, controls, and processes. In the next section, we will see how these controls and processes can be mapped across different frameworks and what strategies can be used to prepare for audits – tasks often led or executed by individuals who have the kind of comprehensive training that certifications offer.

Mapping Controls and Aligning Frameworks for Audits

One of the practical challenges organizations face is dealing with multiple security frameworks, standards, and compliance requirements at once. A company might be simultaneously aligning with NIST CSF internally, pursuing ISO/IEC 27001 certification, adhering to CIS Controls for best practices, and referencing MITRE ATT&CK to ensure threat coverage – all while preparing for external audits or assessments (such as ISO audits, SOC 2 examinations, compliance checks by regulators, etc.). This is where control mapping and alignment become crucial. By mapping controls and requirements between frameworks, organizations can avoid duplication of effort, identify gaps, and streamline audit preparations. In this section, we discuss how to cross-reference and map frameworks (NIST, ISO, CIS, MITRE) and provide examples of mapping tables/diagrams. We try to explain various frameworks through Figure 7-1. We also offer tips for audit preparation, including evidence collection strategies, so that whether it's an internal audit or an external certification assessment, your organization can efficiently demonstrate compliance and security effectiveness.

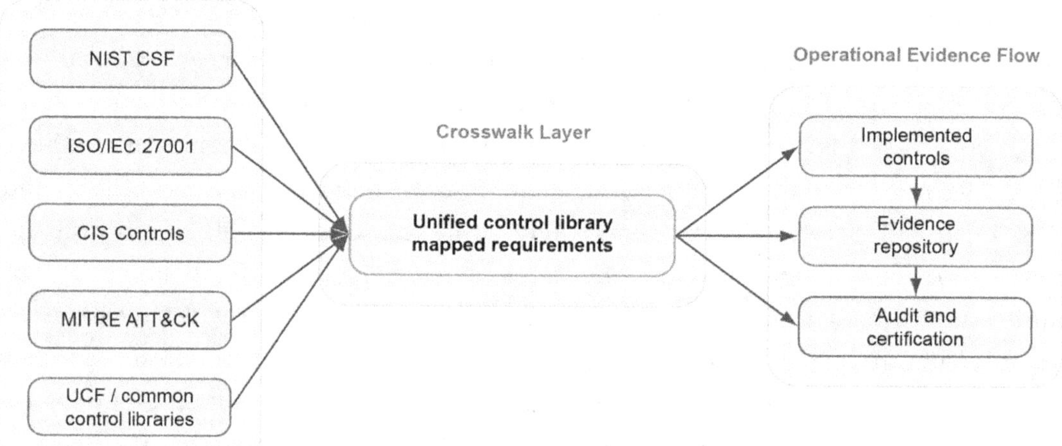

Figure 7-1. *Framework mapping. It shows how multiple frameworks and authority documents can feed into a common control library. Instead of treating NIST CSF, ISO/IEC 27001, CIS Controls, MITRE ATT&CK, and UCF as separate compliance tracks, the organization maps them into unified controls, implemented control activities, evidence repositories, and audit or certification workflows. This approach reduces duplicate testing and helps one evidence artifact support multiple frameworks.*

Cross-Referencing Security Frameworks and Controls

Most security frameworks and standards have significant overlap in their objectives. Cross-referencing (or "crosswalking") frameworks involves creating a mapping that shows how a control in one framework corresponds to a control or requirement in another. This helps in understanding equivalences (e.g., knowing that "audit log monitoring" is expected by all frameworks, even if worded differently) and in reusing compliance evidence.

NIST CSF and ISO/IEC 27001 Mapping: These two frameworks can be mapped at the functional/category level. NIST CSF's Categories and Subcategories can be aligned to ISO 27001 Annex A controls or clauses. For example, NIST CSF category PR.AC (Protect - Identity Management and Access Control) corresponds closely with ISO controls in domain A.9 (Access Control). A mapping might show that CSF Subcategory PR.AC-1 "Identities and credentials are managed" maps to ISO 27001:2022 control 5.15 "Identity management" (hypothetical number for illustration). There are published tables that do this mapping; one source notes, "Specific NIST CSF functions and categories can be mapped to ISO/IEC 27001 clauses and Annex A controls. For example, the NIST CSF 'Protect' function includes activities like access control and security awareness training, which align closely with ISO controls." Indeed, a practical mapping might look like

- **CSF Function**: Identify - Category: Asset Management (ID.AM) → ISO Clauses/Controls: clause 8 (Asset Management) and Annex A.8 controls.
- **CSF Function**: Protect - Category: Data Security (PR.DS) → ISO Controls: Annex A.8 (Asset Management covers data in some part) and Annex A.10 (Cryptography), Annex A.13 (Communications security for data in transit).
- **CSF Function**: Detect - Category: Anomalies and Events (DE.AE) → ISO Controls: Annex A.12.6 (Event logging, detection).
- **CSF Function**: Respond - Category: Response Planning (RS.RP) → ISO Controls: Annex A.16 (Incident Management) corresponds.
- **CSF Function**: Recover - Category: Recovery Planning (RC.RP) → ISO Controls: Annex A.17 (Business Continuity) corresponds.

Performing such mapping, one can create a control mapping table that allows an organization to see "if we are doing X per ISO, we satisfy Y in NIST CSF." This is immensely helpful if, say, management wants to adopt CSF for internal reporting but is also preparing for ISO certification. One can show that by implementing all ISO 27001 Annex A controls, they have covered all CSF subcategories - or conversely, any CSF gap corresponds to an ISO control gap.

CIS Controls Mapping: The CIS Critical Security Controls are often used as a baseline that maps to other frameworks. CIS itself provides an online tool and spreadsheets for mappings to "over 25 different frameworks." For instance, CIS Controls v8.1 to NIST CSF 2.0: The controls are tagged with the CSF Function they primarily support. As seen earlier, a simple crosswalk can align CIS's 18 controls with the five (now six) CSF Functions. For example: CIS Control 1 (Inventory of Assets) aligns with the Identify function, specifically CSF category ID.AM (Asset Management). CIS Control 5 (Account Management) aligns with Protect under PR.AC (Access Control). CIS Control 8 (Audit Log Management) aligns with Detect under DE.AE (Anomalies and Events). CIS

Control 17 (Incident Response) aligns with Respond under RS.RP (Response Planning). CIS Control 18 (Penetration Testing) interestingly aligns with Identify (ID.RA Risk Assessment) because pen testing is a way to identify risks.

Such mapping tables, including examples from CyberSaint and common-control libraries such as the Unified Compliance Framework (UCF), demonstrate alignment. UCF is useful in this context because it helps organizations harmonize overlapping requirements from different authority documents into common controls, reducing duplicate control testing and simplifying audit preparation. These mappings help an organization ensure that if they focus on implementing CIS Controls, they are implicitly covering the CSF. It works the other way too: if an organization uses NIST CSF to identify gaps, they can use the mapping to choose specific CIS Safeguards to fill those gaps. Figure 7-1 shows how multiple frameworks and authority documents can feed into a common control library. Instead of treating NIST CSF, ISO/IEC 27001, CIS Controls, MITRE ATT&CK, and UCF as separate compliance tracks, the organization maps them into unified controls, implemented control activities, evidence repositories, and audit or certification workflows. This approach reduces duplicate testing and helps one evidence artifact support multiple frameworks.

CIS Controls are also mapped to ISO 27001 in available resources. For example, CIS Control 2 (Inventory of Software) corresponds to ISO control on authorized software (Annex A.12.1.2 in the 2013 version about software installation rules). By using these mappings, when undergoing an ISO audit, an organization that has implemented CIS Controls can quickly produce a list: "We address ISO control A.12.1.2 by our implementation of CIS Control 2 with automated inventory and allowlist." This gives confidence that no ISO requirement is missed if you followed CIS.

MITRE ATT&CK Mapping: Mapping MITRE ATT&CK to traditional controls or frameworks is a bit different since ATT&CK is about techniques. However, MITRE and industry collaborators have done mappings like ATT&CK to NIST 800-53 controls. That project, as described, mapped each ATT&CK technique to relevant NIST 800-53 Rev5 controls that would mitigate or detect it. For example, the technique "PowerShell (T1059.001)" might map to controls like SI-3 (Malicious Code Protection), AU-6 (Audit Monitoring), etc., that would help mitigate or log its use. If an organization is using NIST 800-53 or a derivative (such as the moderate controls for FedRAMP), having this mapping means they can say, "We have these controls, therefore we have coverage for these ATT&CK techniques." This approach is part of threat-informed defense, ensuring the controls implemented are actually addressing known threats and not just fulfilling paperwork.

Another useful cross-reference is mapping ATT&CK to CIS Controls. Some companies or tools have done that – e.g., showing which CIS Safeguards help mitigate which ATT&CK techniques. For instance, CIS Control 10 (Malware Defenses) would map to techniques under Execution (like malicious file execution) and so on. By such mapping, one can demonstrate that by implementing CIS Controls, the organization is covered against X% of techniques in ATT&CK (some vendors advertise metrics like 80% coverage of top ATT&CK techniques by implementing all CIS Safeguards).

Unified Compliance and Crosswalking Tools: Given the complexity of managing multiple frameworks, there are both community resources and commercial tools that assist in crosswalking. The Secure Controls Framework (SCF) is a community-driven initiative that consolidates requirements from multiple frameworks into a comprehensive controls catalog, enabling mapping between them. Similarly, the Unified Compliance Framework (UCF) is a commercial common-control framework and mapping database that harmonizes authority documents, such as laws, regulations, standards, and frameworks, into common control statements. Tools like CyberSaint's platform (as mentioned in the excerpt) even leverage AI to automate mapping, so an organization can select frameworks (like NIST CSF, ISO 27001, and CMMC), and it will auto-map their controls and show overlaps. This is valuable because it reduces manual effort and ensures consistency.

For example, an automated crosswalk might reveal: "Control X in our internal policy maps to ISO control A.5.1.1, NIST CSF ID.GV-1 (Governance), NIST 800-53 PM-1, and CIS Control 2." Knowing this, when an auditor asks for evidence of ISO A.5.1.1 (information security policy), the organization can provide the policy document, which also covers NIST CSF governance and was perhaps already reviewed under a NIST CSF self-assessment. The mapping provides one-to-many relationships, so a single internal control can satisfy multiple external requirements. This is the heart of an efficient compliance program.

Mapping Tables/Diagrams Example: A simplified example mapping table might look like:

CIS Control	NIST CSF Category	ISO 27001:2022 Control
CIS 1: Inventory of Enterprise Assets	Identify (ID.AM: Asset Management)	5.9 Inventory of information and other associated assets
CIS 5: Account Management	Protect (PR.AC: Access Control)	5.15 Access control; 5.16 Identity management; 5.18 Access rights
CIS 8: Audit Log Management	Detect, Continuous Monitoring	8.15 Logging; 8.16 Monitoring activities
CIS 13: Network Monitoring and Defense	Detect (DE.CM: Continuous Mon.)	8.20 Network security; 8.21 Security of network services; 8.16 Monitoring activities
CIS 17: Incident Response Management	Respond, Incident Management	5.24 Information security incident management planning and preparation; 5.25 Assessment and decision on information security events; 5.26 Response to information security incidents; 5.27 Learning from information security incidents; 5.28 Collection of evidence
CIS 11: Data Recovery	Recover, Recovery Planning	8.13 Information backup

(Note: ISO control references here are illustrative, as ISO 27001:2022 controls are numbered differently in themes, but, e.g., backup control is one of the technological controls, incident management is organizational, etc.)

Such a table shows the crosswalk clearly. If you were preparing an audit and needed to ensure coverage of ISO controls, you could use the table to check which CIS Controls you must have fully implemented. If CIS Control 13 isn't fully in place, you might be weak on ISO monitoring control, for example.

Using Mappings for Gap Analysis: If your organization must comply with a new framework, mapping helps identify gaps. For instance, if you've implemented all CIS Controls (and have evidence for each Safeguard), and now you have to undergo a MITRE ATT&CK assessment, or you want to ensure threat coverage, you can map CIS to ATT&CK to see which techniques have no corresponding Safeguard. Maybe you find that user training (CIS Control 14) doesn't address some advanced lateral movement techniques - which might prompt adding a specific detection control not spelled out by CIS. On the flip side, if you primarily followed NIST CSF and now a client wants you to get ISO 27001 certified, mapping CSF categories to ISO controls helps pinpoint which ISO controls might not be fully addressed by a pure CSF approach. (CSF is broad, so likely you need to implement more documentation and formal procedures to meet ISO requirements - mapping will highlight those areas, e.g., ISO has specific requirements for supplier agreements that CSF only implies under ID.SC. If you weren't doing that, the mapping would show a gap under the ISO clause for supplier security.)

Audit Preparation and Evidence Collection

Whether it's an internal audit, a customer security assessment, or a formal certification audit (ISO, SOC 2, etc.), being audit-ready is crucial. Audit preparation involves ensuring that controls are not only in place but also well-documented and supported by evidence. Evidence is the proof that what you say in policies and procedures is actually happening in practice. A key maxim in compliance is: "If it's not documented, it didn't happen." Thus, organizations must collect and organize evidence that demonstrates each control or security measure is implemented and effective.

Organizing Controls and Evidence by Framework: If your organization aligns with multiple frameworks, it's wise to establish a unified control matrix that lists all controls and maps them to relevant framework references (as discussed above). During audit prep, this matrix serves as a guide to what evidence is needed for each requirement. For example, you might have a control "User access reviews are conducted quarterly" which maps to ISO 27001 control 5.15 (user access review), NIST CSF PR.AC-4, and CIS Safeguard 5.4. The evidence for that control could be last quarter's access review report and sign-off records. By maintaining a matrix or GRC tool where each control has associated evidence files or links, you can quickly retrieve what an auditor asks for.

Evidence Collection Best Practices: A strong recommendation is to treat evidence collection as an ongoing process, not a one-time scramble. Here are some tips and practices:

- **Document Everything Promptly**: Don't wait until an audit is announced to scramble for screenshots or logs. As soon as a control activity is performed, capture evidence. For instance, when a new firewall rule is implemented as per change management, save the change ticket and a screenshot of the rule. If employees complete security awareness training in April, export the completion report in April and file it. One guide suggests: "Save screenshots or logs when the task is completed, not when the auditor requests it." This prevents missing data (some logs might roll over or get lost) and ensures timestamps are current.

- **Centralize Evidence Storage**: Have a secure, centralized repository for audit evidence (could be a SharePoint site, a GRC system, or even a well-structured folder on a server). Organize it by control or domain. For example, a folder structure might be: "Controls ➤ Access Control ➤ User Access Review ➤ Q1 2025 evidence (report.pdf, meeting minutes.docx)." Another approach is organizing by standard domain: "ISO A.9 Access Control ➤ A9.2.1 User provisioning ➤ evidence files...". The key is that it's logically structured so you can find things. Use versioning and clear naming (include dates in filenames, etc.). And restrict access to this repository to prevent tampering (only compliance team or control owners can add evidence).
- **Use Templates and Checklists**: For recurring evidence (like a monthly server hardening checklist or a quarterly incident response drill record), create templates so that those performing the task know exactly what to capture and save. For example, an "Audit Log Review Form" that an analyst fills in each week, then saves. This standardizes evidence and makes auditors happy because they see consistent records.
- **Automation Where Possible**: Leverage tools to collect evidence automatically. Some modern GRC tools integrate with systems (cloud platforms, HR systems, etc.) to pull data. For example, an integration might automatically fetch a list of all new hires and terminations from HR each month to show user access management is tied to HR events or connect to AWS to get a config snapshot for encryption settings. Automation reduces human error and the "last-minute scramble" described in anecdotal scenarios. Even simple scripts can help (like a script to dump a list of current privileged users from Active Directory every month and store it). Automation not only saves time but also

provides continuous compliance monitoring. Some sources claim that automating evidence collection can reduce preparation time significantly and give real-time visibility. For example, instead of manually checking 100 servers for patch status and screenshotting each, one could use a vulnerability management tool report as evidence of patch compliance.

- **Align Evidence to Controls and Frameworks**: When you map controls to frameworks, also map evidence to controls. This means each control in your matrix should have an entry for "type of evidence" and location. For instance, Control: "Vulnerability scans performed monthly" - Evidence: monthly scan reports (stored at X location) and remediation tickets. If an auditor wants to see ISO 27001 control on vulnerability management, you know exactly which reports to pull.
- **Keep Evidence Audit-Grade**: That means it should be organized, time-stamped, complete, and easily verifiable. Avoid informal evidence like a quick chat screenshot unless absolutely necessary. Instead, use formal records. For example, instead of "Bob said he reviewed the firewall rules," have a change management ticket or sign-off document showing Bob's action and date. Ensure screenshots (if needed) show the critical info (e.g., a screenshot of a configuration should include the date/time from the system if possible to prove it's not an old screenshot). Many auditors appreciate when evidence includes who did the action and when - this ties into traceability.
- **Continuous Compliance vs. Annual Crunch**: Organizations that integrate evidence collection into daily operations find audits to be much smoother. They treat audits as almost non-events because everything is already in place. This is sometimes called "audit-ready at any time." It also aligns with frameworks like NIST CSF or ISO that emphasize continuous monitoring and improvement - you shouldn't be secure only at audit time. Sources echo this: "Make compliance continuous. Strong evidence practices are centralized, automated, and aligned with frameworks, turning audits from seasonal scrambles into routine health checks." Essentially, if you adopt a mindset that you might be audited tomorrow, you'll naturally maintain diligent records.

- **Internal Audits and Pre-assessments**: Conduct periodic internal audits or readiness assessments to identify evidence gaps. For example, do a mock ISO audit internally: pull a sample of controls and see if evidence is readily available and convincing. If not, adjust processes. This not only prepares you for the real thing but also improves security by catching lapses. Internal audits could be aided by internal audit teams or an external consultant acting as a pretend auditor.
- **Traceability Matrix for Audit**: For external audits, consider creating a traceability matrix that maps each audit requirement to the evidence provided. For instance, in an ISO audit, the auditor might have a checklist of 114 controls. You can prepare a sheet that says for each control, list of documents or records ready. Then, as the audit happens, you can quickly pull the specific items. This impresses auditors and saves time.

Audit Dynamics (Internal vs. External)

- **Internal Audits**: Often more advisory in nature, internal auditors verify controls without the pressure of losing certification. Use these to improve. Internal auditors might use frameworks like CIS or NIST as benchmarks even if the org is not formally certified. They will want evidence as well, so treat them seriously – if the internal audit finds evidence lacking, that's a red flag to fix before any external review.
- **External Audits**: If it's for a certification (ISO, PCI) or customer requirement, the stakes are higher. Auditors will expect professionalism in the presentation of evidence. The key here is to avoid last-minute collection. Last-minute scrambling can lead to mistakes (e.g., incorrect or outdated evidence or, worst, attempting to fabricate something which must be strictly avoided). It also stresses staff. Starting preparation months in advance is recommended, with a clear schedule of tasks (e.g., three months out: finalize documentation, two months: conduct an internal pre-audit, one month: gather remaining evidence, etc.). Also, ensure the evidence spans the required period. Many audits (like ISO or SOC 2) expect to see evidence over time, not just one point. For instance, they might check quarterly reviews that happened in Q1, Q2, and Q3, so they have evidence for each instance.

- **Team Roles**: Assign clear roles for audit preparation. Typically:
    - **Control Owners**: People responsible for each control who will ensure evidence for that control is collected and available.
    - **Compliance/Audit Coordinator**: Person (or team) who liaises with auditors, organizes evidence, and keeps the mapping. They often assemble the traceability matrix and double-check evidence quality.
    - **Department Reps**: If an audit spans multiple departments (IT, HR, etc.), have a point of contact in each who understands what evidence that department must supply (e.g., HR provides background check evidence, etc.).
    - During external audits, also designate an "Auditor Contact" or escort for each area - this person will handle questions on a given control area and immediately fetch additional evidence if requested.
- Common Pitfalls and How to Avoid Them
    - **Incomplete or Inconsistent Evidence**: If evidence is missing details (e.g., a screenshot with no date or a policy with no approval signature), auditors may question its validity. Always review evidence with a critical eye: Would an independent person conclude the control was met from this evidence? If not, improve it. For instance, add a cover sheet to a log review that the reviewer signs and dates.
    - **Evidence Gaps ("blind spots")**: Ensure you cover all parts of the scope. Sometimes organizations forget evidence for things like third-party compliance (e.g., did you check your critical vendors' security? This might be a control in ISO or CIS). If you map frameworks, these gaps become visible. Avoid leaving any requirement unaddressed; if something is not applicable, document a rationale.

- **Too Much Evidence**: Surprisingly, providing excessive irrelevant evidence can annoy or confuse auditors. They want exactly what shows the control, not every file on your server. Thus, curate evidence: only give what's asked and what's sufficient. For example, if an auditor asks for "an example of a recent access review," don't send them 100 PDFs of all reviews in the last year - pick one or two that are representative and show completeness. You can have the rest on-hand if they want more.
- **Last Minute Collection and Errors**: We touched on this - when rushed, people might backdate a document or scramble to create a policy on the fly. Auditors can usually detect this (e.g., a policy "last updated yesterday" right before the audit raises eyebrows). It's far better to proactively acknowledge a gap and show a plan than to falsify anything. Plan ahead to avoid being in that situation.
- **Communication Gaps**: During an external audit, if evidence is not clearly explained, auditors might misunderstand and mark a finding. Always provide context with evidence. For instance, if showing a screenshot of an AWS config, you might have a brief note: "Screenshot of S3 bucket settings showing encryption is enabled (AES256) and access logging turned on." This helps the auditor quickly grasp what they're looking at and why it meets the control.

- Collecting Different Types of Evidence: Evidence generally falls into categories:
    - **Policies/Documentation**: These are your written policies, standards, and procedures. They serve as evidence that management has formally addressed a topic. Ensure they are approved and version-controlled (e.g., have signatures or approval records, and dates). Auditors will read these to see if they cover required elements (e.g., an ISO auditor will check if the Information Security Policy addresses all necessary points like asset management, acceptable use, etc.). Keep an index of documents and their latest revision date.

- **Records/Logs**: These show the policy is being followed. Examples: system logs, access logs, change management tickets, training attendance logs, and risk assessment reports. They should be time-stamped and unaltered. If providing logs, sometimes a sample is enough (like showing a few log entries with anomalies and responses).
- **Screenshots/Configuration Settings**: Useful to show technical settings (like a screenshot of encryption settings or a dump of a firewall rule table). These should be annotated or accompanied by an explanation to highlight the relevant part. Also, ensure they show context (like the system name or date).
- **Reports**: Outputs from tools (vulnerability scan reports, compliance tool reports). Make sure these have dates and ideally evidence of review (e.g., a scan report with a manager's sign-off or follow-up actions).
- **Meeting Minutes/Attestations**: Minutes from security committee meetings, risk acceptance memos, and management sign-offs all count as evidence of governance. They show management involvement (which frameworks like NIST CSF Govern or ISO clauses require). If minutes are used, have them signed or at least list attendees and actions decided.
- **Test Results**: If you do DR tests or incident response drills, keep the results and any lessons learned. Auditors like to see that you test your plans and improve.
- **Third-Party Evidence**: This includes things like a cloud provider's ISO certificate or SOC 2 report, penetration test reports by external parties, or certificates of destruction from a shredding service. If your control relies on an external party, have their attestations ready. For example, if using AWS, download their latest SOC 2 report as evidence for certain physical and infrastructure controls.

Evidence and Alignment with Multiple Audits: If you have to undergo different audits (say ISO 27001 and a SOC 2 and maybe client questionnaires), a mapped approach saves effort. Essentially, you can often reuse the same evidence for similar controls. For example, an ISO auditor and a SOC 2 auditor will both want to see that you monitor and respond to incidents. You can maintain one incident log and set of reports, and show it to both – no need to collect separate evidence per audit. If you know the mappings, you might even proactively answer client questionnaires by referencing how your controls meet well-known frameworks ("We have ISO 27001 certification which covers these controls" – and you can attach a few evidences if needed). Many client questionnaires map to CIS or NIST; having evidence file references in those terms speeds up responses.

Continuous Improvement: After each audit (internal or external), take note of any findings or even observations where evidence was weak. Update your evidence collection process accordingly. For instance, if an auditor noted "policy X doesn't state review frequency," update the policy and ensure that it is documented. If they struggled to verify something because evidence was unclear, maybe next cycle collect better evidence for that control. Over time, this makes audits easier and the security program stronger.

In essence, audit preparation is an ongoing aspect of governance. Effective governance frameworks require not just doing the right things, but being able to demonstrate them. By mapping and aligning controls across frameworks, you reduce the complexity of this demonstration because you know exactly what needs to be shown, and you can often cover multiple bases with one set of actions and evidence. By following best practices in evidence collection – timely, organized, and sufficient proof – you transform audits from dreaded, disruptive events into more routine check-ups that validate your program. As one source put it succinctly: "Evidence is everything. Without organized, time-stamped, audit-grade proof, compliance collapses... With organized evidence, audits glide – shortening cycles and reducing findings."

Conclusion

Governance frameworks and security certifications form the twin pillars of a robust information security program. Frameworks like NIST CSF, ISO/IEC 27001, CIS Controls, and MITRE ATT&CK provide structured approaches to managing risk, implementing controls, and understanding threats, while professional certifications like CISSP and CCSP ensure that individuals have the knowledge to put those approaches into practice. In this chapter, we explored each major framework in detail – from the high-level, risk-aligned guidance of NIST CSF and ISO 27001's ISMS, to the prescriptive action items of CIS Critical Controls, and the adversary perspective offered by MITRE ATT&CK. We saw that despite differences in scope and focus, these frameworks share common goals and can be mapped to one another to create a unified, comprehensive security posture.

We also examined how certification domains map onto governance needs: CISSP holders bring expertise in establishing security governance, risk management, and compliance programs, and CCSP professionals extend those principles to the cloud environment. The common thread is aligning security efforts with business objectives and regulatory requirements – speaking both the language of technical controls and the language of executive risk concerns. This alignment is critical in the modern era, where organizations must demonstrate not only that they are secure but that they can prove it through audits and compliance checks.

By mapping controls across frameworks and using unified control sets, organizations can streamline compliance – meaning a control implemented once can satisfy many requirements. We provided examples of crosswalks showing how a single security practice might fulfill NIST CSF subcategories, ISO 27001 controls, and CIS Safeguards simultaneously. With the aid of such mappings (and often tools to manage them), internal teams can reduce duplication and focus on real security improvements rather than siloed compliance tasks.

We then delved into practical audit preparation. The key takeaway is that preparing for audits should be embedded into regular operations. Continuous evidence collection and good record-keeping turn audits from fire-fighting exercises into mere formalities. We highlighted best practices like prompt documentation, centralized evidence repositories, use of automation, and clear role assignments – all of which help maintain a state of "audit readiness." This not only satisfies external auditors but actually strengthens security: organized evidence often reveals gaps that can be fixed proactively, and continuous monitoring of controls ensures issues are caught early.

In an era defined by rapid technological change (cloud computing, AI, IoT) and evolving threat landscapes, having a strong foundation in frameworks and a culture of continuous improvement is more important than ever. The "AI Era" implies that both attackers and defenders are leveraging advanced tools – frameworks like MITRE ATT&CK already catalog techniques involving machine-speed attacks, and defenses are adapting with automation and AI-driven analytics. Amid these changes, frameworks provide a steady anchor, ensuring we cover the fundamentals even as we adopt new technologies. Certifications ensure that the people at the helm of security programs are equipped to make informed decisions and adapt principles to new scenarios.

In practice, a vendor-neutral, well-governed security program might look like this: the organization uses NIST CSF as an overall guide to structure its program and communicate with executives, it has an ISO 27001-certified ISMS to provide assurance to customers and regulators, it implements CIS Controls to drive day-to-day security improvements and measure hygiene, and it references MITRE ATT&CK to validate that its defenses can thwart the tactics used by real attackers. Its security team includes CISSPs and CCSPs who use their broad knowledge to integrate these efforts, ensuring nothing falls through the cracks between strategy, operations, and compliance. During internal reviews or external audits, the team easily maps each requirement to implemented controls and produces evidence, demonstrating a tight linkage between policy, practice, and proof.

Such an organization is not only secure on paper but in practice – it can withstand audits and cyberattacks alike, because it has both the governance (to ensure the right things are done and verified) and the technical vigilance (to ensure threats are detected and responded to). This is the ideal outcome that the convergence of frameworks and certifications aims to achieve.

In conclusion, mastering frameworks and certifications is about translating theory into practice: taking the "what" and "why" from frameworks and leveraging the "how" from technical controls, under the guidance of knowledgeable certified professionals. With the solid groundwork laid out in this chapter, you should be equipped to build or enhance your organization's security program in a way that is structured, measurable, and defensible. By adopting a high-level view of your security posture through frameworks, drilling down to specific controls, aligning everything with business risks, and maintaining diligent documentation, you create a resilient security foundation. This foundation not only protects cloud, data, and identity today but is agile enough to incorporate the advances of tomorrow – truly embodying the foundations of modern information security in the AI era.

Index

A

A. Gupta and S. Mittal, *Foundations of Modern Information Security*,
https://doi.org/10.1007/979-8-8688-2558-3

D

E

F

J

K

L

O

P

Q

R

U

V

W, X, Y

Z

www.ingramcontent.com/pod-product-compliance
Lightning Source LLC
Chambersburg PA
CBHW080738040826
49263CB00023B/552
* 9 7 9 8 8 6 8 8 2 5 5 7 6 *